UNDERSTANDING AND USING
READING
ASSESSMENT
K–12

2nd EDITION

PETER AFFLERBACH

INTERNATIONAL
Reading Association
800 BARKSDALE ROAD, PO BOX 8139
NEWARK, DE 19714-8139, USA
www.reading.org

SO-AYP-841

The International Reading Association attempts, through its publications, to provide a forum for a wide spectrum of opinions on reading. This policy permits divergent viewpoints without implying the endorsement of the Association.

Executive Editor, Publications   Shannon Fortner
Managing Editor   Christina M. Terranova
Editorial Associate   Wendy Logan
Design and Composition Manager   Anette Schuetz
Design and Composition Associate   Lisa Kochel

Cover   Design: Frank Pessia. Book illustration: Thinkstock/Roz Woodward. Front cover photographs (from left): Thinkstock/iStockphoto, Comstock, Jupiterimages. Back cover photograph: Thinkstock/Hemera.

The publisher would appreciate notification where errors occur so that they may be corrected in subsequent printings and/or editions.

Library of Congress Cataloging-in-Publication Data
Afflerbach, Peter.
  Understanding and using reading assessment, K-12 / Peter Afflerbach. -- 2nd ed.
      p. cm.
  Includes bibliographical references and index.
  ISBN 978-0-87207-831-4
  1. Reading (Elementary)--Ability testing--United States. 2. Reading (Secondary)--Ability testing--United States. I. Title.
  LB1050.46.A36 2011
  372.48--dc23
                    2011032679

Suggested APA Reference
Afflerbach, P. (2012). *Understanding and using reading assessment, K–12* (2nd ed.). Newark, DE: International Reading Association.

For
Emma and Rowan

CONTENTS

ABOUT THE AUTHOR

 **P**eter Afflerbach is a professor at the Reading Center in the Department of Curriculum and Instruction of the University of Maryland, College Park. He received his PhD in reading from the University of Albany in 1985. Prior to this, he taught remedial middle school reading and writing in Saratoga Springs, New York; taught high school English in Troy, New York; and was a K–6 Title I reading teacher at Dolgeville Central School in Dolgeville, New York.

Peter's interests include reading assessment, reading comprehension, and the use of the verbal reporting methodology. His work appears in theoretical and practical journals, including *Reading Research Quarterly*, *Cognition and Instruction*, *The Elementary School Journal*, *Journal of Adolescent & Adult Literacy*, and *The Reading Teacher*. Of his most recent books, Peter coedited the *Handbook of Reading Research* (Vol. 4; Routledge, 2010) and edited *Essential Readings on Assessment* (International Reading Association [IRA], 2010). He also serves as an associate editor of the journal *Metacognition and Learning* and a member of the Editorial Advisory Board of *Reading Research Quarterly*.

Peter served on the National Assessment of Educational Progress (NAEP) 2009 Reading Framework Committee and was part of the Common Core State Standards for English/Language Arts Feedback Group. He was a member of the Joint Task Force on Assessment of the IRA and the National Council of Teachers of English (NCTE), which developed the revised edition of the *Standards for the Assessment of Reading and Writing* (IRA & NCTE, 2010). Peter is also the chair of IRA's Issues in Literacy Assessment Committee and was inducted into the Reading Hall of Fame in 2009.

Author Information for Correspondence and Workshops
Peter is available for conferences and workshops and welcomes questions and comments from readers. He can be contacted at afflo@umd.edu.

PREFACE

What do we hope for for our students? In what ways can we help foster their reading development? In this book, we examine reading assessment and how understanding and using reading assessment contributes to students' growth as readers. Helping all students achieve to their potential is challenging work, and doing reading assessment well helps us meet this challenge. A premise of this second edition of *Understanding and Using Reading Assessment, K–12* is that the most consequential and useful reading assessment takes place in classrooms. This assessment is conducted by accomplished teachers through their careful questioning, keen observation, and use of diverse assessment procedures and materials, including reading inventories, portfolios, and performance assessments. Just as we read text to construct meaning, we can, through assessment, read our students to construct a detailed understanding of their strengths and needs.

We know much about reading and literacy: how it develops, how it is nurtured, and how it differs among students. We also know much about reading assessment: We are beneficiaries of a growing body of research and practice that describes how to design, implement, and get the most from our assessments. That we do not always use our robust understandings of reading and reading assessment is troubling. This is due to various economic, social, and political forces that influence the ways and means of reading assessment.

Too often, schools, teachers, and students are under the thumb of high-stakes tests, which provide too thin a measure of all that reading is and dictate the nature of reading and classrooms. In the next decade, it is possible that we will witness a movement away from such tests, and movement toward integrated assessment systems that combine formative and summative reading assessment information. In part, these assessments will be driven by large-scale curricular change movements, such as the Common Core State Standards (Council of Chief State School Officers & National Governors Association [CCSSO & NGA], 2010). These standards are demanding because they require the reading of complex texts and the doing of sophisticated, reading-related tasks. Necessarily, reading assessment will need to provide formative information that helps us guide students through increased reading challenges, and summative information that captures the integrity of both teaching effectiveness and learning outcomes.

This edition of *Understanding and Using Reading Assessment, K–12* includes a new chapter on Response to Intervention (RTI) and early reading assessment. RTI is all around us in elementary reading classrooms, and it presents an opportunity to directly address students' needs through careful assessment. My belief is that successful reading instruction always revolves around detailed and reliable assessment, and RTI is one example of how assessment and instruction can work together to address individual students. I use two very different assessments, the Observation Survey of Early Literacy Achievement (OSELA; Clay, 2002) and the Dynamic Indicators of Basic Early Literacy Skills (DIBELS) Next (Good & Kaminski, 2011) to demonstrate how early reading assessment can vary in form and content and to stress that our early reading assessments shape our vision of what students can do and what they need.

This edition maintains a focus on assessments that are capable of describing and supporting complex acts of student reading, such as those aligned with the Common Core State Standards and the 2009 NAEP reading framework. These assessments, including performance assessment and portfolio assessment, have the promise of combining formative and summative assessments to the benefit of students and teachers. We know how complex reading is, and performance and portfolio assessments offer the opportunity for assessment to capture and describe this complexity.

Since the publication of the first edition of this book in 2007, we have learned more about the nature and power of "the other" in reading: how motivation, engagement, self-efficacy, volition, self-concept, and agency operate in the day-to-day reading of our students. As the evidence base that describes the importance of these other factors builds, our assessments must honor this emerging understanding. Chapter 8 focuses on assessment of "the other" and incorporates recent findings related to factors other than cognitive skills and strategies that can influence reading development, and so should be assessed.

Finally, in this edition, I broaden the idea of what we can do with our reading assessments. I focus on the traditional reporting role of assessment: how it lets us know how students are doing. Also, I stress the need to consider how classroom assessments can be used to support and encourage our student readers, as when our assessments focus on what students can do and provide encouragement for them to continue. I also focus on how reading assessments can be used to help students learn to self-assess and become increasingly independent at gauging their progress across reading tasks. This is one of the hallmarks of the successful reader.

My hope is that this book helps the reader best conceptualize assessment that benefits all students, even as we continue to develop our understandings and uses of reading assessment.

Acknowledgments

Many people contributed to the development of this book. IRA's publications staff has been supportive of all the work included herein.

My colleagues at the University of Maryland, including students and faculty, continue to help shape my thinking about reading assessment and its role in fostering reading development.

The teachers I work with continue to alert me to new ways of thinking about assessment and inspire me with their willingness to stand up for reading assessment that helps students become accomplished readers.

The researchers whose work is cited herein have created a robust and detailed knowledge base that should continue to inform our efforts to improve reading assessment. I especially thank Peter Johnston, who has influenced my thinking about children, learning, and assessment.

Finally, Emma and Rowan, two of my favorite readers, regularly remind me of the importance of reading and knowing what to focus on when we try to assess it.

CHAPTER 1

Important Issues
and Concepts
in Reading Assessment

Imagine for a moment that you spend the day visiting different classrooms in a school district noted for exemplary practices in reading assessment. Throughout the community are children, adolescents, and young adults who are reading and achieving. Reading assessment informs timely reading instruction and plays a vital role in fostering student growth. Teachers are supported in their efforts to best understand and use reading assessment.

The first stop on our tour is kindergarten. Four language-rich kindergarten classrooms occupy an entire wing of the school. Students regularly experience and explore the uses of language: to learn, to inform, to enjoy, and to reflect. The students are involved in classroom discussions and read-alouds. They students create meaning with dictated stories, focus on vocabulary with word walls, and maintain their enthusiasm for language through play with words. In one classroom, we see and hear students mouthing /b/ as they connect speech sounds with the print form of the letter B. The teacher circulates around the room, listening to determine whether students have established an understanding of this relationship. She assesses their ongoing progress in matching print with speech and finds some students struggling to make this connection. Her ability to assess, which she considers central to successful teaching, allows her to provide immediate and focused instruction that meets students at their current level of understanding.

Using the information gathered through careful listening and her assessment of individual students' development of phonics knowledge, the teacher builds toward the teachable moment. She provides additional instruction that focuses on familiar things in and around the classroom to help students cement the connection of the letter B to its corresponding speech sound. We hear, "Bugs. Book bags. Best. Butter. BFF." Smiles spread around the group, and the students and their teacher acknowledge their accomplishments and are ready to move on. Many children in this classroom choose to spend time with books during their independent work time. This inclination to try to read is valued by the school and the teacher. She makes note of students' widespread willingness to try. This is important information, to be included in the students' narrative report cards. Throughout the school day and school year, assessment helps the teacher know her students.

We next enter a fourth-grade classroom. The teacher works with a small group of students while other children read their self-selected books. They choose books wisely for independent reading: A rich classroom library provides choice for the students, and they know well their capabilities as readers. Their self-assessment ability allows them to select books that present an engaging reading experience, including the comfortable challenge of stretching themselves as readers. These students continue to develop the ability to self-assess their reading in relation to the goals of reading and their abilities.

While many students work independently, several work on strengthening the skills and strategies that help them read the texts encountered in fourth grade. A quick paper-and-pencil assessment, in which students are asked to write what they know about key vocabulary words, reveals that several students do not understand *ecosystem*, *symbiosis*, *prey*, and *predator*—words that are key to constructing meaning in the new science unit. The teacher decides that the small group will engage in three tasks that provide both learning opportunities and assessment opportunities related to vocabulary. An enrichment lesson focuses on the common features of ecosystems, and the teacher encourages a small-group discussion of the important vocabulary words. She asks the students to write definitions of the words and answer questions to demonstrate their understanding. Each of these activities provides valuable assessment information—converging evidence of student knowledge and progress. The teacher is sensitive to the fact that several of her students are reluctant to participate, given their shaky self-concepts as readers. Reading assessment that gives students useful feedback while shoring up their self-esteem is important to the students and the teacher. Her feedback to students is directive and supportive. Three sources of assessment information describe the status of her students' growth and knowledge: classroom discussions, the students' writing, and student responses to teacher questions. Combined, these assessments afford her high confidence in her determination that all of the students in the group now understand the key words and concepts of the unit.

Just as important, the teacher of this diverse group of students recognizes the different levels of self-esteem and motivation that each student shows in relation to reading. Students in the small group work to understand the key vocabulary words. The teacher, an advocate of assessing students' attitude toward reading, attends to both the cognitive and affective aspects of learning. She assesses her students' knowledge of words as she assesses their motivation and perseverance. The teacher's careful work here is evident: The students who sometimes struggle at reading meet the reading challenges with positive motivation and complete the lesson with their self-esteem intact. The teacher considers this a critical outcome of her instruction.

Across town, students in a middle school classroom are progressing through an extended language arts period. The students in this class use portfolios, which help them organize their work. Most important, the portfolio provides a context for reading assessment. One pocket holds reading logs and the students' ongoing accounts of their understanding of the stories and their reactions to the stories. Another pocket contains the weekly quizzes that focus on students' knowledge of the literary devices used by authors and the content of the texts that are read. Yet another pocket contains the vocabulary words that the students have independently chosen and determined to be important. Within this pocket, the students regularly sort vocabulary words into and among the categories "I don't know," "Getting to know," and "I definitely know." This self-sorting process demonstrates the ability of students to assess their own learning. The opportunities for students to conduct reading assessment are enhanced by the school district's commitment to provide the time to take full advantage of portfolios. The teacher consults each student's portfolio to regularly gauge student growth. The portfolio is shared with parents at open school night. In addition to demonstrating their children's achievements, the portfolio provides parents with a model of valuable and (for them) nontraditional reading assessment. Finally, the portfolio provides motivation for students, as it helps them see the connection of their consistent hard work to their considerable accomplishments.

The final stop on our tour of reading assessment is a high school. Students are reading primary and secondary source documents, including diaries, newspapers, and textbook chapters related to the American Revolutionary War. The students' reading tasks include establishing a literal understanding of the historical content of the text. Students are expected to investigate when the texts were written, where they first appeared, and who wrote them. Students consider the trustworthiness of the texts they read and the reliability of the historical accounts provided by the authors. Students' success revolves around the reading knowledge and strategies needed for reading in the content area of history. These sophisticated reading strategies build on students' existing reading achievements and their ability to construct literal and inferential meaning from content area texts. The students' work is guided and assessed by a series of performance assessments and their accompanying rubrics. Throughout the year, the teacher refers students to the publicly displayed and often-discussed rubrics for performance assessments in history. The rubrics serve as road maps for students, guiding their performances. The rubrics remind students to search for clues in the text that may reveal an author's biases. The rubrics also provide details that assist the teacher in assigning scores to students' final projects. As such, the rubrics and performance assessment are an example of transparent assessment: They are developed not only to measure but also to educate. They inform students about what is expected to earn a particular grade, and they help students learn how to conduct self-assessment in complex reading tasks.

Upon completion of our tour of the district, we understand that there are stories of success and challenge related to reading assessment across the school district community. Reading assessment is central to knowing students' reading progress and achievement. Reading assessment helps teachers construct understanding of how their students are developing as readers. In doing so, reading assessment provides critical information for making important instructional decisions. The relationship among reading assessment, teaching, and student progress in reading could not be more important.

What undergirds the natural, seemingly seamless approach to reading assessment developed by this district? The assessments derive from detailed and consensus-based understandings of both reading and reading assessment. Assessment is aligned with district standards for reading achievement and content area curricular goals. Assessment is also aligned with the well-researched theories of the development of students' reading skills and strategies. The assessments measure students' self-esteem and motivation as related to reading. They are informed by psychometric standards and issues related to assessment fairness and the consequences of assessment. In addition, reading assessment in this district is planned and systematic. The teachers know reading assessment and understand the strengths, weaknesses, and appropriate uses of different reading assessments. The teachers use reading assessment as it best fits their goals of helping each student become an accomplished reader.

Important Issues and Concepts in Reading Assessment

As we strive to understand and use reading assessment, it is important to consider three questions: First, why do we assess reading? All reading assessment should be conducted with the purpose of helping students achieve in reading. Second, what do we assess when we assess reading? Asking this question allows us to focus on reading program goals and outcomes and what we hope for our students as we teach and support their reading development. Third, how, where, and when do we assess reading? This query anticipates the array of reading assessment materials and procedures that are examined later in this book in individual chapters.

Why Do We Assess Reading?

Reading assessment helps us understand the strengths and needs of each of our students. Although all reading assessments should share this purpose, the manner in which individual assessments provide information and the manner in which we use the particular assessment information will vary. Consider the different formative and summative purposes for assessment that are demonstrated in the following scenarios.

A third-grade teacher uses a reading inventory to gather detailed information about a student's oral reading skills and strategies. The reading inventory provides the teacher with the opportunity for the ongoing analysis of student reading. The teacher determines that the student reads with high confidence but also reads through sentence boundaries. The student does not reread after obvious meaning-changing miscues. The teacher uses this new assessment information to update her understanding of the student and determines that the student needs to concentrate on developing comprehension-monitoring strategies. The teacher uses this information in the next day's instruction, the goal of which is to encourage the student to regularly monitor the meaning-making process that is reading. Using think-alouds, the teacher models the types of questions that good readers ask themselves as they read, including Why am I reading? and Does that make sense? In this case, the answer to the question of why we assess reading is that it provides detailed and timely information that is used by a talented teacher to shape instruction to the student's needs.

Late in the school year, the same third-grade teacher administers a statewide high-stakes reading assessment. The test is used to gather information on students' reading skills and strategies. Results of this test may be used for several purposes. The mean student scores, derived from multiple-choice and short fill-in items, will be used to determine if the school meets federally mandated levels of adequate yearly progress in reading achievement. The test is considered by some to be a judge of accountability, determining if the teacher, school, and school district are working successfully to help students develop as readers and meet state standards in reading. The results of this test are also reported at the individual student level, and parents receive their child's raw scores and percentile rankings in vocabulary knowledge and literal and inferential comprehension. Thus, test results inform parents of their children's general reading achievement levels.

In each of the preceding two scenarios, reading assessment is conducted for specific purposes and specific audiences. One assessment is more direct: The classroom teacher is a practiced expert at using the reading inventory to understand the nature of a student's reading, how it relates to a model of highly efficient reading, and how it anticipates the instruction and learning that the teacher plans for the student. The process orientation of the reading inventory provides a window into the reading skills and strategies that the student uses or needs. The reading assessment information is immediate and fleeting, and the teacher knows how to focus on and interpret the information that the reading inventory produces. The teacher's knowledge of the nature and importance of students' self-monitoring of reading is matched with the teacher's ability to use the reading inventory to provide information related to this important instructional goal. In contrast, the end-of-year test is composed of items that will describe the students' vocabulary knowledge and text comprehension. The results of this test, available several months after students take it, are focused on the products of reading comprehension. The results signal that a certain percentage of students meet state and federal reading benchmarks, and communicate to particular audiences that the teaching of reading in the district is going well and that taxpayers' money has been well spent.

Throughout this book, we will determine that the question of why we assess reading requires us to consider the diverse purposes for assessing reading. These purposes range from determining the development of students' reading, informing instruction, demonstrating teacher and school accountability, and describing a reading program's strengths and weaknesses in involving the home and effectively coordinating home and school efforts, motivating and encouraging students, and teaching students how to self-assess. Representative purposes for reading assessment and the audiences that often request assessment information are presented in Table 1.

The question of why we assess reading is answered in different ways because the natures of reading instruction and reading assessment are influenced by the larger society in which students, teachers, and schools work. Consider that the successful teaching and learning of reading are informed by diverse theories and bodies of research. These theories emanate from domains of knowledge that include cognitive psychology, developmental psychology, linguistics, pedagogy, sociology, anthropology, and critical theory. Each theory may suggest different priorities for reading

TABLE 1 Representative Audiences and Purposes for Reading Assessment	
Audience for Assessment	Purpose for Assessment
Students	• To report on learning and communicate progress • To motivate and encourage • To learn about assessment and how to self-assess • To build independence in reading
Teachers	• To determine the nature of student learning • To inform instruction • To evaluate students and construct grades • To diagnose students' strengths and weaknesses in reading
Parents	• To be informed about children's achievements • To help connect home and school efforts to support children's reading
School administrators	• To determine the reading program's effectiveness • To prove school and teacher accountability
Politicians	• To establish accountability of schools • To inform the public of school progress
Taxpayers	• To demonstrate that tax dollars are well spent

Note. Modified from *Understanding and Using Reading Assessment, K–12* (p. 6), by P. Afflerbach, 2007, Newark, DE: International Reading Association. Copyright 2007 by the International Reading Association.

instruction and reading assessment, which will signal different purposes for doing reading assessment. For example, cognitive psychology provides evidence of the importance of reading skills and strategies, whereas research in motivation provides evidence of the need to engage students to help them develop as independent, committed readers (Afflerbach, Pearson, & Paris, 2008; Guthrie & Wigfield, 1997). A successful reading program has varied, important outcomes that should include students' growth in the ability to use reading skills and strategies as well as students' increased motivation to read. Reading assessment must have strong connections to these outcomes and describe them well.

The assessment of reading takes place in a context that is influenced by social and political forces. There are assessment practices that may be favored politically, practiced locally, widely supported, or widely questioned. Legislators, taxpayers, parents, school administrators, teachers, and students may all claim legitimately that part of the question of why we assess reading is answered: to provide useful information. However, "useful information" varies, from the parent seeking assessment information that will help coordinate classroom and home reading efforts, to the legislator seeking districtwide reading assessment information in anticipation of an upcoming vote for school funding. In these contexts, each purpose for reading assessment must have the potential end result of the betterment of student reading. Ideally, one group's need for particular reading assessment information should not displace another group's need. The standard that assessment will help improve the teaching and learning of reading should help us determine our reading assessment priorities in all cases.

What Do We Assess When We Assess Reading? The Focus of Assessment

Asking ourselves about what we assess helps us focus on the nature and goals of the reading instruction program and the relationship of reading instruction to reading assessment. The answer may demonstrate that our conceptualization of reading achievement, as reflected in the reading assessments used, is broad or narrow. The answer may help us determine whether the diverse goals of reading instruction are adequately reflected in the regimen of assessments that is intended to measure progress toward those goals. Or, the answer may indicate that whereas school district standards and the curriculum conceptualize reading development broadly, reading assessment measures it narrowly. We should plan to assess what we plan to teach.

Effective instruction contributes to the development of students' reading skills and strategies, motivation, and commitment to reading. Effective instruction can broaden students' conceptualization of reading as contributing to success in life. Given the characteristics of successful readers, the array of reasons for reading, and the diverse outcomes of successful reading instruction, should we expect reading assessment to be similarly broad? Does our assessment describe the many beneficial outcomes of becoming a better reader? How are all the important outcomes of reading instruction weighted in relation to the assessment that is conducted in states, districts, schools, and classrooms? An examination of popular reading assessments reveals that there are clear gaps between the rhetoric of why reading is important and what is assessed.

Most reading assessments focus narrowly on one set of important reading outcomes: the cognitive skills and strategies of reading. We are familiar with these outcomes because of our experiences with them in the classroom as teachers and former students. Phonemic awareness, phonics, sight word recognition, and fluency (National Institute of Child Health and Human Development [NICHD], 2000), as well as vocabulary knowledge (Stahl & Bravo, 2010) and literal and inferential comprehension (Snow, 2002), contribute to reading success. Although these are all important elements of successful student reading, they do not fully represent the growth and development that students experience in exemplary reading programs (Afflerbach, Cho, Kim, & Clark, 2010). For example, few reading assessments measure changes in or maintenance of student motivation to read or the range of students' social uses of reading. Many reading assessments sample a small portion of student accomplishment and growth—and by implication, teacher and school success. Bracey (2001) notes that the most consequential type of reading assessment, standardized tests, regularly misses the following outcomes of effective teaching and student learning: *"creativity, critical thinking, resilience, motivation, persistence, humor, reliability, enthusiasm, civic-mindedness, self-awareness, self-discipline, empathy, leadership,* and *compassion"* (p. 158). If we want reading assessment to mirror students' accomplishments, we must avoid reading assessment practice that provides, at best, only a partial reflection of those accomplishments.

The question of what we assess when we assess reading must be asked because it can help us become better at assessment. This question helps us prioritize our reading instruction goals and focus on the most appropriate assessment materials and procedures. Schools use an array of assessments conducted across the school year, from reading inventories at the beginning of the year to standardized, norm-referenced tests at the end of the year. An accounting is necessary to optimize this variety of assessments that are intended to serve different audiences and purposes. When our reading assessments include those mandated by the district, the state, and the federal government and those selected by teachers in schools, an assessment inventory can help us better understand the relationship between the things that a school community values in relation to students' reading development and what is actually assessed. A sample reading assessment inventory, which may be used to investigate the variety, breadth, and focus of assessment, is presented in Figure 1. A reading assessment inventory allows us to rank assessment in terms of the match between our teaching and learning priorities and time demands. An assessment inventory helps us compare what is with what could be. This information may be used to create and enact an ac-

Assessment Type	Assessment is a measure of students'...					
	Cognitive Reading Strategies and Skills	Motivation for Reading	Social Uses of Reading	Independence in Reading	Using Reading in Collaborative Learning Environments	Choosing Reading Over Attractive Alternatives
Tests and quizzes	X					
Portfolios	X	X	X	X	X	X
Performance assessments	X		X	X	X	
Teacher questions	X	X	X		X	X
Reading inventories	X					

X = demonstrated ability of a particular type of reading assessment to serve the indicated purpose. From *Understanding and Using Reading Assessment, K–12* (p. 9), by P. Afflerbach, 2007, Newark, DE: International Reading Association. Copyright 2007 by the International Reading Association.

tion plan with the goal of achieving better alignment among valued and agreed-upon outcomes of reading instruction, what is taught, and what is assessed.

How, Where, and When Do We Assess Reading?

The determination of why we assess and what we assess must be followed by informed decisions of how best to examine and evaluate students' reading development. Indeed, the majority of this book addresses the different means for assessing students' reading. Part and parcel of a description of how to assess reading is the determination of where and when such assessment should occur. This is the point where the logical relationship among why we assess, what we assess, and how we assess should be evident. If we assess students' reading comprehension skills and strategies to determine the general success of a districtwide reading program, year-end standardized and norm-referenced tests may be the first choice of some educational decision makers. Such a test, administered in the last month of the school year, seems well suited to the task. Test scores tell us whether certain cognitive skills and strategies have been learned. In contrast, if we assess individual students' progress to gauge the effectiveness of daily reading lessons, our assessment must be sensitive to the detailed goals of the lessons, and the information provided by the assessment must be immediately useful. Here, we could focus on questions about the contents of the chapter being read, with students' responses providing formative assessment information.

Just as reading assessment should be matched to particular purposes and audiences, how we assess students' reading achievement must be informed by the nature of the reading we expect of them. We are beneficiaries of considerable knowledge about the complexities of reading and the manner in which accomplished student readers develop (Guthrie, Wigfield, & You, in press; VanSledright, 2010). Much of the act of reading has been examined and described in detail, and research reminds us that reading is a stunning and sometimes arduous human accomplishment. Although we are far from any claim that we know all we need to know about reading, our detailed understanding of reading and how it develops should be reflected in our assessments. For example, the value and necessity of learning phonics, or the correspondence between speech sounds and printed letters, is well documented. It follows from this fact that reading assessment should include materials and procedures that allow students to demonstrate their knowledge and use of phonics, where developmentally appropriate. We have many useful approaches to conducting the assessment of students' phonics knowledge. We can ask students to tell us the sounds that different letters make. We can ask students to circle letters or groups of letters that correspond to speech sounds that they hear. We can provide students with exercises in which they circle the words that begin with the same sound as a printed letter. We can have students identify the sounds in words contained in the classroom word wall. We can analyze their spelling.

In contrast, how we assess other reading skills and strategies would appear less well developed. We know that the processes of reading history, reading science, and reading literature share common strategies (Pressley & Afflerbach, 1995), such as determining important vocabulary and synthesizing information. Yet, reading in each of the content areas also demands unique reading strategies (Bråten, Strømsø, & Britt, 2009; VanSledright, 2002). There is limited use of reading assessment that is directly informed by our most recent knowledge of accomplished reading in content areas. We know that performance assessments of reading in the content areas can provide valuable information related to students' reading achievement, teachers' accountability, and schools' goodness (Baxter & Glaser, 1998). We know that authentic assessments of reading are developed, in part, as a reaction to the limitations of multiple-choice, machine-scored tests of reading (Afflerbach, 2005). Unfortunately, such promising assessments have not made inroads to the point that these assessments are regularly called on to tell the story of students' reading achievement. The aggregate results of current reading assessments may thus misrepresent the varied and complex ways in which students have developed as readers. Understanding and using reading assessments demands that we understand the available assessment materials and procedures and that we choose and use them expertly.

Defining *Reading* Is Central to Useful Reading Assessment

Reading assessment must demonstrate clear and direct links to a detailed definition of what reading is. The detail and richness of this definition will figure largely in the process of determining the validity and usefulness of all reading assessments. In this section, my intent is twofold: to describe the process with which I construct a definition of *reading* and to provide a sufficiently detailed definition of *reading*. This description of reading will serve as a reality check for my discussion of various reading assessment materials and procedures. Throughout this book, these assessments must map clearly onto my definition of *reading*. If not, then my definition or my choice of assessment is faulty. The definition of *reading* should inform the goals of reading instruction and the reading assessment program that is developed for a particular classroom, grade, school, school district, or state. We are not wanting for definitions and descriptions of reading, but it is exceedingly difficult to create a consensus definition with which all teachers, parents, students, legislators, and the general public agree. This creates a challenging situation in which there is universal agreement about the importance of reading but not universal agreement on what reading is, how children learn to read, and how reading is best taught and fostered.

I construct my definition of *reading* from several sources. These sources include reading research, state and district standards for reading, recent federal law, and frameworks from national and international assessments of reading. My definition also reflects the knowledge that I have developed as a teacher and researcher of reading, as a parent, and as an experienced reader. In forming this definition, I create the necessary means for critiquing and choosing the types and forms of reading assessment that I examine in this book. I encourage readers to take the time to create a definition of *reading*, for this personalization of the reading assessment context allows us to focus on the most valued aspects of our instruction and student learning, which then provides us the opportunity to compare our reading assessment plans with instructional reading programs. Further, this personalization allows us to develop reading assessments that are best suited to the goals we bring to our reading instruction. It also places us in a strong position from which we may advocate for the assessment of aspects of reading that may be missing or underrepresented in an existing school, district, or state reading assessment program.

To the degree that we have faith in our professional knowledge of reading, this knowledge should inform our conceptualization of reading and students' reading development. Thus, I believe that it is imperative that teachers compare their understandings of what reading is with my definition of *reading* and with others' definitions. Reading assessment can be too narrowly focused and may miss aspects of students' development that are keys to lifelong, accomplished reading. Part of a teacher's prerogative is to augment any definition of *reading* (and reading assessment) that is inherited or mandated in the classroom with his or her professional knowledge.

As mentioned previously, I use several sources of information to build a definition of *reading* that I believe is sufficient to guide my efforts. The definition draws from different traditions of knowledge about reading. First, I refer to my own understanding of reading: Reading is a dynamic and complex process (Afflerbach & Cho, 2009; Pressley & Afflerbach, 1995) that involves skills, strategies, and prior knowledge. Reading is developmental in nature (Alexander, 2005) and consists of identifiable components (e.g., word recognition, comprehension) that interact to make reading successful. Reading development and success are influenced by motivation (Guthrie et al., in press), self-esteem (Chapman & Tunmer, 2003), and prior reading experiences (R.C. Anderson & Pearson, 1984). Hoping to add to this developing definition, I next consult *The Literacy Dictionary: The Vocabulary of Reading and Writing* (Harris & Hodges, 1995). Under the entry for *reading*, there are no less than 20 different takes on the meaning of the word, from Plato to the present. As noted in this dictionary, reading has been conceptualized as a "perceptual act" (p. 206), with this understanding more recently augmented by our knowledge that cognition occurs when we read and that readers actively use skills and strategies to construct meaning. Adding to our understanding of reading is the idea that it is a "social event" (p. 207) that is socially situated. We read, using skills and strategies, in relation to our intellectual and social goals.

Next, I consider reading as defined in the frameworks of two major national and international reading assessments. These frameworks have the advantage of not only describing reading but also describing it in relation to reading assessment. The reading framework for the 2009 NAEP (National Assessment Governing Board, 2009) derives from expert consensus on the nature of reading and defines *reading* in the following manner:

> Reading is an active and complex process that involves:
> - Understanding written text.
> - Developing and interpreting meaning.
> - Using meaning as appropriate to type of text, purpose, and situation. (p. iv)

The NAEP framework portrays reading as a dynamic and goal-oriented process that involves skills, strategies, prior knowledge, and the reader's purpose. I am encouraged when I read this portrayal of reading related to such a high-profile test because the framework appears to cover important aspects of reading and shares much with what I believe is an accurate representation of reading.

A dynamic, strategic, and goal-oriented conceptualization of reading also serves as a foundation for the Program for International Student Assessment (PISA), which is used to assess reading achievement in 74 countries (Organisation for Economic Co-operation and Development [OECD], 2011). The PISA framework provides further details on the nature of reading and anticipates the types of reading assessment that are necessary to gauge student growth in reading across the school year: "The capacity of an individual to understand, use, reflect on and engage with written texts in order to achieve his/her goals, to develop his/her knowledge and potential, and to participate in society" (OECD, 2010, p. 23). This further explanation of reading in relation to the PISA framework is critical, in my opinion, for built into this definition of *reading* are reader motives and the subtexts for why we read and what we read. This definition acknowledges that we read to do things and that we must read critically in a world that is swimming in information.

We can appreciate the complexity and accomplishment in reading that the NAEP and PISA reading frameworks describe. However, there is one major wrinkle. The NAEP (conducted at 4th, 8th, and 12th grades) and the PISA (conducted with 15-year-old students) are based on the premise that the majority of students who take the tests are capable of reading. The majority of these students can decode language, recognize words, read fluently, identify the concepts that are represented by vocabulary words, comprehend, and critically evaluate. The challenge, then, is to create a definition of *reading* that accommodates the development that students undergo as they learn to read. We are fortunate to have considerable research information related to the development of reading ability in young children (Clay, 1979; Gamse, Jacob, Horst, Boulay, & Unlu, 2008; Heath, 1983; Metsala & Ehri, 1998; Wagner & Torgesen, 1987). We also have recent research syntheses that describe the importance of particular reading and language knowledge in helping students learn to read and continue their development as readers (NICHD, 2000). This research demonstrates that success in reading is attributable, in part, to the development of skills and strategies related to phonemic awareness, phonics, fluency, vocabulary, and comprehension. Each of these areas contains developmental benchmarks and trajectories that are helpful to me as I construct an account of successful student reading.

At this point, my definition of *reading* includes the ideas that we read to construct meaning and that we must use particular skills and strategies to do so (Afflerbach et al., 2008). These skills and strategies are developmental in nature. My experiences as a teacher and as a parent remind me that cognitive skills and strategies are central to success in reading, but they do not guarantee success. When I compare my evolving definition with what I know about reading and what I value as important outcomes of reading instruction, I find that there are several missing pieces. They include students' motivation to choose to read, whether it is in the face of what might be attractive alternatives (e.g., Facebook, soccer, television), and students' motivation to persevere with reading when the going gets tough. Another missing piece is how reading experience and reading accomplishment make ongoing contributions to a student's personality development and sense of self. My hope for all students is that they become lifelong, committed readers, and if reading instruction helps them do so, that is an important accomplishment. I certainly would like part of my reading assessment plan to describe this feat.

As I contemplate the nature of reading and what is currently assessed, I am reminded of the need to develop assessments that measure the complexity of student achievement. Too often, reading assessment seems to focus on the measurement of thin accomplishments while missing the opportunity for detailed accounting of rich reading growth (Davis, 1998). For example, we might ask students to determine the main idea of a text that describes the economic concept of opportunity cost. Determining the main idea is an important reading ability, but it is relatively constrained if we compare it with reading assessment that asks students to apply the main idea related to opportunity cost to an economic decision that the student makes (e.g., How should I spend my allowance? How should I spend this $10 bill that I found in my laundry?) to explain the relation of the main idea to other important economic concepts, or to critique the author's stance toward the main idea.

As to my definition of *reading*, I am confident that it includes a breadth of conceptualization that informs my reading instruction goals and the nature of the reading assessments I will use: *Reading is the act of constructing meaning from text. We use skills, strategies, and prior knowledge, all of which are developmental in nature, to understand what we read. The act of reading is supported by reader motivation and positive reader affect. We read to help us achieve our goals, within and outside of school.*

In summary, the definition of *reading* that we construct must reflect an accurate understanding of what reading is, for this definition becomes a benchmark for judging reading assessments in our classrooms. We must assess our assessments to determine if they get into the nooks and crannies of students' strengths and needs and students' immediate and long-lasting achievements in reading. We must build, maintain, and revise our understandings of what reading is to make informed decisions about the quality of our reading assessments.

A Model of Reading Assessment

Just as we need a clear definition of *reading* to help us determine what we must assess, we also need a clear understanding of how assessment works so that we can develop informed reading assessment materials and procedures. *Knowing What Students Know: The Science and Design of Educational Assessment* (Pellegrino, Chudowsky, & Glaser, 2001) describes the integral components of successful assessment materials and procedures. The authors describe three requisite components of accurate and useful assessment: cognition, observation, and interpretation. We touch on aspects of this model whenever we assess, although we may not have considered them in such formal terms.

The cognition component of reading assessment focuses on the skills and strategies used by students as they develop as readers. To the degree that we understand what developing students do when they read, we can use this information to specify the things we would like to assess. We have research related to particular cognitive aspects of reading: the skills and strategies that students use to decode and understand words and construct meaning. This research contributes to the building of detailed theoretical constructs that reflect successful reading, which in turn informs our instruction. For example, we know that the ability to summarize a text is an important comprehension strategy (Snow, 2002) that is frequently applied by successful student readers in school reading tasks. Research provides considerable detail on the nature of summarization strategies (Pressley & Afflerbach, 1995), the usefulness of the strategies, and the manner in which they are used in classrooms (Berkeley, Mastopieri, & Scruggs, 2011; Block & Pressley, 2002). We know that students must be able to ignore unimportant text information and recognize and synthesize important text information, using processes that determine connections, similarities, and repetitions within the text. Students must be able to clearly synthesize and state the content and the purpose of the text read. This contributes to a clear sense of what we want students to learn and how we might teach them. Once a text is summarized, it can be used in the creation of student work or to challenge another text (Luke, 1994). In this case, reading strategy research clearly describes the cognitive details of summarization.

Our ability to describe the detailed nature of summarization and other important aspects of reading should inform the second component of our reading assessment model: observation. The observation component of reading assessment must accurately represent our knowledge related to the domains of reading and assessment. As research contributes to our evolving understanding of how reading works, a concurrent evolution is taking place in educational measurement. That is, theories of how to assess and evaluate student progress are themselves informed by research in assessment and educational measurement. This work has contributed to an expanded conceptualization of how we can assess those things that we deem critical for reading success. Applied to summarizing text, we can think about reading assessments that create situations that reflect classroom reading practice and require students to use summarization strategies:

- Do we ask students to construct a summary as opposed to choosing the correct summary in a multiple-choice format?
- Do our assessments allow for different interpretations of the text or a single, "correct" meaning?
- Do we ask for retellings of text that can be checked against a detailed list of the text's contents?
- Do we ask for accounts of several related texts?
- Are summarization assessment tasks related to the types of summarization regularly done in the classroom?

The observation component of the assessment model reminds us that an effective assessment clearly reflects our understanding of how students read in relation to a particular task, text, and setting. This component will also relate to the measurement possibilities that are available to help us observe and record such learning and knowledge. Related to the nature of assessments, what are our options and alternatives? We may consider constructed-response questions, think-alouds, short fill-in responses, and answers to questions as the means to gather and then observe students' work with summarization. Or, we may require students to perform tasks in which success is contingent, in part, on the students' ability to summarize text. Our analysis of the text that students read tells us that their summaries should include specific information, along with information that is attributed to individual differences in prior knowledge for the text topic. A final consideration focuses on what we can and should add to assessing the cognitive—in this case, summarization:

- What noncognitive factors may serve to support students' summaries?
- Do we assess changes in students' motivation to read?
- Do we assess changes in students' self-concepts as readers?
- Do we assess the attributions that readers make for their performances?
- Do we do so in both formative and summative assessments?

Interpretation is the third component of Pellegrino et al.'s (2001) assessment model. Assessment is always related to acts of inference (Johnston, 1987). So far, we have designed an assessment that focuses on students' summarization ability, combining our understandings of reading and assessment. One product of this process is the assessment results themselves. Our faith in our understanding of the nature of summarization and our faith in the assessment materials and procedures that we have developed to assess summarization figure largely in the faith we have in the inferences that we then make about student achievement and ability.

All reading assessment involves interpretation. Assessment done well allows us to make inferences, from students' performances in a particular place and time on an assessment task, about the more broad abilities and talents that are related to the performances. This basic process of reading assessment, generalizing to students' reading performances from a sample of their reading, demands that our inferences be accurate and born of high confidence. The importance of accurate inferences from valid assessment information cannot be understated, given that we assess reading to help students become better readers. However, we are only able to make inferences about those things that we sample. An incomplete assessment agenda, including one that ignores how students develop in terms of motivation, perseverance, and self-esteem in relation to reading, will limit the inferences that we can make about students' reading development, our own effectiveness, and the value of the reading curriculum.

The helpful model of assessment proposed by Pellegrino and colleagues (2001) focuses on cognition as the important aspect of learning and instructional outcomes. However, in relation to the model, we can conceptualize reading assessment with other aspects of reading besides those that are cognitive. We can determine that students' motivations, self-esteem, and developing sense of the self as a reader are important. In such instances, we must develop assessments with the rigor and attention to detail that are equivalent to those that measure cognitive skill and strategy growth. An assessment of students' motivations for reading must demonstrate our clear understanding of the construct of motivation, specify what aspects of motivation are to be assessed, inform the development of the observation instrument, and guide our interpretation of results:

- Do our high school students choose reading over attractive alternatives?
- Do middle school students discuss books at lunch?
- When asking parents for a birthday present, would second graders ever ask for a book?

Having considered the three elements of cognition, observation, and interpretation separately, it is important to stress that we must consider each of these components separately and then in relation to one another. As we contemplate what happens when students summarize text, we must think about the nature of an assessment that would capture and describe this important reading ability. Also, we must think of the interpretations and inferences that we can and cannot make about students' reading and summarization, based on our understanding of reading and the assessment we have planned.

Determining the Suitability of Reading Assessment: The CURRV Model

Our final consideration for this chapter is the suitability of reading assessments:

- What is the optimal mix of reading assessments that we use across a school year?
- How do we choose one assessment over another, given our limited resources?
- On what basis can decisions about the suitability of a reading assessment be made?

The CURRV model (Leipzig & Afflerbach, 2000) requires us to examine a reading assessment with five criteria to determine if it is appropriate for measuring and describing our students' learning. This model supports us in understanding and using reading assessment and allows us to examine the (1) *consequences*, (2) *usefulness*, (3) *roles* and responsibilities, (4) *reliability*, and (5) *validity* of a reading assessment. The knowledge gained from applying the CURRV model brings us closer to an informed use of reading assessment.

TABLE 2
**The CURRV Model's[a] Framework: Questions to Help Determine
the Suitability of a Reading Assessment**

- What are the positive consequences of the use of this assessment?
- What are the negative consequences of the use of this assessment?
- What is the usefulness of this assessment to teachers, students, and others?
- What are the specific roles and responsibilities for the teachers, students, and administrators associated with this assessment?
- What are the reliability issues related to this assessment?
- What are the validity issues related to this assessment?

CURRV = *consequences, usefulness, roles* and responsibilities, *reliability,* and *validity.* From *Understanding and Using Reading Assessment, K–12* (p. 18), by P. Afflerbach, 2007, Newark, DE: International Reading Association. Copyright 2007 by the International Reading Association.
[a]"Determining the Suitability of Assessments: Using the CURRV Framework," by D.H. Leipzig and P. Afflerbach, 2000, in L. Baker, M.J. Dreher, and J.T. Guthrie (Eds.), *Engaging Young Readers: Promoting Achievement and Motivation* (pp. 159–187), New York: Guilford.

The CURRV model (Leipzig & Afflerbach, 2000) was developed, in part, as a reaction to the historical practice of using only the criteria of reliability and validity to argue for the quality of reading assessments. Reliability and validity are traditional and critical aspects of assessment. Yet, they are psychometric principles that cannot help us ultimately determine whether an assessment is suitable for particular teachers, their students, and specific reading situations. The CURRV model retains the criteria of reliability and validity and adds three necessary considerations:

1. What are the consequences of the reading assessment?
2. What is the usefulness of the reading assessment?
3. What are the roles and responsibilities related to effectively using the reading assessment?

The five different components of the model allow us to analyze different reading assessments and make choices and suggestions based on our understandings of the nature, strengths, and weaknesses of these assessments. The model allows us to judge the situational appropriateness of an assessment. A sampling of the questions that the CURRV model allows us to ask of a reading assessment is presented in Table 2.

Consequences of Assessment

All reading assessments have consequences. If we return to the question of why we assess, we are reminded that a reading assessment must have the primary consequence of helping students continue their development as readers. Yet, not all reading assessments may effect this change. We must consider all of the possible consequences of a reading assessment, positive or negative. Students may experience immediate and continual support in their learning to read as a consequence of careful classroom-based assessment. High-quality reading assessment will help them become better readers. They may feel increased self-esteem as readers when they receive high-stakes test scores that demonstrate their learning. Students could become motivated to read more as a result of encouraging and accurate teacher feedback. In contrast, students may lose class time for reading because of time being reallocated to test preparation. Inappropriate assessment will not provide the type of information that best shapes classroom instruction to students' immediate and long-term needs. A teacher's insensitivity to a student's response to a question stifles engagement. Additionally, a history of low test scores and other reading assessment feedback may teach students to avoid reading. Ultimately, their motivation to read suffers.

The positive or negative consequences of different types of reading assessments influence teachers. Reading inventories and careful teacher questioning provide important information with which accomplished teachers practice the art of teaching. These assessments allow teachers to adjust instruction and influence student learning in a dynamic manner. Performance assessments allow a teacher to better understand the depth and breadth of student achievement related to content area reading and learning. High test scores garner a salary increase for some teachers and may help build parental and community support for teachers and schools. In contrast, inappropriate assessments take away valuable class time from the teaching of reading without yielding valuable information. Curricular decisions made in relation to high-stakes tests may constrict the curriculum: Both the content of what is taught in reading blocks and the time to teach it shrink. Assessing our assessments from the perspective of their intended and unintended consequences will help us determine the suitability of reading assessments for the particular teachers and students involved in particular reading tasks.

Usefulness of Assessment

A second aspect of the suitability of a reading assessment, closely related to consequences, is the usefulness of the assessment. If the criterion of usefulness were applied to the mix of reading assessments selected and mandated in schools, the assessment landscape might look different. The array of assessments that exist in many classrooms represents a legacy of tradition and habit, insight and oversight. Reading assessments accompany districtwide initiatives and are mandated under federal and state laws. Some are developed by individual teachers, and others are inherited from earlier times. There may be no strategy for coordinating reading assessment efforts. Thus, it is important to take stock of available assessments so that they might be considered in terms of their usefulness.

The array of reading assessments may or may not be broad enough to cover the range of student ability and achievement that exists in our classrooms. A useful assessment would be one that allows the teacher to gather accurate and usable information about students' reading. As teachers, we need reading assessments that allow us to address the different audiences for the information garnered. We need assessments that provide both formative and summative information. We need assessments that focus on the processes and products of student reading. We also need assessments that are sensitive to the breadth and depth of students' accomplishments in reading at the different levels of reading achievement.

A focus on the usefulness of reading assessment allows for decision making about necessary assessments and those that are expendable. Using criteria for usefulness, including how well the assessment describes student achievement, how easily the assessment information is communicated, and how well the assessment works with a particular teacher's immediate and long-term goals, can help us rank reading assessments. This ranking according to usefulness then allows us to make sometimes difficult decisions about which assessments are first-order and keepers, which are optional, and which we might do well without. Please note that in some of the chapters that follow, I combine our consideration of the consequences and uses for particular assessments as guided by the CURRV framework because they are tightly interwoven.

Roles and Responsibilities Related to Assessment

The third component of the CURRV framework (Leipzig & Afflerbach, 2000) reminds us that our use of reading assessments must be accompanied by a clear understanding of the related roles and responsibilities. Knowing what we must do to optimize the use of a particular assessment helps us prepare professionally and contributes to our informed use of particular assessments. It is especially important to focus on the roles and responsibilities created by reading assessments when we are considering moving beyond the traditional and familiar forms of reading assessment. For example, teachers' roles and responsibilities related to testing include reminding students to take the tests seriously, familiarizing students with the tests' formats, and following the tests' standardized administration procedures. Students are responsible for adopting a serious approach to the tests and preparing to take them.

All assessments demand attention to specific roles and responsibilities. Teachers must play the role of educator when new assessment materials and procedures are used. For example, performance assessments can offer distinct advantages over many machine-scored, multiple-choice tests because the performance assessments are capable of describing detailed student learning and achievement. Not all parents are aware of this fact, and teachers may be charged with informing parents about the potential advantages of performance assessments. In addition to the need to communicate these potential advantages to parents, we must become familiar with the important components of different reading assessments. If we adopt a series of performance assessments to measure students' reading and learning in the content areas, then we must be able to use rubrics to score students' complex performances. In addition, we should be able to use rubrics to help students anticipate the nature of the performance expected of them and to provide models for student learning. We should also be prepared to use performance assessments and rubrics to help students develop their self-assessment abilities (Afflerbach, 2002a).

Reliability of Assessment

The reliability of a reading assessment relates to the accuracy or precision of the assessment instrument and process (Kerlinger, 1986). When we assess students, we generate information from which we want to make inferences about the students' learning and performances. Reliability theory posits that the information we gather through assessment is comprised of two components: (1) the true component, which reflects the reality of the student's reading achievement; and (2) the error component, which signals the part of an assessment result that does not reflect the student's reading achievement. We must be vigilant in recognizing and controlling the error component. If we recall the model of assessment presented by Pellegrino and colleagues (2001), we can immediately appreciate the need for high reliability. If our assessments are unreliable, then the inferences we make about our students' learning and achievements may be erroneous and ultimately worthless. We may miss a student's need for developing critical reading strategies, mistakenly teach decoding skills to a student who already has them, or fail to recognize an increase in a student's motivation to read.

Standardized testing provides a paradigm, of sorts, for reliability. Considerable effort is placed into the development of such tests to reduce the error of measurement that is present in all assessments. The application of reliability theory to assessments other than standardized tests is an important and necessary practice. Teachers must strive to determine that their assessment practices are consistent and focused on the important aspects of student learning. The goals of evenhandedness in dealing with different students and of clear and fair communication with our reading assessments are imperative. When we assess student reading, we must have confidence in the reliability of our assessment. Otherwise, our assessment information is not worth consulting.

Validity of Assessment

The fifth component of the CURRV model (Leipzig & Afflerbach, 2000) is validity (Messick, 1989). In addition to the voluminous research and theory related to the validity of assessment, there is the intuitive test: We want our assessment efforts to matter, and we must ask questions related to validity before we invest valuable time in any assessment. There are several types of validity. For our purposes here, it is important to consider the construct validity and ecological validity of a reading assessment. (Within the chapters, I only discuss the particular forms of validity that pertain to the chapter topics.)

How do we conceptualize reading? The construct of reading represents our best theory of what reading is. If we view reading as a series of skills and strategies, then we likely believe that phonemic awareness and reading comprehension are critical to students' development as readers. We should also make every effort to assess students' growth and achievement related to their comprehension and phonemic awareness. If we believe that reading achievement can be influenced by student motivation, then we should consider a reading curriculum that addresses student readers' motivation. We should also develop assessments that help us understand growth in student motivation, in relation to the construct of reading. When we invest time in ascertaining the links between our assessment, curriculum, standards, and constructs, we may arrive at the determination of construct validity for an assessment without surprise.

An additional consideration is ecological validity. Neisser (1976) uses the term to refer to the extent that a theory can tell us something about what people do in real and significant situations. An application to assessment requires us to focus on the degree to which an assessment item, a series of items, and tasks reflect what students do when they read in the classroom. Schmuckler (2001) describes ecological validity as a test of "whether or not one can generalize from observed behavior in the laboratory to natural behavior in the world" (p. 419). This description leads us to two questions:

1. Does student work on an assessment generalize to what is normally done in the classroom?

2. Does student work in the classroom generalize to important tasks and accomplishments in the world outside the classroom?

An example of reading assessments with contrasting ecological validity might include a reading inventory conducted while a student reads orally from a self-chosen text, and a series of comprehension questions that follow a two-paragraph reading selection on a standardized, norm-referenced reading test. A talented teacher conducting a reading inventory can, in this instance, gather information from a student reading texts that are part of the school curriculum and that are read in a normal manner, reflecting the classroom routine. One challenge to ecological validity might be that if a student does not regularly read orally, the demand of doing so compromises the assessment's validity. Compare this with the ecological validity of a multiple-choice, machine-scored reading test. There may be a very limited relationship between daily classroom reading instruction routines and students' reading behaviors, except for those classrooms where test preparation is a focus, with test-like reading materials and assessments used regularly. When the reading and reading-related tasks demanded on an assessment vary greatly from the reading and reading-related tasks done regularly in the classroom, we may see considerable challenges to the notion of ecological validity.

The Plan for This Book

The CURRV framework (Leipzig & Afflerbach, 2000) described in this chapter is used as an organizing principle for the remainder of the book. That is, subsequent chapters focus on particular types of reading assessment, including reading inventories, teacher questioning, portfolios, performance assessments, and high-stakes tests. These chapters begin with a brief introduction and historical overview of the particular assessment, followed by a detailed accounting of the characteristics of the assessment. We then examine the consequences, usefulness, roles and responsibilities, reliability, and validity of each type of assessment as it is situated in a particular teacher's classroom. The consideration of these different types of reading assessment is done in relation to the reading development that most students experience across their school careers. Thus, we determine the suitability of an assessment in relation to students' development as readers. In addition, Chapter 6 focuses on RTI and early reading assessment. In the chapter, I describe the role of assessment in RTI. Then, I focus on two representative early reading assessments that have distinct differences in how they represent reading and in the nature of the assessment information they provide. Finally, Chapters 8 and 9 focus on important issues that are not given the attention they deserve: how reading development other than cognitive skill and strategy growth may be assessed and the accommodation of learners in reading assessment.

The array of reading assessments now available to teachers and students is broad. To this end, I acknowledge that successful reading assessment programs sample and choose from this wide assortment and tailor these assessments to the programs' particular needs. It is not uncommon to encounter individualistic approaches to portfolios and performance assessment, hybrid assessments that combine positive features of checklists and performance assessment, and diverse approaches to the omnipresent issues that surround high-stakes testing. Thus, my chapter-by-chapter approach to understanding and using reading assessments may appear artificial in some respects. Guiding my plan here is the goal of presenting each assessment separately and providing details related to the assessment, while noting the ways in which it might be complemented by other, valuable reading assessments.

Throughout this book, issues are framed in relation to the educational, social, and political factors that exert varied degrees of influence on reading assessment. There are sharp divides in how different stakeholders, from teachers to legislators, conceptualize reading, the teaching of reading, and reading achievement. It follows that there are disparate ideas related to the nature and role of reading assessment. I attempt to represent reading assessment in relation to the frames of reference and agendas that different people bring to the assessment arena, for consideration of any reading assessment divorced from the school and societal contexts in which it is used does not pass the reality test. Further, I attempt to represent the thinking and rationale behind particular reading assessment initiatives and programs. My purpose here is to anchor reading assessment to the classrooms and the society in which our students read and are assessed. Each chapter ends with a section called "Enhancing Your Understanding," in which I provide questions and tasks that invite the readers of this book to apply the knowledge they gain from each chapter to their own assessment practices.

Each chapter is followed by a section called "Reading Assessment Snapshot." Each snapshot addresses an important reading assessment issue that pertains to some or all of the assessments covered in this book. For example, the reading assessment snapshots include examination of the distinctions between formative and summative assessments, confounds in reading assessment, technology and assessment, and task analyses of our assessments as a check on their suitability.

Throughout this book, I stress the need to examine reading assessment in relation to our current understanding of the reading process, students' development, and the culture of schooling. I reflect on Huey's (1908) observation, made over 100 years ago: "To completely analyze what we do when we read would almost be the acme of a psychologist's achievements, for it would be to describe very many of the most intricate workings of the human mind" (p. 6). When we are successful in our attempts to assess the range of students' development in reading and use this information to help our student readers thrive, we will have accomplished a similarly remarkable, and necessary, feat.

The Purpose and Intended Audiences for This Book

My purpose is to help readers understand and use reading assessments. Through reading this book, readers will become familiar with different types of reading assessments, and together we examine important issues in reading assessment. Never has there been a more promising time for the implementation and productive use of assessments to help us understand students' growth in reading. Yet, this promise is challenged by the frenzy of testing that daily threatens to change effective classroom teaching and assessment into a narrow, mechanistic approach to schooling. It is my hope that this book will help readers become familiar with the characteristics of different types of reading assessments and become accomplished in the assessment of reading. Herein, we consider the suitability of different reading assessments for particular purposes and audiences. In doing so, we consider the means for developing, conducting, and using reading assessments to help foster students' reading achievements.

This book is intended for those who are interested in developing a more detailed understanding of different reading assessments, their characteristics, their usefulness and possible consequences, and their requirements. As such, this book can be used in undergraduate and graduate teacher-preparation courses that focus on reading assessment. This book may also be useful in graduate courses that include a comprehensive overview of reading assessment materials and procedures. Finally, this book is inspired by and intended for K–12 teachers.

Summary

Using assessments well demands our knowledge and vigilance. The informed use of reading assessments may be accomplished when we attend to the issues discussed in this chapter. First, we must regularly ask the following questions:

- Why do we assess reading?
- What do we assess?
- How do we assess reading?

Second, all of our work in reading assessment must be guided by a detailed understanding and definition of what reading is and a clear conceptualization of reading assessment. We are fortunate that an evolving understanding of reading is paralleled by an evolving understanding of the manner in which we might best assess reading. A model of reading assessment provides general and useful guidelines for us to assess assessments. Finally, we must examine the suitability of a reading assessment. The psychometric standards of reliability and validity are central to any successful reading assessment. Yet, these aspects of assessment must share the stage with our consideration of the consequences, usefulness, and associated roles and responsibilities of particular reading assessments. Equipped with these important understandings of assessment, we are now ready to begin our consideration of the different types of reading assessments.

ENHANCING YOUR UNDERSTANDING

1. Chart an inference that you make from a reading assessment about a student's reading development. Where does the information that you use to make the inference come from? What degree of confidence do you have in the inference? How could you gather further, complementary information about the student and the inference?

2. Assess your assessments. Are there assessments that provide information about student reading that is not otherwise obtainable? Are there assessments that you cannot live without? Are there assessments that are not worth the time and effort put in them, in relation to the quality or type of information they provide?

3. Talk with your students about a particular assessment. Do they understand what it is? Do they understand how it works and why it is valuable?

4. Develop an assessment inventory. Identify the different types of reading assessments that are used in your classroom, grade, and school. Describe their frequency of use and their usefulness.

Task Analysis

How can we determine that student work within an assessment is clearly related to the specific reading skills, strategies, and attitudes that we teach and hope to measure? How can we determine that our assessment is clearly focused on the knowledge that students gain from reading? How can we be certain that what we ask students to do in a reading assessment is a legitimate request? Conducting an assessment task analysis can provide confidence that we are getting what we ask for from our assessments.

Effective assessment is aided by the process of piloting, or trying out, the assessment. The pilot phase of an assessment allows us to determine if the assessments we create or choose actually elicit particular student thinking and student work. We can walk through the very assessment tasks that we demand of our students. By taking the assessment ourselves, we become aware of what the assessment task demands of our students. We must also be sensitive to the developmental differences that influence our work on a task and our students' work on the same task.

A common result of a detailed task analysis is a realization of the necessary commitment of time and resources to create and use truly worthwhile assessments. We may determine that our "reading" assessments involve student capabilities that are not necessarily specific to reading. If students write to demonstrate what they have understood in a textbook chapter or are called on to verbalize their constructed understanding of a poem, we need to consider how writing and speaking figure in the assessment. In summary, task analysis is a critical part of assessment development and determining the congruence of an assessment with its purported purpose, or verifying that we are getting what we ask for.

CHAPTER 2

Reading Inventories

Students in our classrooms possess a complex array of reading skills and strategies. Students vary in their ability to recognize words, unlock word meanings, read fluently, comprehend text, and monitor the construction of meaning. Moreover, students exhibit differences in how they coordinate reading skills and strategies in an effort to understand what they read. Each of these reader characteristics is important for us to know for every student. Assessment that helps us understand and appreciate the diverse growth that students experience and the reading challenges that they face must be a priority in each classroom. Reading inventories provide us with the means to assess and evaluate many of these diverse aspects of students' reading performance and growth.

An inventory, according to the *Merriam-Webster* (2011a) online dictionary, is "an itemized list of current assets...a list of traits, preferences, attitudes, interests, or abilities used to evaluate personal characteristics or skills...the act or process of taking an inventory." Harris and Hodges (1995) define the term *reading inventory* as "a checklist or questionnaire for assessing reading interests, habits, books read, etc." (p. 211). In this chapter, I conceptualize the reading inventory assessment as a set of materials and procedures, ranging from commercially published reading inventories to teacher-designed and -conducted reading inventories. Reading inventories may vary in their origins and the depth and breadth of the information they can provide, and each may share theoretical bases and practical applications. Thus, I focus on the commonalities of these related reading assessments and note their differences.

A Brief History of Reading Inventories

Reading inventories, in one form or another, have existed for as long as teachers have been interested in better understanding their students' reading development. Teachers who carefully analyze their students' oral reading, check their students' fluency, encourage their students to retell what they have read, and ask a series of comprehension questions gather useful assessment information that helps inventory student reading behaviors and achievement. The popularity and history of reading inventories is a testament to their usefulness (Paris & Carpenter, 2003; Pikulski & Shanahan, 1982; Walpole & McKenna, 2006). Contemporary reading inventories can provide information related to each of the five target areas identified by the No Child Left Behind Act (NCLB; i.e., students' phonemic awareness, phonics, fluency, vocabulary, and comprehension), as developmentally appropriate. In addition, some inventories provide information on students' prior knowledge for particular texts and students' metacognitive processes. Typical components of reading inventories include graded word lists, graded passages that can be read orally or silently by the student or read aloud to the student, retelling rubrics, and comprehension questions.

A key feature of most inventories is the means to identify a student's independent, instructional, and frustration reading levels. *Independent* signifies an approximate reading level on which students can read successfully on their own, *instructional* suggests a reading level on which students can read successfully with a teacher's support, and *frustration* represents reading situations in which students will not be successful, with or without teacher support. The conceptualization of these levels is often traced to the work of Betts (1946), as is the idea of gauging a student's reading level in relation to text difficulty.

Although the characterization of independent, instructional, and frustration levels has been constant over the past 50+ years, students' performances in reading inventories should be examined in relation to our continually evolving knowledge of reading. How we interpret students' oral reading and comprehension-question performance should be informed by our most recent research understanding. In the following example, a student's oral reading includes rereading of words and clauses:

> *Text:* The former president bowed in gratitude to the hosts.
>
> *Student reads aloud:* The farmer president....The former president bowed in great....The former president bowed in gratitude to the hosts.

We can develop different interpretations of this student's reading using different lenses, polished by research and teaching knowledge, to explain the student's reading behavior. The reader may be considered needy, unable to get the text in a single reading. Words are repeated and sections reread, and there are substitution miscues, including *farmer* for *former*, and *great* for *gratitude*. The reading is not fluent. Alternatively, we can infer that the reader has important strategies based on the student noticing a reading processing difficulty (i.e., misreading particular words) and his or her rereading strategy as part of addressing the difficulty. This rereading, according to current conceptualizations of reading, indicates that the student is being metacognitive (Paris, 1983; Veenman, 2005). We infer that rereading is initiated by the student's realization that comprehension is not occurring to the degree that it must in relation to the reader's goal. We know the value of metacognition and self-corrections for students' reading, and our interpretation of reading inventory data derives from particular reading research and theory. The student must work toward accuracy and speed in reading, but underlying this performance is the student's clear focus on making meaning from the text.

Reading inventories build on our understanding that children are mindful users and processors of language and that the examination of their oral reading can shed light on how they use language to construct meaning (Betts, 1946; Clay, 2000; Goodman & Goodman, 1977). For example, miscue analysis (i.e., the examination of developing readers' oral reading, including their missteps and hesitations) emanates from a perspective that readers strive to make meaning from text. It is not expected that children will read text perfectly because few people, including expert readers, do so. Careful attention to the miscues and processes that are part of oral reading can illuminate those aspects of students' language processing that are working smoothly and those that need further development. Moreover, the process-oriented assessment provides an opportunity to observe the interaction and coordination of different reading skills and strategies that might otherwise be assessed separately, in piecemeal fashion. Thus, research and assessment converge in inventories around the idea that reading is interactive, with the goal of the construction of meaning. The assumption is that most student readers are mindful processors of information who work with specific goals, and our understanding of students' performance on a reading inventory should be so informed.

Fundamental to this approach is a respect for what children try to accomplish in learning to read. Use of the term *oral reading miscue* precludes use of the term *oral reading mistakes*. This word choice results in an assessment perspective that is forward looking: Examination of miscues, along with those aspects of reading done well, provides assessment information of considerable usefulness. It is anticipated that students are on a developmental path to become better readers. The talented teacher uses a student's miscues in oral reading to construct an accurate account of what a developing reader can and cannot do. Informed by cognitive, psycholinguistic, and child development theories, assessment information from reading inventories can provide rich information about students' ongoing reading achievement.

Throughout their history, reading inventories have offered an opportunity to gather comprehensive information about the processes and products of student reading. In doing so, reading inventories allow us to examine students' individual skills and strategies and the degree to which they are developed and coordinated in acts of reading. Few assessments offer the potential to provide as much useful information as reading inventories, which helps explain their past and current popularity and future prospects.

Characteristics of Reading Inventories

Commercial reading inventories typically contain graded word lists, reading passages, and a series of comprehension questions and requests to retell that are used to gauge students' understanding of text. Reading inventories also provide us with opportunities to assess silent reading and listening comprehension. Each of these components may provide useful diagnostic reading information for a particular student. A listing of typical components of reading inventories and the related information they provide is presented in Table 3.

In this section, we review the constituent sections and procedures of reading inventories in the order that teachers and students commonly use them. I note that the sequence is necessarily flexible to allow for accommodation of different students, their varied reading achievement levels, and our specific diagnostic assessment needs.

It is imperative that the placement of students in a specific task in the reading inventory be guided by our best estimate of their current reading ability, as each word list and reading passage is intended to represent an approximate grade-level difficulty. When in doubt, it is best practice to underestimate a student's achievement levels, therefore

TABLE 3 Representative Components of Reading Inventories and the Diagnostic Information They Provide	
Reading Inventory Component	Provides Information Related To
Word lists	• Sight word vocabulary • Mediated word recognition processes • Self-corrections at the word level

Reading passages
• Oral reading
	• Word recognition
	• Decoding
	   Phonics
	• Sight word vocabulary
	• Fluency
	   Rate of reading
	   Accuracy
	   Prosody
	• Comprehension
	   Retelling
	   Literal understanding
	   Inferential understanding
	• Metacognition
	   Monitoring
	   Fix-up strategies

• Silent reading	• Comprehension
	   Retelling
	   Literal understanding
	   Inferential understanding

• Listening	• Comprehension
	   Retelling
	   Literal understanding
	   Inferential understanding

Note. From *Understanding and Using Reading Assessment, K–12* (p. 30), by P. Afflerbach, 2007, Newark, DE: International Reading Association. Copyright 2007 by the International Reading Association.

TABLE 4
A Typical Sequence of Administration of a Commercially Published Reading Inventory

1. The teacher estimates the student's reading achievement level.
2. The student is placed in the appropriate level of the graded word list(s).
3. The student reads the graded word list(s).
4. The teacher determines the student's oral reading passage placement.
5. The student reads passage(s) orally until his or her frustration level is reached for word recognition, fluency, or comprehension.
6. The teacher determines the student's silent reading passage placement.
7. The student reads the passage(s) silently until his or her frustration level is reached for comprehension.
8. The teacher determines the student's listening placement.
9. The student listens and answers questions until his or her frustration level is reached for comprehension.
10. The student is tested via specific subtests.[a]

Note. Modified from *Understanding and Using Reading Assessment, K–12* (p. 31), by P. Afflerbach, 2007, Newark, DE: International Reading Association. Copyright 2007 by the International Reading Association.
[a]These subtests may include parts of speech, such as consonant blends and long and short vowel sounds, and may be included in the published reading inventory or added by the classroom teacher.

increasing the probability of the student experiencing initial success with the inventory. This initial placement is crucial because it contributes to a positive reading inventory experience for the student. The placement of students in a zone of current ability allows the reading inventory to best provide detailed information related to independent, instructional, and frustration levels of reading. An overview of the typical sequence of administration of a commercially published reading inventory is presented in Table 4.

Word Lists and Reading Inventories

Students often begin a reading inventory with the graded word lists, and placement of students should be guided by the teacher's knowledge of each student's approximate reading ability and achievement level. Each word list in commercially published reading inventories is composed of 10–30 single words that are designated at an approximate grade level and listed in order of increasing difficulty. The word lists can range in approximate difficulty from preprimer to high school level. The grade-level distinction for a particular word is based on the frequency of occurrence of the word in common instructional materials and the regularity of the word's sound–symbol correspondences. It is assumed that more frequently occurring words are easier to recognize. For example, the first five words in the primer-level word list of the Qualitative Reading Inventory–5 (Leslie & Caldwell, 2010) are *keep, need, going, what,* and *children,* and the final five words of the second-grade word list are *breathe, insects, weather, noticed,* and *money.*

Word lists serve several purposes. Performance on the word lists provides information about students' decoding ability, which is particularly helpful in our determination of those students who need continued attention to word recognition skills. Word list reading also provides us with information on a student's sight word vocabulary. Students read the word list until they encounter continued difficulty, suggesting that they have reached a ceiling in their performance.

McCracken (1966) proposes that approximate reading levels can be derived from students' performance on word list reading. Specifically, independent level is 90% and above for words read correctly, instructional level is 70–85%, and frustration level is less than 70%, or more than 3 words missed for every 10 encountered. Although the specific criteria for continuing or discontinuing students' reading of words varies across reading inventories, these percentages are useful, approximate guidelines for determining when a student should stop word list reading.

We then calculate the number of words correctly pronounced and determine the level of this baseline performance. Based on an immediate appraisal of the student's performance on word list reading, we choose the appropriate difficulty level in an initial oral reading passage, and all subsequent decisions for placement in reading passages are made in relation to this initial word list reading performance. Each student task in a reading inventory is sequential and interdependent. That is, what a student does on the word list reading determines the level at which the student begins oral reading.

Reading Passages With Reading Inventories

Having completed the word list reading, the student then begins oral reading of passages. As we listen to the student reading aloud, we make observations and take notes. We attend to the student's oral reading miscues and oral reading fluency. Oral reading miscues are determined by examining the student's oral reading in relation to the printed text, with miscues representing the student's verbalizations that do not match the text. Fluency is determined by the number of words read correctly per minute. Analysis of the student's oral reading miscues may provide details about his or her specific reading skills and strategies. Miscue analysis requires that we learn to identify specific reader behaviors and then record these behaviors accurately. The typical miscue analysis rubric allows for noting important reader skills, strategies, and behaviors that may be reflected in the omissions, repetitions, substitutions, and insertions that a reader makes. Figure 2 contains examples of these miscues and illustrates the symbol system used to signify particular miscues in a student's oral reading.

Experienced teachers can create a record of a student's oral reading behavior as it occurs. The recording of miscues and the ability to assign particular status to each miscue improve as we become more familiar with the materials and procedures of the reading inventory and the types of miscues that students make. Many accomplished

Printed sentence read by student: The cowgirl rode into the sunset on her horse.

Omission	• *Student reads:* The cowgirl rode into sunset on her horse.
	• *Miscue notation:* The cowgirl rode into ⟨the⟩ sunset on her horse.
Repetition	• *Student reads:* The cowgirl rode rode into the sunset on her horse.
	• *Miscue notation:* The cowgirl rode into the sunset on her horse.
Insertion	• *Student reads:* The cowgirl rode into the sunset on her spotted horse.
	• *Miscue notation:* The cowgirl rode into the sunset on her ^spotted horse.
Substitution	• *Student reads:* The cowgirl rode into the sunset on her house.
	• *Miscue notation:* The cowgirl rode into the sunset on her ^house horse.
Self-correction	• *Student reads:* The cowgirl rode into the sunset on his on her horse.
	• *Miscue notation:* The cowgirl rode into the sunset on ^on his c her horse.
Notes	• *High meaning-change miscue:* Substitution of *house* for *horse*
	• *Low meaning-change miscue:* Omission of *the*

Note. Modified from *Understanding and Using Reading Assessment, K–12* (p. 33), by P. Afflerbach, 2007, Newark, DE: International Reading Association. Copyright 2007 by the International Reading Association.

teachers find it helpful to tape-record reading inventory sessions, as the opportunity to listen again to a student's reading allows the teacher to check his or her original coding of miscues and may help the teacher gain further insights into the student's reading ability and strategies.

Oral reading continues for as long as the student meets acceptable criteria for oral reading accuracy, comprehension-question response accuracy, and reading rate. As the student scores within the parameters of instructional- or independent-level reading (95% and 98% accuracy and correctness, respectively), oral reading can continue until a ceiling is hit (i.e., the student is unable to read accurately and fluently and/or cannot answer a minimum number of comprehension questions correctly). This is the point where a student's learning area, or zone of proximal development (Vygotsky, 1934/1978), is overreached, and the task demands are too difficult.

Through examination of the student reader's performance, we can use miscue analysis to create a detailed portrait of the reader. For example, we may detect patterns of guessing words, reading without regard to punctuation, challenges to decoding final consonant blends, and other important issues, depending on the student. However, analysis of oral reading may indicate that a student is using context to self-correct and varying the rate of reading to accommodate the relative difficulty of the text. Each occurrence provides the opportunity for us to add to our understanding of student readers, and this information can be used to create effective instructional plans.

Reading inventories supply assessment information for both reading products and reading processes. The reading inventory provides a focus on oral reading followed by investigation of students' comprehension of text. Oral reading provides the opportunity for teachers to examine the processes of decoding, word identification, meaning construction, and metacognition in situ. The skill and strategy use that we witness and record is embedded in an act of reading. We are not examining consonant blends as they appear on a consonant blend worksheet; we observe how students blend consonants as they read text and as this important process relates to other reading skills and strategies. We are not examining answers to comprehension questions to determine only the state of passage comprehension; we also are privy to the word identification and meaning construction processes that contribute to comprehension. Comprehension processes may be glimpsed through miscue analysis, and comprehension products are tapped by the series of literal and inferential questions and student retellings.

Reading inventories also provide measures of reading rate and fluency. Across several oral readings, fluency in real time can be observed and calculated. This information, combined with the approximate grade levels of each oral reading passage, can be used to represent students' reading fluency by grade level. Thus, oral reading is a veritable storehouse of important information about students' reading strengths and needs. Whereas many reading assessments focus on the products of students' reading, such as their responses to comprehension questions, reading inventories provide us with detailed process information. (For more on this important process and product distinction, see the Reading Assessment Snapshot for Process and Product Assessment at the end of Chapter 3.)

Like the word lists, the reading passages in reading inventories vary in difficulty. Passages are assigned specific grade-level equivalents, such as 1.0, 3.5, or 5.0. These numbers represent an approximation of the passages' grade-level difficulty, based on readability formulas. Currently, the Common Core State Standards address grade-level difficulty in terms of text complexity, which represents a more detailed appraisal of a text's structure, levels of meaning, conventionality of language, clarity, and related knowledge demands (CCSSO & NGA, 2010). In either case, students' reading performance can be described in relation to these graded reading passages. For example, reading inventory results may document that a fourth-grade student is reading at a 4.5 independent grade level orally and a 5.0 independent grade level silently and that the student's listening comprehension is at a 6.5 independent grade level. Most reading inventories contain several passages at each grade level so that students can demonstrate their reading proficiency on oral, silent, and listening comprehension tasks. That is, having read orally a passage and answered comprehension questions listed at the 3.5 grade level, a student may do so silently with a different passage that is also rated at a 3.5 grade level of difficulty.

Because passages in reading inventories are rated for difficulty through the use of readability formulas, teachers must be careful to check the approximation of reading difficulty that the reading formulas present. The texts included in reading inventories, like those encountered in daily instruction, may privilege particular students and discriminate against others because of the presence or absence of particular prior knowledge, which may lead to an inaccurate account of students' reading achievement level. The inferences we draw from different students' performances in reading these texts may be faulty, as performance is a result of reading ability and prior knowledge, although performance is often attributed solely to reading ability. Thus, reading inventory passages most often represent a judgment on the developer's part that the familiarity of text content is acceptable—not too familiar to privilege particular groups of student readers and not too unfamiliar that it prevents readers from using some prior knowledge in constructing meaning. As teachers administering the reading inventory, we must check this assumption.

Retelling and Comprehension Questions

Following each oral reading passage, students are expected to demonstrate their comprehension of the text. The reading process information that we collect during oral reading is thus complemented by product information: students' understanding of the reading passages, as determined by students' comprehension-question responses and retellings. There are two widely used practices that help teachers understand the nature of students' comprehension: (1) retelling and (2) comprehension questions. Retellings allow students to use their own words to give an account of the passage they have just read. By using retelling checklists, we can determine the nature of students' comprehension by combining relevant parts of their retellings with their comprehension-question responses. As the student retells, the teacher must focus on the content of the retelling and its relation to the existing comprehension questions. This involves knowing the gist of each of the comprehension questions and determining that the student's retelling answers the particular questions.

The passages in reading inventories are followed by sets of related comprehension questions, typically ranging from 5 to 10 in number. Questions may be designated as focusing on details or main ideas and on literal or inferential comprehension. When students are encouraged to immediately follow their oral or silent reading with a retelling of the passage, we can determine a student's sense of the text, including his or her understanding of the text's content and structure. Retellings also allow students to preanswer the comprehension questions that accompany commercially published reading inventories spontaneously, without the prompting provided by questions.

In each of the cases cited in this paragraph, question type designation (i.e., literal or inferential) is intended to provide details about students' comprehension beyond whether or not they got the correct answer. For example, a student answering the minimum acceptable number of comprehension questions correctly may be demonstrating literal comprehension but not much inferential comprehension ability. This distinction can provide us with valuable assessment information. Several commercially published reading inventories provide retelling checklists that are tied to the comprehension questions. By using the checklists, we can determine the nature of students' comprehension, combining relevant parts of students' retellings with their comprehension-question responses.

Students answering a minimum acceptable number of questions can continue with their reading, while a score below the cutoff suggests that continued reading at the present or more difficult text level will not be fruitful. Should a student need to answer 7 out of 10 comprehension questions correctly to be considered for reading text at the next level, we see the importance of an accurate determination of comprehension. Because students' retellings are not necessarily in the language of the scoring guide, there may be times when it is challenging to determine if a portion of the retelling answers a particular question. In such situations, asking the question for clarification is important. We must know the parameters for acceptable student responses to the questions that are asked, how to map student retellings onto the existing comprehension questions in the reading inventory, and when a retelling or an answer to a specific question is not counted for credit.

Students' apparent comprehension of reading passages can be influenced by the manner of administration of the reading inventory. We can allow lookbacks—that is, opportunities when students are allowed to review the text while answering comprehension questions—to determine if an apparent comprehension strength or weakness is attributable to the availability of the text. For certain student readers, the challenge of a series of 6–10 comprehension questions may be due, in part, to the fact that memory is involved. Lookbacks help diminish the demand on students to remember all that they have read for answering comprehension questions. Flexibility with the use of lookbacks is recommended; successful readers are adept at returning to text they have read to identify and remember important information. In each case, it is important for us to determine the degree to which students' text lookbacks on a reading inventory reflect regular classroom practice and the importance of having assessment information about students in either situation.

Following oral reading, retellings, and answering comprehension questions, we analyze the nature of the responses and the number of correct responses, making the decision for the student to continue oral reading at the next level of difficulty or to switch to silent reading. Teachers use several sources of information to make this decision, including the student's rate and accuracy of reading and the nature of the student's comprehension of the oral reading passages. Once a performance criterion is not met (i.e., the student exceeds the maximum number of permissible oral reading miscues, does not reach the minimum number of acceptable comprehension questions, or both), oral reading is completed, and silent reading of passages should begin.

Many commercially produced reading inventories include literal and inferential comprehension questions. It is important to determine if an inventory includes higher order thinking questions and if the texts that students are required to read are suitable for asking such questions. The determination of how well (or if) a student can answer questions that demand application, synthesis, and evaluation of information is a crucial use of diagnostic assessment information (Afflerbach, Cho, & Kim, 2011). However, the relatively brief texts that are found in most reading inventories may not lend themselves to higher level thinking questions. Should this be the case, it is important to determine if higher order thinking questions can be developed for the particular reading inventory passages.

Silent Reading and Listening Comprehension

Some students read silently and comprehend text at levels higher than their oral reading and comprehension levels because silent reading does not have the considerable public performance requirement of oral reading. However, silent reading requires the student reader to be independent in the ability to process text, detect difficulties as text is read, and address these difficulties. We do not have the opportunity to assist a student with difficulties encountered in silent reading because silence is not revealing of the nature of the challenges. Silent reading, which is the normal mode for most readers, is also silent as to the work that readers do while reading. Silent reading excludes our opportunity to gather information about word recognition, vocabulary, and comprehension processes that is provided by oral reading, so our focus is on how well students have comprehended the passages and their rate of reading. Students read silently, provide a retelling, and answer comprehension questions. Progress through the increasingly difficult silent reading passages is dependent on scoring at or above a level of 70% on the comprehension questions.

A third aspect of comprehension, listening comprehension, can be measured by the reading inventory. With listening comprehension, the teacher reads the selection, and the student listens. When the teacher finishes reading, the student is asked to retell the passage and answer specific comprehension questions. The student's listening comprehension achievement level is often a future marker of instructional and then independent reading comprehension levels. The teacher, as the reader, deals with decoding and word identification, fluency, and reading rate, leaving the student with the task of listening, processing spoken language, and constructing meaning.

Reading inventories provide diagnostic information from word lists and in relation to the acts of silent and oral reading and listening comprehension. Given the range of value of this information, it follows that adopting a single reading inventory and learning

TABLE 5
Representative Questions That Experienced Teachers Can Ask of Reading Inventory Information

- Do the word lists and their grade-level designations reflect the approximate achievement levels of my students?
- Are the graded word lists and graded reading passages well coordinated?
- Do the graded word lists help in the accurate placement of students in their first reading passage?
- Are there opportunities to examine students' oral reading fluency?
- Does the reading inventory tend to overestimate or underestimate students' reading ability when compared with other reading assessment information, such as standardized test scores and students' regular text comprehension performance in class?
- Are there comprehension questions that do not appear to tap important aspects of the text (i.e., questions focused on information not central to understanding the text)?
- Are there comprehension questions that are vaguely worded and unclear for students?
- Do the text passages contain content that is more familiar to some of my students?
- Are there comprehension questions that are answered correctly by students when other indicators suggest that students have not comprehended well?
- Are there comprehension questions that can be answered because students have much prior knowledge for the text content and not because they understand the text?
- Are there opportunities to check students' critical and evaluative comprehension?

Note. From *Understanding and Using Reading Assessment, K–12* (p. 37), by P. Afflerbach, 2007, Newark, DE: International Reading Association. Copyright 2007 by the International Reading Association.

the texts, questions, and nuances of that particular inventory makes assessment sense. As we become familiar with the inventory, we are in a good position to critically evaluate and use the information that the reading inventory provides. Sample questions that experienced teachers can ask of reading inventories are presented in Table 5.

Teacher-Initiated Reading Inventories

Teacher-initiated reading inventories share several features with commercially produced reading inventories because they both seek to describe the detail of student readers' reading achievement in a developmentally appropriate manner. As with commercially published reading inventories, students' oral reading can be analyzed via teacher-initiated reading inventories to gather useful information about aspects of reading development. We can focus on students' oral reading fluency, decoding, sight word vocabulary, frequency and nature of oral reading miscues, vocabulary knowledge, metacognition, self-correction strategies, and reading comprehension strategies. Teacher-initiated inventories can be characterized by flexibility and adaptability, as they may be conducted during the course of a student's normal reading routine during the school day. For example, we may work with a student during an elective reading period or while the class is involved in silent reading. Teacher-initiated reading inventories can focus on the text that a student is reading as part of the school curriculum, or on a self-selected text. They can include oral and silent reading, along with listening comprehension, and provide valuable information from miscue analysis and the analysis of comprehension ability.

Part of the appeal of teacher-initiated reading inventories is that they can revolve around students' authentic classroom reading, reading that would otherwise take place in the routine of the classroom. Thus, conducting the reading inventory does not disrupt classroom reading. The reading inventory can focus on the texts that students choose to read, offering the chance to see motivation at work, or on texts that students must read, such as a social studies text, a science text, or a short story. Student reading achievement is examined in relation to actual school reading material. When reading inventories focus on students' self-selected texts, we might expect a relatively strong showing of reading proficiency because students may be working with a considerable amount of prior knowledge for the text's subject, may be motivated to read well because they were allowed to choose the text, or both. Alternately, we may create a reading inventory consisting of selected texts and reading passages that yields important information about the students. A first attempt at selecting passages can be informed by the type of texts that students typically read in class, with attention to both informational and narrative texts. Over time, our experience with these texts can contribute to ongoing refinement of the questions that are asked of students and the interpretations that are made from reading inventory results.

There are several challenges inherent in this approach to reading inventories. First, we must be familiar with the texts that students are reading, to the degree that if students are asked to retell what they read and if they are to answer comprehension questions, we can determine how accurately a retelling reflects the passage. Second, we must also construct a series of comprehension questions that focuses on important text content and the student's purpose for reading. Should we be interested in creating an "arc of questions" (Wolf, 1987, p. 4) that provide information on students' literal, inferential, and critical thinking, then this is additional work to be done. (For more on arcs of questions, see Table 7 in Chapter 3.)

Running Records

Clay (1979, 2002) characterizes learning to read as the patterning of complex behavior and advocates the use of running records to gauge students' development of this behavior. Running records share with reading inventories the focus on readers' decoding and meaning-making processes, a system for identifying oral reading processes, and the use of this information to create hypotheses about students' reading strengths and weaknesses in order to inform instruction and assess text difficulty. (A more detailed account of the OSELA [Clay, 2002] and running records' role in this survey is one focus of Chapter 6.)

While conducting running records, teachers combine the reading inventory's detailed, reading process–oriented information with portability: Running records can be conducted in conjunction with many classroom reading tasks. Although running records are a centerpiece of Reading Recovery, an early intervention program for struggling readers, skillful teachers can conduct and create a running record with the texts that students are reading in class. The assessment is authentic because it focuses on an intact act of reading and provides both reading process and product information. The assessment emanates from the life of the classroom itself. Running records require no special set of reading assessment texts and student tasks because assessment happens within the already occurring work of the school day. Running records reflect an important perspective on teacher–student relationships in reading assessment. That is, they are conducted while we sit with students (Johnston, 1987) to best understand their strengths and needs. This flexibility helps running records gain high marks for the authenticity of the reading texts and tasks and the context in which the assessment is conducted.

Clay (2002) does not advocate for using recording devices while conducting running records, suggesting that it can become a crutch for teachers; that is, they may become too reliant on the recordings. Although this recommendation may be sensible for some teachers, I recommend that we consider the trade-offs involved in using or not using a recording device. In my experience, a simply operated device requires minimal attention and preserves a valuable record of students' interactions with text. I compare this with my experiences working with many students who speak English in a manner different than I do, who are soft talkers, or who may trail off in the middle of reading a sentence or paragraph. Such students regularly challenge my ability to accurately record and interpret their oral reading. I also am concerned about the need for all of our classroom assessments to demonstrate high reliability. If recording helps me with this reliability, then I will choose to use it.

Using Reading Inventory Assessment Information

Reading inventories, whether commercially published, teacher developed, or accompanying reading intervention programs, can offer rich information from which we infer students' reading strengths and challenges. As anticipated by Pellegrino and colleagues (2001), comprehensive and detailed results allow for comprehensive and detailed inferences about students' reading needs and strengths. As the reading inventory is analyzed, teachers can interpret students' work on individual portions of the inventory and on their overall work. Patterns of accomplishment and need can be identified. The results of reading inventories and the inferences we make about students from these results should be combined with our ongoing account of how and how well each of our students reads. Accomplished reading teachers are continually updating their ideas about students' strengths and needs, and reading inventory results offer an opportunity to add rich and detailed information to a teacher's conceptions of individual students.

I believe it is helpful to consider students' independent, instructional, and frustration reading levels in relation to Vygotsky's (1934/1978) theories of learning and the zone of proximal development. The zone of proximal development is the area in which we can expect student growth, aided by our focused instruction and support. Figure 3 depicts the reading levels juxtaposed with a student reader's zone of proximal development.

The reading levels help us create boundaries within which we can expect a student reader's independence and success, growth with assistance, and difficulty. This helps us better understand students' reading achievement from a teaching perspective.

The frustration level represents reading and reading-related tasks that are so far beyond the student's current level of competency that there is little chance (save luck) that his or her reading will be successful. This is a level with which students should have only brief experiences: Prolonged work at the student's frustration level may provide little diagnostic information but much grief. Instructional-level reading occurs within the zone of proximal development; it is here that the accomplished reading teacher helps the student build on current reading competencies for new learning and continued reading development. For example, a student reading successfully at an instructional level may receive our occasional help related to vocabulary, word pronunciation, and comprehension. Independent reading signifies student success without

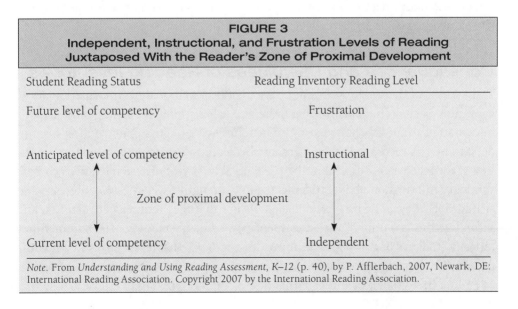

FIGURE 3
Independent, Instructional, and Frustration Levels of Reading Juxtaposed With the Reader's Zone of Proximal Development

Student Reading Status	Reading Inventory Reading Level
Future level of competency	Frustration
Anticipated level of competency	Instructional
Zone of proximal development	
Current level of competency	Independent

Note. From *Understanding and Using Reading Assessment, K–12* (p. 40), by P. Afflerbach, 2007, Newark, DE: International Reading Association. Copyright 2007 by the International Reading Association.

a teacher's help because the student is reading at a current level of competency. At this level, the reader is fully capable of reading and answering questions about the text. Reading inventories help us identify both the general range in which students can experience success and learning, informing our understanding of their zones of proximal development related to reading and providing us with diagnostic details to foster students' reading growth.

Reading Inventories in Tasha's Second-Grade Classroom

Tasha's (all teacher and student names are pseudonyms) classroom is populated by a diverse group of students. They vary in their reading experiences and reading achievement levels. As is her preference and the school district's practice, Tasha uses a reading inventory to gather detailed information about each of her students at the beginning of the school year. This complex and demanding undertaking is supported by the school district and building principals, who understand the value of the formative assessment information that reading inventories yield. Tasha and her colleagues use a commercially published reading inventory, the Qualitative Reading Inventory–5 (Leslie & Caldwell, 2010), and the teachers' accomplished use of the inventory is supported by professional development that focuses on the procedures involved with administering, scoring, and interpreting the inventory and using the information it yields.

Tasha considers the inventory a rich source of information that helps her better understand her students' reading development. Through this understanding, she is in a strong position to provide effective instruction and identify texts and reading situations that are developmentally appropriate for her students. Across the year, Tasha can depend on the reading inventory to provide information on an important range of student reading skills and strategies.

Consequences and Usefulness of Reading Inventories

Tasha's uses of the reading inventory are to collect and analyze information at the beginning of the school year, learn more about her students' reading, and use this information to inform her reading instruction. She begins constructing her understanding of incoming second graders by reading the narratives written by the first-grade teachers at the end of the previous school year. These narratives contain summary information about students' reading strengths, weaknesses, interests, and attitudes. However, Tasha's experience tells her that the summer between first and second grades is a time of varied influence on students' reading. The summer may reflect a student's ongoing growth in reading, indicate that a student is in a holding pattern (i.e., starting second grade with approximately the same skills and strategies as ending first grade), or indicate that a student is regressing to a level below that attained at the end of first grade. Students' independent reading levels, habits, and opportunities to read all influence what a beginning second grader brings to school. Tasha needs to know the current state of her students' reading skills and strategies. She needs a means of considering these skills and strategies on a developmental trajectory for each student. The reading inventory and its designation of student reading levels allow her to do so.

Tasha values the notes provided by her colleagues because they offer a starting point for understanding her new students. She uses the notes to create hypotheses about her students' reading development. Throughout the school year, she strives to collect information through observation and questioning that will help her investigate her hypotheses about her students. She values reading inventories because of the amount of high-quality and immediately useful data that they provide. The assessment information from reading inventories is a detailed complement to information gathered with other reading assessments. The different sources of information provided by the reading inventory allow Tasha to triangulate this information with what she has learned about her students through her initial observations of and conversations with her students and comments from the previous year's teacher. This means that there is more than one source of evidence. With information about her students' reading abilities from different assessment sources, Tasha builds both inferences and confidence in her inferences.

Sam, like his fellow students, begins the school year with a folder that includes teachers' notes from prior years, observations, and reports of instructional approaches to reading, in addition to summative reading assessment information. Tasha appreciates this information as she begins to develop a portrait of Sam as a reader. She uses the reading inventory information to create initial hypotheses about his strengths and needs and to consider suitable reading instruction. Prior to second grade, Sam demonstrated a commitment to reading. He is enthusiastic and eager to please, according to his first-grade teacher's year-end notes. He has a sight word vocabulary that is about average for the end of first grade, and he exhibits comprehension that is on grade level. Based on Sam's reading of several short passages, Tasha notes that he does not always attend to the ends of words, which contributes to patterns of miscue when he reads. She also notes that he is developing self-correction strategies.

Tasha considers the initial reading inventory information and then compares this with the assessment information she collects across the school year. She checks her on-the-fly application of the shorthand for miscues against the tape recording of Sam's oral reading. Her goal is to seek and identify patterns of reading behavior in his work. The reading inventory reveals that he does well at recognizing short, common words and the beginnings of longer words but that he does not consistently attend to the endings of the words in text. A result is that he substitutes words for those printed in the text, such as *home* for *house* and *fear* for *feat*. A related pattern is that Sam's substitutions are guesses aided by the semantics of the passage. That is, he substitutes words after meaning, which indicates that he is reading with an overall goal of constructing meaning. Rarely does he substitute or insert nonsense words. Tasha believes that the reading inventory provides converging evidence that Sam is consistently focused on self-correction.

Tasha is adept at using the information gained from the reading inventory to plan instruction for Sam and his classmates. Within the reading program, she builds in exercises in which he is encouraged to attend to the ends of words, processing more of the visual information to determine words instead of guessing, as he did before. Tasha also helps Sam maintain his healthy focus on reading as meaning making by encouraging him to ask himself, Does that make sense? at the end of sentences and paragraphs.

Across the school year, Tasha incorporates a blend of commercial reading inventory materials and procedures with running records to establish a consistent opportunity to gather information about Sam's reading. This information is always fresh, being analyzed and used within days, if not minutes or hours, of being collected. She uses assessment results to inform the teachable moment, focusing her instruction on Sam's zones of proximal development.

The precious and limited time that is available for reading assessment demands that we choose our assessments wisely. Tasha is convinced that her time and effort with reading inventories are well spent. They provide detailed information about the skills and strategies, and processes and products, of her students' reading.

Roles and Responsibilities Related to Reading Inventories

The effective use of reading inventories requires that the teacher is expert at classroom-based assessment. Although Tasha's path to becoming a reliable user of reading inventories is arduous, she is convinced that no other reading assessment can so closely inform her instruction. The carefully crafted, administered, and interpreted reading inventory provides teachers and students with valuable accounting of how reading develops in relation to the cognitive skills and strategies and the metacognitive routines that contribute to reading achievement. Gathering and using reading assessment information with reading inventories is particularly demanding of Tasha's teaching expertise. Reading inventories work well when we are familiar with their contents and structure and when we are expert at giving and interpreting reading inventories. The reading inventory is an assessment with much potential, and Tasha puts much effort into developing her ability to conduct and use the reading inventory in a consistent and accurate manner. Thus, a prime responsibility for us is to pursue professional development that helps us become familiar with reading inventory materials and processes and then master the components and sequences.

Because successful reading inventories hinge on close interaction between the student and the teacher, it is imperative that we attend to the nature of this interaction with students as a reading inventory is conducted. If our typical oral reading interactions with students include providing occasional words that pose problems for the students, we must be aware of how doing so during a reading inventory changes the information we get. For example, a student's inability to recognize and say a key vocabulary word as it appears in text might, in another scenario, pose a major block to comprehension. Tasha understands that if she provides the word, following adequate wait time on her part and thinking time on the student's part, she has changed the very reading process that she seeks to assess. This is an example of how the authenticity of the assessment can influence the validity and reliability of the assessment.

The regular use of the Qualitative Reading Inventory–5 (Leslie & Caldwell, 2010) increases Tasha's familiarity and facility with the inventory. Over the years, the inventory is increasingly helpful and powerful because Tasha becomes fluent in how she understands and uses it. She has learned and practiced the particular components and procedures, including using the shorthand for designating particular miscues, understanding the sequence of graded word list reading, oral reading, silent reading and then listening comprehension, and using guidelines for determining independent-, instructional-, and frustration-level reading for each student.

Tasha also pays close attention to her students' speech and pronunciation. The interpretation of oral reading depends on a clear understanding of what exactly students are saying. Given the language diversity in her classroom, the array of students, and their accents, dialects, and manners of speaking, Tasha has the responsibility to accurately determine what students are saying. As noted earlier, the use of a tape recorder helps Tasha revisit her students' spoken words and better understand them.

Throughout each administration of the reading inventory with every student, Tasha uses the opportunity to examine her use of wait time and her attitude toward the different students in her class. She is especially sensitive to those students for whom reading is a regular struggle. Her hoped-for balance is to provide enough wait time to allow all students the opportunity to use their existing skills, strategies, and knowledge while she is there with helpful information and support when needed. Wait time is related not only to student reading but also to Tasha's stance toward her students.

Tasha believes that the series of questions that follows each passage provides good coverage. The questions focus on main ideas and details and require students to demonstrate literal and inferential comprehension. Having used the inventory for three years, she believes that it should be supplemented with her own questions that focus on author purposes, students' critical evaluation of the text, and how students use what they learn from reading. Thus, Tasha creates questions that help her understand student comprehension and that can influence her instructional decisions. Although limited by the reading inventory passages because they are relatively short and not exceedingly complex, she develops additional questions and tasks that are linked to the passages and represent a convergence of the reading inventory with her instructional program and goals.

Reading inventories are comprehensive assessment instruments that demand attention and effort on the part of the student. The time on task required during a comprehensive reading inventory means that teachers must be alert to student fatigue. Reading inventories may be novel to the student in form and length, demanding consistent, on-task behavior with little downtime between assessment events. As the teacher develops familiarity with the reading inventory materials and procedures, this knowledge is useful in making decisions about continuing a particular segment of the inventory, moving on to another part, or taking a well-advised break. For example, if a student completes three oral reading passages with few miscues and excellent comprehension, moving to silent reading rather than continuing until a too-difficult oral reading text is encountered makes sense.

Reliability of Reading Inventories

The reliability of reading inventories depends on our expertise in collecting, coding, and interpreting the results of the inventory. We must know how to make accurate initial placements of students, the appropriate challenge levels for our student readers, the shorthand that allows us to record reading behavior, and the means to analyze and diagnose students' reading. The inability to do so reduces reliability and compromises the inferences drawn from the reading inventory information.

Tasha's experience with the inventory provides her with knowledge about its strengths, weaknesses, and idiosyncrasies. When she was first learning to use reading inventories in a reading diagnosis and remediation college course, she was encouraged to tape-record her students' reading so that she might have a backup to her initial record of student reading behaviors. The tape recordings allowed Tasha to return to each oral reading and word list performance and bring scrutiny to her original notations of students' oral reading miscues, retellings, and answers to comprehension questions. Tasha has reduced her reliance on referencing the tape-recorded reading of her students over three years. Yet, she continues to make recordings because she believes that it enhances the reliability and consistency of her interpretation of her students' reading behavior. In turn, this strengthens the confidence she has in her inferences made from the assessment. The tapes give permanence to students' performances, and having them allows Tasha to examine in fine-grained detail some student reading performances that were difficult to interpret in real time or were misinterpreted in the first place.

Tasha develops her ability to listen, observe, and record student reading behaviors with increased accuracy. She also builds knowledge of the tasks, reading passages, and comprehension questions that accompany each reading selection. As the commercial reading inventory is developed, piloting helps focus attention on the difficulty of the passage, the accompanying questions, and the prior knowledge that a student needs to answer questions correctly, independent of reading the passage. Tasha views her work with the reading inventory as an ongoing project, as she finds particular questions that are unusually easy or difficult for her students to answer. She also is comfortable making inferences about what students comprehend, based on their retellings of the passages they read. In each of these instances, Tasha adds to the reliability of the reading inventory by bringing her professional knowledge into the process of conducting and interpreting the inventory.

Published reading inventories consist of preselected reading passages and comprehension questions. Recall that the reading passages are selected using a method that seeks to mediate the amount of prior knowledge that students may have for particular passages. In general, commercially published reading inventories aim for a middle ground of texts that will be somewhat, but not overly, familiar for most students. This aspect of the inventory can introduce measurement errors related to readers' prior knowledge for the reading passages and the degree to which comprehension questions can be answered with or without reading the text. For example, consider the student who is asked to read a passage that discusses farm life. The 10 comprehension questions that follow focus on literal and inferential comprehension of the text. Given what we know about the constructive nature of comprehension, will all students in Tasha's class have the appropriate prior knowledge to construct the meaning that is anticipated by the questions? Will students who live on farms and are familiar with farming have an advantage in answering the questions?

Reading inventories that use classroom reading materials may avoid this issue. That is, when the texts that are used to gather reading assessment information are the very texts that students are reading as part of the school day, teachers may already be aware of the prior knowledge that students possess and are developing and the manner in which they use this prior knowledge. It is expected that students will use their prior knowledge. Thus, the influence of prior knowledge on comprehension can be anticipated and explained.

Validity of Reading Inventories

The goal of reading is the construction of meaning, and an assessment that allows us to better understand the processes by which student readers construct meaning is valuable. How does the reading inventory help us understand students' development in relation to the construct of reading? Reading inventories can provide valuable information about each of the five target areas identified by NCLB: phonemic awareness, phonics, fluency, vocabulary, and comprehension. The inventories can do so in a developmentally appropriate manner. When we read, we use reading skills and strategies in a coordinated effort to construct meaning (Afflerbach et al., 2008). Skill and strategy work in concert, not in isolation. The reading passages and routines in reading inventories are designed to help us observe such: We build understanding of readers' strengths and needs in reading as the students are actually reading. The reading inventory focuses on both reading processes and reading products and thus gains high marks for construct validity.

Commercial reading inventories vary in their ecological validity. The graded reading passages may or may not reflect the type of reading that students do in the classroom. Reading passages are relatively short, and they are selected, in part, with the intent to present students with passages for which they have neither too much nor too little prior knowledge. Similarly, the retelling and comprehension-question segments of commercial reading inventories may or may not reflect the daily routine and work of the classroom. Commercial reading inventories permit the observation and assessment of reading in a holistic sense. We can gather information about decoding and word recognition, fluency, vocabulary, and comprehension within the same assessment session, and we may be able to better understand how each is contributing to the construction of meaning of text. Or, we may develop an understanding of the areas that are preventing students from constructing meaning.

The materials and procedures used in teacher-developed reading inventories and running records may contribute to high ecological validity. Running records, conducted as students read text that they would be reading anyway, reduce the differences between the assessment and the classroom routine. Also, reading inventories conducted by teachers as students read and use texts as part of their normal school day minimize the differences between reading done for assessment and all other reading that students do. Running records and reading inventories are often strong examples of authentic assessment: reading assessment that is done with materials that are typical in the classroom, and assessment procedures that are minimally invasive.

Summary

There are few reading assessments that provide detailed descriptions of readers' skills and strategies and how these act in concert to help readers make meaning from text. Reading inventories provide details about student reading in relation to specific reading grade levels and independent, instructional, and frustration reading levels. Further, the inventories help us focus on the processes and products of student reading: the meaning that is constructed and the tools that students use to construct this meaning. Few assessments are as demanding of teachers and students as reading inventories, but few give such valuable return on our efforts.

ENHANCING YOUR UNDERSTANDING

1. Working with a reading inventory, tape-record a student reading and practice coding his or her oral reading.

2. Practice recording oral reading behaviors and then use this information to inform your ideas about the student reader and then your instruction related to the student.

3. Practice making initial placements for students in word lists, oral reading, silent reading, and listening comprehension passages, based on information you have recently gathered about the students.

4. For a classroom-based reading inventory, choose reading selections that can accommodate the range of student reading achievement in your class. Next, develop appropriate comprehension questions that you can ask students following their reading.

Formative and Summative Assessment

Effective assessment programs combine formative and summative assessment. Formative assessment is used to help us shape or form an understanding of students' reading development and learning across lessons, units, marking periods, or academic years. Formative assessment provides information that helps us develop instruction that in turn provides experiences that further influence students' development. For example, a third-grade class participates in a hands-on science lesson in which important instructions must be read, followed by scientific inquiry. The teacher's questioning and observation of all of the students indicates that some of them do not understand the written instructions and cannot conduct the scientific inquiry. This formative assessment information may be immediately useful to the teacher who is focused on students' ability to read, understand, and follow written instructions and use scientific inquiry strategies. Formative assessment captures the students' needs and alerts us to immediate teaching and learning opportunities.

In contrast, summative assessment provides a summary of student achievement. Summative assessment can help us take measure of student achievement in relation to reading curriculum goals and district or state learning standards. High-stakes tests are examples of summative assessments, as their results can be used for comparing students and determining which ones meet achievement benchmarks. Unit tests in science provide summative accounts of student learning, as do the year-end tests that students take. These summative assessments can be used for comparing students with other students, and actual and expected student achievement levels.

The designation of formative or summative assessment is determined, in some instances, by the manner in which a particular assessment is used. Some assessments can be used in both a formative and summative manner. For example, consider a series of questions that follows reading in social studies. Students' responses to these questions allow us to make inferences about students' learning. Our immediate analysis of students' answers to such questions can suggest that we need to teach to the moment, that we should spend valuable class time on reteaching and clarifying an important concept, such as democracy, or checking on students' understanding of a related vocabulary word, such as *citizen*. These same sets of questions may be part of a regular, ongoing assessment routine. The answers to the questions describe students' understanding of important course content. A student's answers figure into the weekly grade and are then used in determining the report card grade for social studies. Thus, the same assessment may serve both formative and summative assessment purposes. There is a clear need for a balance of formative and summative reading assessments in the classroom, and it is crucial to identify assessments that provide the immediate, constructive information for formative assessment and those assessments whose information might also serve in the summative assessment role.

Finally, formative and summative assessments may require different levels of teacher expertise for appropriate use. High-stakes tests do not require much on the part of the teacher, beyond making sure that test directions are read clearly and that each student is treated fairly. In contrast to such summative assessments, keeping close track of the important questions to ask during classroom lessons, interpreting students' responses to those questions, and using those responses in a formative manner requires considerable teacher expertise.

CHAPTER 3

Teacher Questioning as Assessment

Questions are deeply ingrained in the routines of the school day, in which the questions serve a variety of functions. Questions help us understand students' ongoing and summary understanding of text, their metacognitive development, and the manner in which they use what has been learned from reading. Through questioning, teachers seek an account of how well students are reading. The form and content of our questions should be informed by our knowledge of students and the curriculum and our goals for instruction. These questions help us understand what students learn from reading, how their reading is progressing, and what they need. The types of questions we ask of our students can be as broad as our conceptualization of what students learn from what they read and how they think. Questions help us model good assessment practices for our students. In each and every case, we must be sure that we are asking the right questions and making full use of the student responses that our questions elicit.

A Brief History of Questioning

Throughout the history of schooling, questioning has been associated with teaching and learning. Socrates is credited with developing a method of rigorous questioning in the fourth century BC that serves two purposes: (1) using the question as a guide to inquiry and thinking and (2) using questions to determine what the person who answers the question knows. A teacher poses questions that encourage students to think in new ways and that provide the opportunity to assess students' learning from text. For example, after a fifth-grade class reads a textbook chapter on immigration, the teacher uses Socratic questioning to help students focus on their family histories of immigration and then how the reasons for immigrating as described in the chapter apply to these histories. The Socratic method also serves as a challenge: As teachers, we should pose questions that assess different types of learning, provoke thought, and are worthy of response.

How we think about reading, the purposes of reading instruction, and the development of the students we teach should influence the nature of the questions we ask. A century ago, behaviorism posited that we read with the text acting as the stimulus and verbatim recall as the paradigm of response (Watson, 1913). Such a view of reading suggests that giving back text when responding to questions is a desirable benchmark of the accomplished reader. However, our evolving understanding of the mind and reading (Huey, 1908; Snow, 2002; Thorndike, 1917) should be reflected in an evolution in the types of questions we ask of student readers. Cognitive psychology has demonstrated that readers use prior knowledge, combined with skills and strategies, to construct meaning (Pressley & Afflerbach, 1995). We also know that students are capable of complex thinking. We should ask questions that honor these understandings. Moreover, our increasing understanding of the socially situated nature of cognition (Lave & Wenger, 1991) and the increasing demands on students to develop complex literacy abilities for success in life should influence our theory and practice of asking questions (Afflerbach, Cho, & Kim, 2011).

Questions have been the focus of considerable attention over the past century (Bloom, 1956; Guszak, 1967; Pearson & Johnson, 1978), and it is important that we consult this knowledge as we plan to use questions in our classrooms. In assessment, questions are generally regarded as a means to access student knowledge. Stevens (1912) found that roughly two thirds of the questions asked in observed classrooms focused on recitation and memory of facts. In this case, students who are expected to memorize text information often prove up to the task and accurately answer low-level comprehension questions. Durkin (1978) examined fourth-grade classrooms and interviewed teachers about their reading comprehension instruction. She found that many teachers equated comprehension instruction with asking questions about text, as if posing the question somehow taught students how to answer it. In fact, this study signified the need for rethinking how reading is taught and making clearer the relationships between reading, teaching, and answering questions. The study also concluded that because questions are not an adequate means for teaching, then there is a need for the explicit instruction of reading strategies.

Questioning is prominent in present-day classrooms but occurs most often in the initiate–respond–evaluate (IRE) discourse form. This form describes classroom practice in which teachers initiate classroom talk by asking questions, students respond to the questions, and then the teacher evaluates students' responses (Cazden, 1986; Mehan, 1979). Following is an example of the IRE form:

> Initiate (Teacher):   What is a compass rose?
> Respond (Student):   It's the part of a map that shows directions.
> Evaluate (Teacher):   Yes, that's correct.

IRE discourse often focuses on known-answer questions, in which the students' task is, in part, to figure out what the teacher wants to know. In reading lessons, IRE questions often focus on literal and simple inferential comprehension of text. It is not that such comprehension is not important—it is critical. Yet, failure to move beyond such questions to determine students' comprehension is a missed opportunity to both promote and evaluate their more complex thinking. Further, the IRE discourse pattern, or form of questioning, locks us into a manner of speaking and reduces our opportunities to use language in the classroom to encourage students and expand their thinking (Johnston, 2004).

Categorizing and Classifying Questions

A history of good question asking is informed by theories of learning. These theories help us conceptualize how our questions may tap particular types of knowledge that students gain from reading. As learning theories are generated and our understanding of learning and how to assess it evolves, different approaches to asking questions also evolve. For example, Bloom's (1956) taxonomy of learning and work related to the taxonomy (Krathwohl, 2002) support the proposal that learning can range from a relatively simple understanding (assessed with a literal comprehension question) to a complex evaluative understanding (assessed with questions that focus on students' critical appraisal of what is learned).

Bloom's (1956) taxonomy of learning defines six levels of increasingly sophisticated human learning and performance that relate to our reading. If we believe that our reading instruction should help students learn to generalize from what they read, critically question the authors of the texts they read, and apply what is learned from reading, Bloom's taxonomy offers a theoretical means to categorize our reading assessment questions in relation to these instructional goals. From relatively simple to increasingly complex, the taxonomy charts possible outcomes of students' reading and associated learning. The taxonomy can serve as an aid to our efforts to develop a rich and appropriate array of questions to ask students as they read. Table 6 focuses on the different types of learning in Bloom's taxonomy and suggests the focus of our questions that can help us understand the nature of students' learning in relation to each level of the taxonomy.

TABLE 6
Different Types of Questions Related to Different Categories in Bloom's Taxonomy of Thinking[a]

Category of Bloom's Taxonomy	Questions Can Focus On
Knowledge	Recognizing, remembering
Comprehension	Understanding
Application	Using, applying
Analysis	Determining attributes, comparing and contrasting
Synthesis	Making hypotheses, planning, speculating
Evaluation	Rating, judging

Note. Modified from *Understanding and Using Reading Assessment, K–12* (p. 53), by P. Afflerbach, 2007, Newark, DE: International Reading Association. Copyright 2007 by the International Reading Association.
[a]*Taxonomy of Educational Objectives: The Classification of Educational Goals, Handbook 1: Cognitive Domain*, edited by B.S. Bloom, 1956, New York: David McKay.

In spite of our knowledge of how to ask students diverse and appropriate questions about their reading, the increased prevalence of high-stakes tests (Afflerbach, 2005) is a major influence on questioning practices in classrooms. These tests are scored within the constraints of the question–response format, meaning that the cost of scoring students' responses to questions often dictates the type of questions that are asked. Compared with students' constructed responses to questions, machine-scored responses are relatively easy and cheap to score and are favored over those items that require scoring by human beings. Further, these tests restrict the practice of having students regularly answer divergent thinking items or extensive constructed-response items. Such items are useful when we are interested in students' understanding of text and when we acknowledge that there may be more than one correct answer to the question. A result is that to the degree that there is teaching to the test, there is also teaching to low-level questions. There is the tension of scientific research informing us about the depth and breadth of student learning that is possible in high-quality classrooms, the need for assessment questions that help us describe this learning, and the requirement that millions of students be assessed in reading with tests that are incapable of describing this breadth and depth.

Recently, the U.S. Department of Education funded two consortia: the Partnership for Assessment of Readiness for College and Careers (PARCC) and the SMARTER Balanced Assessment Consortium (SBAC) in the Race to the Top Comprehensive Assessment Systems Competition. Each of these consortia is developing assessments that will align with the Common Core State Standards. As the Common Core State Standards focus on increasingly complex thinking and achievement goals, related assessments must follow suit. Assessment questions and related tasks that are capable of prompting and describing higher level student performance are required. This may help move test questions to a place where they better represent the kinds of thinking students do when reading.

To compound the problem of tests that present a limited range of questions, we are creatures of habit. Assessment practice may be more a reflection of tradition than of principled decision making. Teachers not only ask questions but are also surrounded by questions. We receive a steady diet of questions: those that follow reading selections and those on quizzes, unit tests, and year-end examinations. This diet is often restricted, lacking examples of alternatives to test-like questions. Unfortunately, as tests receive more and more attention, classroom practices that help prepare students to take and succeed on high-stakes tests focus on question types that appear on tests. Why would we ask middle school students to develop a theory of why poverty persists in East Africa when the high-stakes test question requires choosing, from alternatives, the capital of Somalia? Teaching to the test is, in effect, teaching to an impoverished notion of what questions can tell us. Perhaps the new generation of assessments can improve this situation.

Pearson and Johnson (1978) characterize questions as textually explicit, textually implicit, and scriptally implicit. Each of the characterizations is important for us to understand because they describe the types of reading, thinking, and answering that students must do to be successful. Consider the following paragraph:

> Rowan smiled with satisfaction as her horse vaulted her over the last jump. She knew that the prize would be hers. After crossing the finish line, she did a celebratory gallop past the spectators. The judges awarded her the trophy for First Place, Steeplechase. The trophy was silver with a young rider and horse jumping over a fence. As Rowan got into the car with her parents, she thought of the place in her room where she would proudly display her award.

Textually explicit questions require students to locate answers that have exact wording in the texts they read; the answers are right there in the text. For example, the question, "What trophy did Rowan win?" can be answered, "First Place, Steeplechase." Textually implicit questions require students to gather information from at least two different parts of the text to successfully answer the question. Here, a representative question is, "Why did Rowan gallop past the spectators?" and an acceptable answer is, "She was celebrating winning the trophy." Scriptally implicit questions require students to integrate information from the text with information in their prior knowledge to successfully answer questions. A representative question is, "Do you think Rowan's parents are proud of her, and why?"

The three distinctions of question type help us determine the type of comprehension and thinking that the student is capable of. They mark the growth of the reader from someone who can give back correct information from text to one who is manipulating knowledge contained in different parts of the text with his or her own prior knowledge. The question types may also provide information related to what and how much prior knowledge a student has or needs for a particular text. Each of the question types can reflect the ongoing development of how students read, think, and understand. The preceding examples also help illustrate how a student with little or no prior knowledge for the text content may be at a disadvantage in answering the same set of questions.

The work of Bloom (1956), Pearson and Johnson (1978), and others offers us frameworks for thinking about our questions. Categorization schemes for questions help us understand the type of thinking and learning that are reflected in students' answers to our questions. Thus, the schemes help us understand what exactly we are asking students to do with our questions. The frameworks challenge us to consider what kinds of questions we ask and the frequency with which we ask them. Reading questions must focus on the content of what is read, but the different frameworks remind us that questions can ask for verbatim responses, ask us to make generalizations from text, ask us to read between the lines, such as when we try to determine an author's purpose or intent, and ask us to evaluate the content and form of the texts we read. Each type of question plays a valuable role in helping us understand the important ways in which student readers develop.

Instructional Perspectives on Questioning

Over the past 25 years, we have seen approaches to questioning that may serve the double duty of helping teachers gather assessment information about their students while helping students learn to ask important and appropriate questions themselves. These programs and models include the K-W-L strategy (Ogle, 1986), question–answer relationships (QARs; Raphael & Wonnacott, 1985), and questioning the author (Beck, McKeown, Hamilton, & Kucan, 1997). Ogle, working with theories of cognition and metacognition, developed the K-W-L strategy, which requires students to ask themselves the following questions:

- What do I *know* about the text?
- What do I *want* to learn from the text?
- What did I *learn* from the text?

The strategy is popular not only as a questioning routine but also as a means of helping students develop strategic approaches to reading. In fact, this strategy is a strong example of questioning that guides students' strategy use and reading, in addition to promoting text-based comprehension. The K-W-L strategy can help us assess both students' learning from text and their strategic approaches to reading. Our evolving understanding of how students think and learn should privilege particular types of questioning practice, especially as we consider the complex curricular goals and sophisticated student thinking that are hallmarks of high-quality instructional programs.

QAR strategies (Raphael & Wonnacott, 1985) help students understand the connections between questions that are asked by the teacher or test and the answers that students give in response. In effect, the QAR approach helps students become metacognitive about the relationship of the meaning that is constructed through reading with the comprehension questions we ask them. The approach is built on the assumption that it is important for student readers to know where their answers come from and the suitability of using different sources of information for answering different types of questions. The four categories of QARs are right there, think and search, author and me, and on my own. *Right there* means that students should be able to find the content for their answers to questions from one source in the text. *Think and search* means that student readers should find information from different sources. *Author and me* requires students to use prior knowledge related to the text in combination with inferences they make about the text. Finally, *on my own* means that although the question is related to the text, the student's answer may or may not be related, and answers emanate from students' prior experiences and knowledge.

Questioning the author (Beck et al., 1997) is a means for teachers to help students learn good questions to ask of authors of the texts they read and for teachers to gauge the development of students' ability to read critically. Questioning the author helps the reader approach texts from a purpose-driven perspective. Students may ask themselves,

- Why did the author write this?
- What is the author trying to tell me?
- How well does the author succeed at the task of writing well?
- What are the strong and weak points of the author's writing and argument?
- Are there alternative approaches to the author's portrayal of the issue?

Knowledgeable students ask such questions. One result of questioning the author should be that students better appreciate talented authors' approaches to writing, which in turn may influence students' own writing. This approach also helps students make accurate attributions for their comprehension of text. Challenges to comprehension may be the result of poorly written text, and students who understand this and can identify such texts when they are reading them are in a good position to make the correct attributions for their own performance.

Many questions that are asked of students focus on literal and simple inferential comprehension. Such questions will always play an important role in reading assessment. However, they do not fully represent the types of questions that are important to ask of students, nor do they help us assess reading, learning, and thinking at more complex levels. Consider the critical and evaluative questions that we may ask of students. Students and other citizens in democratic societies must be able to ask questions about the accuracy and trustworthiness of texts. Readers should determine the obvious and hidden agendas of the authors who create texts. Advertisements, editorials, political campaign documents, and other forms of persuasive text must be addressed with critical questions. Such questions help us determine if students understand the different purposes for authors writing particular types of texts, the apparent accuracy of accounts of factual information, the strength of an author's argument and claims, and the form and content of the text (Bråten et al., 2009; Muspratt, Luke, & Freebody, 1997).

Characteristics of Effective Questions

If we envision success for our students in and out of school, does this success revolve around answering literal comprehension questions? Does it involve a student's ability to read between the lines, stand in critical judgment of authors and their works, and use that which is read and understood in tasks and performances? The answers to these questions must influence how we conceptualize and use questions in our classrooms, and this conceptualization and use of questions must be informed by the most recent and compelling theory, research, and practice related to asking questions. We want our questions to help students demonstrate their present understanding of texts read in school as well as anticipate their future success in life.

Questions are used to determine what a student has learned from reading a text. They are also used to help us best understand the thinking and reasoning that students do in relation to their reading. We must examine our curriculum and goals of instruction to help determine the types of questions we ask of our students. If we ask them to read so that they can give us back information from the text, then factual questions are suitable. If we want students to demonstrate that they know facts and opinions and know when an author is being persuasive, then we need to ask questions that reveal the students' knowledge related to persuasive writing and content learning.

Appropriate questions result from careful and often complex analyses of the important components of teaching and learning. First, good questions are tied to the text. They seek to identify student learning that occurs as a result of and in relation to reading. Good questions represent an inquiry into clearly defined areas of learning. We want our questions to focus on important points of learning and attainable goals. Questions should be aligned with our personal and districtwide learning goals and curriculum. Our questions should reflect a clear understanding of how students learn and develop, how knowledge is constructed in particular content areas, and how reading operates.

Slack (1998) developed a list of factors to consider when developing questions and determining a sequence for the question-asking process. Figure 4 presents a checklist based on these factors that we should consider as we seek to construct effective questions. Examination of the checklist demonstrates that we must focus on both the content and the form of our questions so that they are appropriate, accessible, and answerable.

FIGURE 4
A Checklist for Asking Appropriate Questions

_____ I ask questions that are appropriately phrased and understood by students.

_____ I ask questions that are at an appropriate level for the materials being covered.

_____ I ask questions that require students to think at various intellectual levels.

_____ My questions follow a logical sequence.

_____ Student responses are used to guide my next question.

_____ My questions are consistent with the intended goals or objectives of the lesson.

_____ I ask questions that assess student understanding.

_____ I ask processing questions if a student's answer is incomplete or superficial.

_____ I encourage students to answer difficult questions by providing cues or rephrasing.

_____ I avoid closed-ended questions that restrict students' demonstration of learning.

Note. Adapted from "Questioning Strategies to Improve Student Thinking and Comprehension" (p. 28), by J.B. Slack, 1998, unpublished manuscript, Southwest Educational Development Laboratory, Austin, TX. Adapted with permission.

As we develop assessment questions, we must remind ourselves that our questions model for students a specific manner of thinking about learning and knowing. Our questions teach students about particular stances that they may take toward knowledge.

Consider the following five questions. Each could be asked as students complete a chapter on the American Revolution in their social studies textbook.

1. Where did Colonial troops defeat General Cornwallis?

2. What is the theme of this chapter?

3. Why did the author choose these examples to illustrate the main idea?

4. Was the author successful in his strategy?

5. How do you judge your performance on these questions?

The first question is informed by the perspective that students should learn and memorize historical facts. The information exists on the written page and is to be learned and remembered by the reader. The second question asks students to synthesize a theme based on their literal understanding. The perspective that readers should be inquisitive about the things they read and be aware of authors' strategies and intent informs the third question. The fourth question asks students to make a critical judgment about the author's ability. Finally, the fifth question asks student readers to look inward and provide an account of metacognitive processes. Each question is worth asking, and each yields responses that tell us much about a student's reading development. The challenge is to balance our question asking so that in relation to our teaching goals, no type of question is ignored, and no type of question predominates.

The questions that students encounter related to their reading can shape their stance toward reading and knowledge and their very beliefs about the authority of the text. Just as important, the questions we ask of students consistently communicate what we value. Low-level questions asked across an entire school year send students a consistent message that memorization and retrieval of information from text are important. More challenging questions invite students to problem solve, problem find, and partake in complex thinking. Across the school career, our questions, whether high-level or low-level, help shape students' epistemologies because we send consistent messages about the nature of knowledge, what is important in the texts we read, and what correct interpretations of texts should be.

Examining Different Types of Questions

In this section, we examine the types of questions that we may ask in relation to students' reading. It is common to think of reading assessment questions as focused on comprehension because this is a primary role of questions. However, the means by which we measure and describe students' comprehension of text should not be limited to a series of literal and inferential comprehension questions. We should consider questions that help us understand if students are able to apply what they learn from reading, generalize from what they read to their lives, and adopt critical and evaluative stances toward texts and their contents.

Introduced earlier in this chapter, the IRE approach to questioning and assessment can be a direct path to ascertaining the different types of student learning. For example, we can ask students questions like, What is the capital of Kansas? and What is a tectonic plate? and effectively evaluate their responses. A more complex IRE question might be, How is the French Revolution like the American Revolution? As the question becomes more complex, so must our evaluation and assessment. In fact, IRE questions can be used to assess student learning and performance at diverse levels of thinking and understanding. In contrast to the promise of gearing our questions to increasingly difficult levels of thinking and learning, the IRE structure predominates, and classroom questions related to reading are relegated to relatively low levels of thinking.

Several caveats are necessary for teachers considering the IRE structure in questioning routines or identifying it as an already prevalent mode of classroom discourse. First, IRE is teacher dominated: The teacher determines what questions will be asked and then asks them. In the extreme, the teacher can become the sole model of the types of questions asked and the placement of questions within lessons. If we ask an array of questions that revolve around what is understood from reading, using that which is understood, and reacting critically to texts that are read, it may well be that students are getting a healthy sampling of the important types of questions to ask. However, if we continually ask lower level questions (i.e., those that require students to only identify literal information and make simple inferences), this does not help students better understand how different question types encourage different types of thinking.

Second, the IRE pattern establishes the teacher as the sole determinant of the appropriateness of students' responses. The teacher is the single person with the correct answer to the question. Over time, this classroom routine and the approach to knowledge that it represents can suggest to students that our knowledge and understanding of content is all that matters, that divergent thinking is not appropriate, and that there is a single arbiter of students' answers to reading questions. Third, the IRE pattern represents a teacher monopoly on assessment. When we do all the question asking and are in charge of all the answers, there may be missed opportunities for students to learn to do question asking, peer evaluation, and self-evaluation. If the teacher generates the questions and then evaluates student responses, there are missed opportunities for students to learn these important reading-related strategies.

Questions That Are Planned or Spontaneous, Divergent or Convergent

Classroom assessment questions can be spontaneous or planned, and divergent or convergent. Spontaneous questions follow the flow of reading in the classroom and are prompted by our careful observations and monitoring. Spontaneous questions help teachers assess students' understanding as it is developing. These questions help us make determinations of the degree to which students have read, understood, and learned from text. The questions provide information that helps the teacher decide to reteach, elaborate and enrich, or move ahead during the reading lesson. Spontaneous questions are well suited to helping us obtain useful information. We do not plan for students to encounter difficulties with our introduction and explanation of plate tectonics, but we should plan to have contingency questions that guide us to a detailed understanding of individual students' developing knowledge and current needs. Contingent and spontaneous questions fuel our ability to identify and capitalize on teachable moments.

Conversely, planned questions can provide coverage of important school learning in relation to goals of the lesson, as determined a priori. We go into the questioning routine knowing what we want to check with our assessment questions, and these must be targeted at important anticipated outcomes. Key vocabulary and the concepts they represent, main ideas, and supporting details are all examples of appropriate foci for planned questions. Planned questions can also prompt critical thinking. Students' responses to such questions help us determine their understanding of key concepts. When our students read an article about plate tectonics, we are interested in their understanding of earthquakes, the Richter scale, and the San Andreas Fault, as well as the tectonic plates themselves. As teachers, we may develop familiarity with aspects of the curriculum that pose challenges within particular lessons for particular students. For example, we may determine over time that the tectonic plate article is engaging but that students' understanding of how tectonic plate movement leads to earthquakes is elusive. Our attention to these challenges means that we can build a repertoire of planned questions, informed by our observations of student performance, that focuses on the relationship between tectonic plates and earthquakes. Student readers will benefit from a mixture of spontaneous and planned questions. The talented teacher approaches reading assessment with ideas for both.

We may ask students divergent or convergent questions. Convergent questions are made with the expectation that different students' responses, when accurate, will be similar or identical. There is often one correct response expected with convergent questions. For example, we can ask, Where is the San Andreas Fault? and be confident that there is a single correct answer to the question. In contrast, divergent questions encourage a classroom of students to each answer the same question in suitable, and what may be different, ways. We can ask, Why would people build homes close to the San Andreas Fault? Determining the quality of the responses may be more difficult with divergent questions because the questions invite different paths to solutions, different explanations for phenomena, and different criteria for explanation. Thus, the means to evaluate responses to divergent questions should be developed with the understanding that answers may vary and still be appropriate.

Question Comprehensibility, Wait Time, and Passage Independence

When we ask questions, we are often interested in how well students have comprehended the text. Our questions are texts themselves, and we must query, what is the comprehensibility of the questions we ask? We typically think of difficulty in reading in relation to the match between the reader and the text, the degree to which a text contains new and difficult material, and the motivation that a reader may or may not have for reading. Assessment questions are a specific genre of text, and we must scrutinize the questions we ask for how well students understand them. A difficult question can confuse students who, through more appropriate questions, might demonstrate comprehension of what they read. When we construct questions, we should consider the vocabulary of the question and the complexity of the prompt. If the vocabulary demands of our question are greater than, and in addition to, the vocabulary demands of the learning we seek to investigate through questioning, then we need to revise our questions. (For more on making accommodations, see Chapter 9.) We should also anticipate the sense that a student might make out of a question that does or does not coincide with our intention.

Between a teacher's posing a question and a student's response to that question exists wait time. Every question that we ask may warrant wait time, from a seemingly simple literal comprehension question to a complex critical and evaluative one. We should not expect that comprehensive answers spring fully formed from students' minds. Thoughtful answers require thought, and thought requires time. Wait time will vary from question to question and from student to student. The amount of time needed to answer a question is influenced by several important factors, including the focus of the question, students' comprehension of the text, the comprehensibility of the question, the complexity of the thinking required to give an adequate response, and students' individual differences. The wait time allowed for students' responses to questions should vary based on our best estimate of these factors. In effect, it is our responsibility to probe the question and understand the demands that it creates for students, so we can develop legitimate estimates of how much time a student needs to adequately think about and answer the question. This estimate will have parameters so that we have a general sense of what a question demands and what our individual students require in terms of time to respond.

Sometimes, students can answer our questions without comprehending the related text. Thus, our questions should be vetted for text independence. Students may be able to provide correct answers when they have not comprehended the text addressed by the questions. This situation is prominent in multiple-choice question situations in which students with no idea of the correct answer respond correctly, without any understanding of the text: The lucky guess helps. Also, students may come to a correct answer by faulty reasoning. Finally, students can answer correctly by using their prior knowledge related to the text's topic rather than their comprehension of the text. Asking students to provide reasons for their answers serves as a check on their answers and helps us best understand what a student was thinking when giving a particular answer.

A further consideration for our questioning is the demand that the response creates. Following our questions, students may be required to speak or write a response. The response format is one that must be considered as questions and sets of questions are created. Multiple-choice questions require the reader to choose the correct answer, often from among four or five possible answers. A well-developed multiple-choice question can provide valuable information about things students learn. Or, our questions may prompt students to provide constructed responses, which were called fill-ins in the not-so-distant past. Brief constructed responses require students to provide short answers, typically ranging from one to three sentences. Extended constructed responses can demand that students provide sentences, paragraphs, or sets of paragraphs. In each instance, our estimation of the item format that will best provide useful information is important. Like oral responses, written responses may have considerable wait time demands for the students to not only find and retrieve information from their long-term memory but also draft, revise, and construct the response to the question.

Good questions evolve over time because teachers who ask the questions pay attention to how students respond. A question and answer that seem excellent from our teaching perspective must be checked against students' performance and perspectives on the same, especially in culturally diverse classrooms. As questions are introduced into the classroom routine, we must ascertain that they work. We cannot be content with determining if a student's response to a question is correct or incorrect. We must uncover the student thinking that led to the response to the question. Only the examination of this thinking will allow us to determine if what we anticipate as a typical thought process and question response is what students actually do when responding to the question.

Assessing Responses to Questions in Retellings and Discussions

Earlier in this chapter, we discussed the IRE discourse structure, which focuses on individual questions. Yet, in many classrooms, there may be opportunities to assess students by listening to their retellings and discussions of the texts they read. We can obtain information related to students' understanding of text by examining the classroom context that surrounds reading:

• Do students discuss their understanding of stories and informational texts?

• Are they empowered to do so?

- Do students give retellings that help us fill in the gaps of our understanding of their comprehension?
- As a prelude to systematic questioning, what can a reader who is unprompted tell about what was read?

(Oral retellings of what students read are also examined in Chapter 2.)

There are considerable benefits to student discussions of the things they read (Wells, 1989). As we become sensitive to the content and structure of students' discussions, we can find answers to our questions without asking them. Of course, done successfully, this demands that teachers are able to observe and analyze students' discussions in relation to a set of questions. Task analysis of the important things that students do when they read, practice with listening to students, and matching discussion to questions can make this an important part of the classroom assessment routine.

Teachers who are knowledgeable about questioning and have the time to do so can create a series of questions for the texts their students read in class. More often, questions are included in commercially produced curricula, and it is important to scrutinize those questions. We must consider when and where the question we would ask was created. When questions are developed far from the here and now of reading in our classrooms, there may be a reduced chance of a particular question being the best one. Questions can guide or follow thought. The questions that accompany textbooks in social studies, science, music, art, and literature are, hopefully, talented question writers' best estimation of what is needed to focus students on important content and elicit their responses. The questions tend to track knowledge, attending to how well students learn predetermined content. The questions are based on anticipated student work and outcomes, which may or may not be close to the work of particular students in our classrooms.

Approaches to questioning in commercially produced materials vary considerably. These questions anticipate an average level of understanding and insight, and they assume uniform progress among students. The questions, through their focus, predetermine the important information in the texts that students read and also predetermine the correct or acceptable answers. Teachers should always check the stated goals of the lesson and accompanying questions against their own priorities. For example, will a set of questions tell us much about a student's learning and remembering of key details and main ideas but little about how the reader can judge the trustworthiness of the author? Careful examination of the questions that accompany commercial reading materials can help teachers make decisions related to the questions' suitability. A question, or a set of questions, may be all that is needed by the teacher to determine that important learning is being assessed in an appropriate manner. In such cases, questions can be used as provided in teachers' manuals. In other cases, questions may focus on only part of what the teacher considers to be important learning related to the reading. Such questions should be augmented by the teacher's quest for more information. There may be questions that are directed toward eliciting important information, yet they do not present the best question for a particular student in a particular context. At different times in the school year and for different readers, the following questions are entirely appropriate:

- What is the theme of this essay?
- Do you think the author makes a convincing argument? Why?

Questioning in Joan's Fourth-Grade Classroom

The students in Joan's classroom represent a diversity of reading achievement levels and reading interests. Throughout the school year, she sets as a personal professional development goal the ability to ask the right question. Yet, what is the *right* question? For Joan, it is determined by a complex set of factors: a student's developmental level as a reader, the content of the text, the type of thinking that is important to model and then require of the student, and the testing landscape in the school and district. Although these factors are at first burdensome for Joan as she formulates and chooses questions and determines when to ask them, she is confident that the questions in her classroom are worthwhile for her students and reflect important teaching and learning. Her fourth-grade students are in their last year in a largely intact classroom, without any pullouts for particular content areas, which allows Joan to approach her question-asking strategies across the school day and across content domains. She observes students reading and thinking in science, social studies, mathematics, and English, which provides her with a continual source of information related to her students' current state of development and corresponding instructional opportunities. She has the luxury of knowing her students across the school day and the responsibility of attending to the detail of their development so that her teaching and accompanying questioning are appropriate.

Joan is a strategic question asker. She knows that a good question-asking practice is not just a matter of having a range of questions that may evoke different types of student thinking and reveal different types of comprehension and learning. Good questioning is also dependent on the interactive dynamics between the teacher and the student, and the question and the answer. For example, in leading up to a relatively complex question that requires students to propose an explanation (e.g., How can global warming be slowed while people continue to use electricity and automobiles?), Joan knows that her students must demonstrate a literal understanding of the scientific findings related to global warming research. Assuming that this understanding exists without first questioning the students to ascertain this could render the subsequent questions worthless.

To reach her goals for questioning, Joan relies on an "arc of questions,…in which simple factual inquiries give way to increasingly interpretive questions until new insights emerge" (Wolf, 1987, p. 4). The questions help her address her students' learning about global warming and their development related to that learning, and the

66

questions are complementary, building on one another. While the set of questions is intended to help students demonstrate their knowledge and thinking at increasingly complex levels, it also has a diagnostic feature. More simple questions (e.g., What is one cause of global warming?) are asked prior to more complex questions (e.g., How can global warming be slowed or stopped?). This sequencing allows Joan to tailor her questions to individual students. She finds it useful to think about an arc of questions in relation to her students' current levels of reading ability and content area knowledge, along with Bloom's (1956) levels of thinking. Table 7 contains examples of questions that Joan includes in her arc of questions, and indicates their increasing complexity and relationship to Bloom's taxonomy. This arc of questions represents Joan's comprehensive and hierarchical questioning routine and demonstrates her attention to using questions to help shape and assess her students' thinking.

TABLE 7 An Arc of Questions in Relation to Bloom's Taxonomy[a] and Joan's[b] Classroom	
Scenario: Students are reading from different texts to learn about global warming.	
Bloom's Taxonomy Category	Joan's Question to Her Students
Knowledge, or recalling data or information	What is one cause of global warming?
Comprehension, or understanding the meaning, translation, interpolation, and interpretation of instructions and problems; stating a problem in one's own words	How does global warming occur?
Application, or using a concept in a new situation or unprompted use of an abstraction; applying what was learned in the classroom to novel situations in the workplace	What might happen with global warming as the number of automobiles increases?
Analysis, or separating material or concepts into component parts so that the organizational structure may be understood; distinguishing between facts and inferences	What proof of global warming is offered by those people who claim it is a potentially deadly problem?
Synthesis, or building a structure or pattern from diverse elements; putting parts together to form a whole, with emphasis on creating a new meaning or structure	What would you include in a comprehensive plan to reduce global warming?
Evaluation, or making judgments about the value of ideas or materials	Are the alternative explanations for global warming that are given by those who are opposed to taking action against global warming credible, and why?

Note. Modified from Understanding and Using Reading Assessment, K–12 (p. 66), by P. Afflerbach, 2007, Newark, DE: International Reading Association. Copyright 2007 by the International Reading Association.
[a]Taxonomy of Educational Objectives: The Classification of Educational Goals, Handbook 1: Cognitive Domain, edited by B.S. Bloom, 1956, New York: David McKay. [b]Pseudonym.

Consequences and Usefulness of Questioning

Joan believes that it is important for students to apply what they learn from reading to identify and solve problems, to engage in generative thought, and to be critical consumers of the information contained in the texts they read. She surveys questions and determines those that tap literal and simple inferential comprehension. As she categorizes her instructional goals in relation to Bloom's (1956) taxonomy, she can determine the degree to which the questions she asks of students focus on the different types of learning within the taxonomy. A result is robust questioning. Students need to not only establish accurate literal understandings of text but also complement that understanding with the ability to answer questions about authors' motives, persuasive features of texts, and the degree to which claims in the text are supported with evidence. A more typical approach of using literal and inferential questions would not provide assessment information that is as rich as that provided by robust questioning.

There are several critical consequences and uses of the questions that Joan develops for her students. First, the questions help her understand how well students learn course content. The questions tap students' literal, inferential, and critical understandings of the texts they read. Second, the questions, having tapped students' literal and inferential comprehension, then require students to demonstrate diverse approaches to thinking and increased sophistication in their thinking. Questions help Joan understand how students use that which they comprehend. Importantly, questions serve to both provoke thinking and assess it. For example, Joan asks how students might adopt different perspectives to comment on the portrayal of global warming in their science text. Without the question, it is unclear how many students would be moved to this type of thinking. With the question, Joan also has a means for judging students' approaches to the thinking. Her questions provide process and product information about students' reading development, information that can be used in both formative and summative assessments.

The consequences for Joan's students are substantial. They are continually asked to demonstrate their understanding of text through an array of questions that target literal and inferential understandings. These questions describe the extent to which students understand the text, and also serve as practice for the high-stakes tests at year-end, which are heavily weighted to measure students' literal and inferential comprehension. Provided with diverse types of questions, the students in Joan's class get consistent models of how to think and are learning to ask questions of themselves as they read. These questions fall into two broad categories—comprehension and meta-comprehension—and help students independently determine the degree to which they understand the texts that they read.

Over time, the variety of questions that are asked in Joan's classroom (and in grades prior to and after fourth grade) have another serious consequence for students: They learn that what they read is often worthy of investigation and challenge. Questions model for students different ways of thinking and stances toward reading and knowledge. As fourth graders, these students are bombarded with advertisements and other types of propaganda encountered in newspapers and magazines and on the Internet. Questions that uncover a hidden intent of text, an author's strategy for being persuasive, and the trustworthiness of the text help students navigate their daily, personal lives and help us prepare students for critical reading throughout their lives.

Roles and Responsibilities Related to Questioning

Across a school career, the type and frequency of questions used in classrooms can have a profound influence on students' thinking, their engagement with learning, and their epistemologies. Consider the student who receives an exclusive mix of literal and inferential comprehension questions across elementary school. This student may become adept at giving back text to answer literal comprehension questions and at combining literal information from text with prior knowledge to achieve inferential comprehension. The steady stream of questions focuses on knowledge checking, an important outcome of our reading. Unfortunately, this student may not have the opportunity to begin to question the authority of the text, challenge an author's claims, or determine the subtext that underlies an author's explicit and implicit arguments. In U.S. society, where there is consistent initiative to convince people that they need to buy things and where truth is hard to find in political campaigns, our students must be able to ask questions of texts so that they are in a powerful, and not powerless, position as readers. The Common Core State Standards (CCSSO & NGA, 2010) require such student thinking and related questions that aspire to critical and evaluative reading.

Joan is convinced that good teaching in fourth grade results not only in students learning in the content areas but also in further development of students' ability to think and reason. Future grades' curricula in middle school and high school will demand that students master literal and inferential comprehension of texts so that students may critically evaluate the texts. Joan knows that the application of knowledge learned from reading is not only demanded in the upper grades but also central to much of the reading that students will do outside of school. She is responsible for certifying that her students learn from text in each of the content areas and can apply the knowledge learned. She is responsible for helping her students prepare for high-stakes tests that will determine their futures. She is also responsible for instilling the ideal that good questions beget more good questions: Students who are asked diverse and necessary questions learn new ways of thinking and can internalize and use these same types of questions in their future.

Joan's questions are informed by her ideas of good practice. She makes sure that she provides adequate wait time for all of her students to construct appropriate responses and that her questions are comprehensible for her students. She conducts task analyses in relation to her questions, always double-checking to see that what she anticipates being involved in the process and product of student answers is actually there. Joan resists the idea of questioning becoming a comfortable habit in her classroom. She knows that questions can lead to the establishment and reinforcement of power relationships in classrooms. Questions can be used to acknowledge particular students' contributions or lack of contribution to the class. For Joan, asking, What's the right question? sets the parameters of her roles and responsibilities. She is focused on determining how and to what degree students are learning content from their reading. She regularly asks questions that focus on what students understand from the textbook chapter on earthquakes, the primary source texts in social studies, and the short story in English. She also checks for her students' ability to understand math word problems.

Joan continually monitors her questions: She believes that most good questions need a tryout period. To refine and polish her questions, Joan pilots them in her classroom, which allows her to apply her knowledge from the task analysis to help troubleshoot those questions that she believes are important but seem to be causing difficulty for her students. She structures her question-asking routines so that they include opportunities for her students to learn how to ask important questions of themselves. She models, explains, and discusses with her students why we ask questions, where questions come from, how they then connect to our learning goals and tasks, and how student responses to questions are evaluated. In addition, she amends the questioning routine that accompanies the commercially produced materials to include questions that direct students to the nature of questions, knowledge, and power.

Reliability of Questioning

As a teacher who creates many different types of questions for her students, Joan follows a detailed routine for ascertaining the reliability of her questions. At the heart of this routine is a task analysis of what exactly students must do to understand and respond to the questions. (For more information on task analysis, see the Reading Assessment Snapshot for Task Analysis at the end of Chapter 1.) The task analysis is conducted with the goal of creating questions that provide reliable information. The analysis allows Joan to go through the motions that her questions will demand of her students and to experience firsthand what answering the question entails. She considers first the comprehensibility of the question: Will her students understand it? Is this literal question more challenging than the text that students must read to answer the question? Next, she examines the fairness of the question: Does it privilege certain students who already know something about the content of the assigned reading? Is the question straightforward and not confusing? Can the question be answered without reading the text? Next, Joan checks for confounds. (For more information on confounds, see the Reading Assessment Snapshot for Confounds in Reading Assessment at the end of Chapter 9.) Will a student's speaking or writing ability influence Joan's interpretation of that student's reading achievement? Joan examines each question to determine the things that students must know and do to answer the question well. She considers the complexity of the question in relation to her students and estimates the necessary wait time for each to answer.

The reliability of her assessment also depends on her interactions with the students during questioning. When asking questions during a lesson, Joan can discuss, model, and suggest things that lead students to insights and correct answers. This is a regular part of her question asking during class. In contrast, she is consistent in her treatment of students when asking summative assessment questions. She does not provide hints or clues when questions are related to unit tests because she knows that students must be prepared to take consequential, high-stakes tests.

Validity of Questioning

Joan's questions must pass two stringent tests related to construct validity. The first test focuses on her conceptualization of reading comprehension as including literal, inferential, and critical or evaluative comprehension. She makes sure that her array of questions honors the construct of comprehension by asking questions that provide students with opportunities to demonstrate these different levels of thinking. The typical arc of questions in Joan's classroom reflects her knowledge of what it means to understand text. Students must construct literal and inferential meaning of the things they read while understanding why texts are written, authors' acknowledged and unspoken agendas, and how the contexts in which we read can influence what we take from a text.

A second test relates to the thinking done by students as they answer questions. Bloom's (1956) taxonomy suggests increasingly complex and sophisticated thinking, and the array of questions in Joan's classroom reflects this construct. Thus, her questions serve the dual role of providing detail on what her students learn and providing a model of diverse and sophisticated thinking. They also reflect ecological validity, in that Joan strives to instill further inquisitiveness in her students by posing and modeling good question asking.

Summary

There are many types of questions that we may ask when we assess our student readers. These questions should be informed by our knowledge of theories of thinking, our students, strategies, cognitive development, the role of the reader, and the curriculum. Across history, questions have been central to reading assessment. We ask questions because we want to know about our students' learning and progress. Questions are central to assessing and evaluating students' reading comprehension, yet many questions do not reflect our detailed understanding of the suitability of particular types of questions for particular learning goals and reading curricula.

Our questions should reflect the nature of learning and thinking that we expect of our developing readers. Questions are influenced by diverse factors, including their structure, syntax, and vocabulary. Also, an effective questioning practice reflects our attention to factors that include wait time, the questions' relation to retelling and discussion, and the development of a series of questions that represent a range of comprehension levels and the range of content that we are interested in assessing.

ENHANCING YOUR UNDERSTANDING

1. Videotape a reading lesson. Examine your questions: the type of question, the comprehensibility of the question, the wait time, the clarification, teacher dominance, and the relation to different learning goals. Who asks questions, and who answers them? How much class time is involved?

2. In relation to the information in this chapter, would you characterize the mix of the types of questions you ask as optimal? Why?

3. Create an arc of questions in a particular content area that helps you understand student achievement from the level of literal understanding through critical analysis and application of what is understood from reading.

4. Think of a recent, personal learning experience. How did you know how you were doing? How did you know how well you did upon completion of the task? What can this teach you about good questions to ask of students' reading, assessment, and self-assessment?

Process and Product Assessment

Useful reading assessment revolves around the quality of the inferences we can make about students from assessment information. The accuracy and suitability of these inferences are influenced by the relationship of the assessment to instruction and student learning. With this in mind, it is important to consider how assessments focus on the processes or products of student learning and achievement.

Process measures help us examine the means by which students learn and achieve. These processes might involve determining the match of the letter *B* with the spoken sound /b/, reading fluently, or constructing meaning from text. For example, a teacher observation conducted during reading instruction can provide detailed and immediate assessment information related to the processes that fourth graders use as they work with the K-W-L procedure (Ogle, 1986). The teacher observes students making note of the things they *know* and the things they would like to *learn* from the text to be read. The teacher observes students monitoring their work, so they can effectively answer the *L* section of the K-W-L exercise: What did I *learn*? The teacher's observation is process centered, so the inferences made about students derive from a more direct view to those processes.

In contrast, product measures are removed in several ways from the acts of instruction and learning. First, product assessments focus on learning that is assumed to be, in some sense, complete. This means that our inferences about students and their learning may be limited to the nature of the products that are the end result of the processes. We may consider completed performance assessments, students' final drafts of writing, or correct or incorrect responses to test questions. In these cases, our inferences are necessarily backward looking; that is, we can determine that learning occurred or did not occur, based on the student's response, but from that point on, we have little or no information to understand how the product was created. We may lack the understanding of how, what, and when particular processes were or were not used. Product measures reveal little or no information about the processes that students used or tried to use in creating the products. Thus, we are not often in a position to use product assessment in a diagnostic manner. We are also not in a position to use product assessment for formative assessment because product assessment has little explanatory power to guide our inferences and instruction.

It is important to become familiar with both product and process assessment and the types of inferences that we are required (and permitted) to make, based on the assessment information. Whatever the nature of the assessment, the quality of the inferences we make from product or process reading assessment must be high—a suitable result of our understanding of the nature of the assessments we use and the inferences that are justified from the data they provide.

CHAPTER 4

Portfolio Assessment

Across the school year, we hope to determine that students ably comprehend the texts that they read, use what they comprehend to undertake learning-related tasks, and are increasingly focused on conducting their own assessments. Portfolio assessment, when done well, helps us in this work. Also, portfolios are the rare breed of assessment that supports student learning while describing it.

An examination of definitions of *portfolio* helps us understand how portfolios have developed as assessments. *Webster's New Collegiate Dictionary* (1973) describes a portfolio as "a flat, portable case, usually of leather, for carrying loose sheets of paper, manuscripts, drawings, etc.: a briefcase" (p. 1404). This description focuses on the physical characteristics of portfolios used by artists and authors and the possible contents of these portfolios. Portfolios have a heritage in the fine arts, where they help individuals organize, reflect on, present, and discuss their work. Portfolios provide flexibility: The keeper of the portfolio can determine its contents, how it is used, and the manner in which the contents are presented to different audiences for different purposes. The *Merriam-Webster* (2011b) online dictionary defines *portfolio* as "a selection of a student's work (as papers and tests) compiled over a period of time and used for assessing performance or progress."

The Literacy Dictionary (Harris & Hodges, 1995) defines *portfolio* as "a selected, usually chronological collection of a student's work that may be used to evaluate learning progress" (p. 190). This definition focuses on how portfolio contents may be organized to allow for the examination and assessment of work over time. Tierney and Clark (1998) describe what we might expect if we were to sample successful portfolio assessments of reading from different classrooms: "If one created a portfolio on portfolios, there would be enormous variety in what might be represented and some variation in what might be considered key elements, undergirding assumptions, and possibilities" (p. 474).

In all cases, effective student portfolios reflect specific curricular and assessment goals in classrooms, schools, and school districts. Portfolios succeed when they are informed by clearly stated needs and purposes related to teaching and learning reading. Successful portfolio assessment is well organized, and the structure of the portfolio helps guide student assessment work. Portfolio assessment is an example of authentic assessment and is characterized by its close relationship with instruction and learning and its ability to provide a detailed account of students' achievement in complex school tasks and performances. Portfolio assessment should be used with sensitivity to how portfolios will make their best contribution to students' and teachers' work in classrooms, schools, or districts.

A Brief History of Portfolio Assessment

Our consideration of portfolio assessment in reading is informed by lessons learned over several decades. The history of the use of portfolio assessment in reading is preceded by reading assessment that includes cumulative and diverse indicators of students' achievement. Fifty years ago, the careful collection and coordination of student work to demonstrate student learning was not necessarily called portfolio assessment, although the intent was to describe richly how students develop as readers and literate individuals. Contemporary advocates posit that portfolios are a means to assess and support students' development in reading (Tierney & Clark, 1998), and the promise of describing and supporting student work has led to the development of successful schoolwide (Au, 1994) and districtwide (Valencia & Place, 1994) portfolio assessment programs.

Portfolio assessments can be used at the district and state levels to provide useful information, but the school resources needed to develop and conduct such assessment are substantial (LeMahieu, Gitomer, & Eresh, 1995). Currently, success stories and the accompanying enthusiastic support for portfolios are most often found in pockets within schools and schools within districts (Hebert, 1998). These successful portfolio programs are the result of teachers working to establish reading assessment that honors the quality of teaching and students' learning in classrooms (Tierney, Carter, & Desai, 1991). The adequate yearly progress requirements demanded by NCLB are tied, in each state, to a single indicator of student achievement. No state uses portfolios to describe how students develop as readers in relation to adequate yearly progress. Using portfolios in this role is too costly for states to undertake.

However, new assessment initiatives related to the Common Core State Standards may effect change. Two assessment consortia receiving Race to the Top funding from the U.S. Department of Education have proposed significant changes for students' literacy assessment. For example, the PARCC (2010) proposes to link reading with Common Core State Standards for Writing:

> The Partnership intends to align the task rubrics with the CCSS [Common Core State Standards], which require students to draw evidence from literary or informational texts to support analysis, reflection, and research, and produce coherent organized writing appropriate to purpose and audience. In addition, the through-course components may ask students to write an argument, write with the intent to inform or explain, or write a narrative.[6] Further, the extended component might require students to conduct a research project to gather and synthesize information from multiple sources. (p. 50)

This description invokes portfolio assessment and suggests that literacy assessments will become more complex over the next decade and, thus, may require portfolio approaches to assessment.

Similarly, the SBAC (2010) intends to assess student learning in relation to the Common Core State Standards

> in ways that require more student-initiated planning, management of information and ideas, interaction with other materials and/or people, and production of more extended responses (e.g., oral presentations, exhibitions, product development, in addition to more extended written responses) that reveal additional abilities of students (Darling-Hammond & Pecheone, 2010) not captured by the other item types included in the summative assessment. (p. 53)

Portfolios are ideally suited to the "student-initiated planning, management of information and ideas, [and] interaction with other materials and/or people" described by SBAC.

Although the prospect of portfolios playing a larger role in reading assessment is intriguing, the remainder of this chapter describes portfolio reading assessment whose promise is realized in individual classrooms and schools. This focus on the local use of portfolio assessment does not preclude the hope that portfolios might figure prominently (and soon) in large-scale, consequential assessment programs. Rather, this focus is offered with the belief that a thorough understanding of portfolio assessment, the successful local use of portfolios, and the clear demonstration of portfolios' benefits may contribute to their more widespread use.

Characteristics of Portfolio Assessment

Successful portfolio assessment is marked by key characteristics. Portfolios provide both formative and summative assessment information. A portfolio may contain students' written papers, tests, quizzes, reports, rating sheets, teacher and peer commentary, and journals, along with creative, multimedia products, including videotapes, audiotapes, CDs, and DVDs. Portfolios provide samples of students' ongoing work—the steps by which students progress to increasingly accomplished reading. To accommodate this range of contents, portfolios can assume diverse shapes, sizes, and materials, including folders, boxes, binders, containers, and electronic files. The availability of digitized portfolios means that students' complex performances and projects can be stored with relative ease, and unwieldy projects may be tamed by the use of a digital portfolio (Kimball, 2003).

Valencia and Calfee (1991) characterize three general functions of portfolios: documentation, evaluation, and showcase. The documentation portfolio presents a detailed account of student work and progress across time. Items within a portfolio, selected by the student and the teacher, may include completed tasks and projects, as well as tests, quizzes, checklists, and graded work with teacher comments. For example, in relation to a unit on ecosystems, a student's portfolio contents may represent vocabulary learning, observation of the schoolyard ecosystem, charts with numbers representing counts of plants and animals, preliminary drafts and a final copy of a persuasive essay on why people should care about their local environments, quizzes, and unit tests. Both student and teacher perspectives on learning are present in the documentation portfolio, and the portfolio items represent the array of learning processes and products across a particular time frame, be it a marking period, school year, or content area unit of study. As with all effective assessment, the purpose and contents of the portfolio are carefully aligned.

The evaluation portfolio is marked by the standardization of its contents and the processes by which those contents are evaluated. For example, a portfolio that requires each student to include common contents, such as a set of constructed responses, a reflective journal, and a semester project, brings consistency to the work that students include in the portfolio. Learning and achievement, assessed in a standardized manner within the portfolio by quizzes and tests, may be compared across students. This requires teachers and students to use consistent criteria for including and judging portfolio contents. Results may be used to determine individual student achievement, reading program effectiveness, and teacher accountability.

The showcase portfolio encourages individual students to select and represent their best work. This portfolio demands that students be capable of reflecting on their work and self-assessing their progress (Afflerbach, 2002a; Black & Wiliam, 1998). Students can employ a broad array of items, including papers, projects, and multimedia presentations, to demonstrate the nature of their achievements. A result is that the contents of showcase portfolios may be individualistic. Although the contents of different students' showcase portfolios may vary, the means by which students select, critique, and comment on their good work may be comparable.

It is important to note that the three portfolio functions outlined are not mutually exclusive. Insightful planning can lead to a reading portfolio that addresses all three purposes of documenting, evaluating, and showcasing student work. Also, portfolios can represent the work of a 1st grader just as well as they represent the work of an 11th grader (Kingore, 2008). There should be no arbitrary minimum age limits placed on students who might benefit from the portfolio experience. As demonstrated in this chapter, the nature of the curriculum, the learning goals, and the expectations placed on students should all be considered when a determination of whether to use portfolios is being made.

Portfolio Assessment in Jennifer's Fifth-Grade Classroom

Jennifer is in her third year of using portfolios in the hands-on science unit on ecosystems. The unit is representative of a complex curriculum and teaching and learning goals and reflects careful attention to literacy and science standards (CCSSO &

NGA, 2010; IRA & NCTE, 1996; National Research Council, 1996). A goal of the unit is the development of students' understanding of the general characteristics of ecosystems. Across the unit, students are expected to read and understand several different types of text. These include a science textbook chapter on ecosystems; documents downloaded from the websites of scientific institutions, particularly museums and zoos; articles from local newspapers; and the written work of fellow students. Students are also expected to read and interpret different types of graphs, figures, and tables found in traditional and online texts. Finally, students are encouraged to lead their own portfolio conferences with their teachers and parents (Austin, 1994; Bailey & Guskey, 2001).

The science curriculum requires fifth-grade students to not only read, understand, and remember information but also use what they understand to demonstrate and extend their learning. Reading complements the work of the unit: The fifth graders observe the ecosystem that includes the field behind the school, identify the components of the ecosystem and their interrelationships, collect samples of plants and animals, inventory the different life-forms, and hypothesize about threats to the ecosystem and the means to protect it. The nature of the curriculum and the work that is expected of students require reading assessment that is sensitive to students' achievement and teachers' accomplishments within the ecosystems unit.

These tasks and learning goals relate directly to the grade 5 reading standards for literacy in informational text that are contained in the Common Core State Standards. Specifically, the portfolio assessment in Jennifer's classroom helps describe student learning as related to the following categories of the Common Core State Standards (CCSSO & NGA, 2010, p. 14):

Key ideas and details

- Explain the relationships or interactions between two or more individuals, events, ideas, or concepts in a historical, scientific, or technical text based on specific information in the text.

Craft and structure

- Determine the meaning of general academic and domain-specific words and phrases in a text relevant to a *grade 5 topic or subject area.*

Integration of knowledge and ideas

- Draw on information from multiple print or digital sources, demonstrating the ability to locate an answer to a question quickly or to solve a problem efficiently.

Consequences and Usefulness of Portfolio Assessment

In this section, I combine our consideration of the consequences of and uses for portfolio assessment as guided by the CURRV framework because they are tightly interwoven within Jennifer's classroom. She is dedicated to using portfolios in diverse ways: Portfolios help coordinate assessment and document student learning, support students' reading achievement, and foster students' self-assessment and their appreciation of their accomplishments. Portfolios also help describe student growth that is not cognitive.

An important point is that the form and function of portfolios is flexible. In this sense, the physical space of a portfolio must reflect the psychological and social spaces that the portfolio's contents and processes represent. For example, a portfolio intended to help a student construct a semester project based on diverse reading assignments must be planned and structured to accommodate the student's work: to hold a collection of sources, writing drafts, and the development of a related media project.

Portfolios help Jennifer and her students document learning and achievement. The fifth-grade science curriculum focuses on reading as a tool that students use for learning about ecosystems. Readers are expected to comprehend their science texts and use the knowledge they gain through successful reading. For example, students must use the textbook description of symbiotic relationships to identify and describe one such relationship in the local ecosystem. At the same time, students continue to develop their reading strategies. Students increasingly understand how science texts are structured and how to summarize and synthesize information in the science texts that they read (Chambliss & Calfee, 1998). Jennifer's students are learning how to identify an author's claims and search for the evidence in support of the claims. The students continue to progress in their thinking about and discussion of different science texts in relation to one another: The students are required to locate and read two texts on the Internet that focus on food chains, the effects of pollution on food chains, and how this affects entire ecosystems. These fifth graders are gaining the strategies and knowledge that distinguish proficient and advanced levels of reading achievement from basic levels (National Assessment Governing Board, 2009).

Coordinated and consistent means of assessing development in each of these areas of growth are important. Also, students' academic and personal achievement must be documented to earn ongoing support for the portfolio assessment program that is in place. Portfolios allow for the coordination of the variety and range of reading assessments, and in doing so, portfolios help demonstrate the detail and depth of student learning. The portfolios in Jennifer's class help her understand her students' growth in vocabulary knowledge, the understanding of ecosystems and related concepts, the ability to self-assess when using a checklist, and the critical inquiry of texts. In this sense, portfolios serve as an umbrella under which different reading assessments may be gathered and used.

The portfolio also helps students gather and organize evidence and make claims about their progress across a marking period. The portfolio is a repository of work and thought, carefully arranged by the student to document learning. In Jennifer's class, students include before and after conceptual maps of the schoolyard ecosystem, and these demonstrate how student understanding has grown from an initial list-like account of single things (e.g., rain, wind, snow, sun, trees, weeds, birds, bugs, mammals, reptiles) to a more complex portrayal of their interrelationships within the ecosystem.

The portfolio allows for regular and systematic opportunities for students to document their progress. As we consider the complexity of the reading and related tasks that students must increasingly undertake, we must anticipate the nature of student work so that it allows teachers and students to gauge progress at important points in the constructive process of gaining new knowledge. In Jennifer's class, a student presentation on the varied bird visitors to the schoolyard documents his learning about how to observe and record wildlife. The presentation also helps Jennifer demonstrate her ability to understand and describe this student's academic growth and communicate this knowledge effectively to an interested audience, as noted in the portfolio.

Portfolios provide a place for Jennifer and her students to coordinate assessment efforts. It is one thing to amass reading assessment information across a unit or marking period, but it is quite another thing to bring organization and structure to this information. Each of us can identify students in our classrooms who have a knack for organizing and keeping track of their work. Yet, other students are not so inclined. Portfolios can contribute to the collection of diverse and coordinated information related to students' reading development. Portfolios also demand a plan for coordinating this information. Learning how to manage a portfolio effectively is an important teaching and learning goal and yields benefits throughout the school year. Guidelines for portfolio use in the fifth-grade science classroom are provided in Table 8, which illustrates how curricular goals and processes toward attaining those goals are accommodated within the portfolio.

Within the unit-long inquiry into the nature of ecosystems in Jennifer's class, her students do a lot of work to meet the demands of the accompanying assignments. The students' portfolios hold work in progress, including notes from library books and Internet searches on the interdependency of organisms. Each portfolio contains digitized photo files of ecosystems, either taken in the schoolyard or downloaded from appropriate websites. As they investigate, students keep a log of the websites they visit and the information they provide in relation to the search request for "grassland symbiotic relationships." Each portfolio holds the student's initial draft narrative account of diversity within the schoolyard ecosystem, with subsequent revisions. The portfolio provides a place for students to store and use the information they collect for, in this case, a written report. The portfolio also holds the finished written presentation texts, along with earlier drafts and versions.

Helping students coordinate the indicators and products of their accomplished reading and providing the work space for this reading are unique contributions of portfolio assessment. The portfolio holds a record of how the student writer presented

TABLE 8
The Relation of Different Sections of the Portfolio
to Different Goals of the Portfolio

| | Goals of the Portfolio | | | |
Section of the Portfolio	Document and Coordinate Learning	Support Learning	Encourage Self-Assessment and Appreciation of Reading	Describe Noncognitive Aspects of Reading
Checklist	X		X	X
Vocabulary	X	X	X	
Writing project	X	X	X	
Self-assessment			X	X
How do we know?	X		X	

Note. From *Understanding and Using Reading Assessment, K–12* (p. 77), by P. Afflerbach, 2007, Newark, DE: International Reading Association. Copyright 2007 by the International Reading Association.

his or her work, how classmates reacted to the work, and how the student used peer feedback to improve his or her writing. Here, the portfolio serves as an organized repository for students' reading and reading-related work. The portfolio documents the depth and breadth of student learning, and the coordination of the portfolio's contents contributes to its usefulness. Moreover, the portfolio serves to connect reading with related literacy activities: writing, discussion, and reflection.

Teachers may determine that variability in students' particular uses of the portfolio is to be expected and encouraged in classrooms, while the standardization of aspects of the portfolio is also a worthy goal. To this end, portfolio use in different classrooms within a school, or different schools within a district, may be marked by a set of common procedures, contents, and goals. Portfolios can provide us with a set of standardized experiences with portfolio assessment that proves useful throughout students' school careers, from kindergarten to 12th grade.

For example, an instructional priority in Jennifer's school district is the development of critical reading (for more on assessment and critical reading, see Chapter 3). Portfolios assist in this effort by providing a dedicated place for students to document their work as they address the question, How do we know? across grade levels and content areas. The intent is to have all students regularly reflect on this question in relation to the sources of information (i.e., where texts and the information they contain originate), the different purposes of texts and their authors, and the reliability of the information found in texts. Jennifer's fifth graders answer the question in relation to their classmates' written descriptive accounts of the schoolyard ecosystem. Within this section of the portfolio, students at each grade level keep track of questions they have about things they read; the evidence that authors provide to support their claims; and examples of facts and opinions gathered from textbooks, newspapers, magazines, and webpages. In all cases, the reading portfolio serves as the reminder and forum to address the important question, How do we know? Across students' careers, the portfolio serves as a tool that helps students both learn and demonstrate their learning.

In Jennifer's class, portfolios provide a supportive context for student reading. Early in this chapter, I claimed that portfolio assessment can both describe and support student achievement. How might this work? There is much science content to be learned and used in the ecosystem unit, and Jennifer views the portfolio as a tool that supports the reading and reading-related work of her students. For example, one section of the portfolio is dedicated to the checklists that are used by her fifth-grade students throughout the year. One checklist, shown in Figure 5, helps her students conduct a scientific observation and analyze and apply the information they gather through their observation.

The checklist serves to remind students of the individual steps for observation of the ecosystem: preparing for the observation, beginning the observation, recording information gathered through the observation, and concluding the observation. The checklist section of the portfolio provides a set of reference points that helps students keep account of their work. In addition, checklists provide a consistent source of information that helps students build a mental model of how to conduct scientific observations. It is an external reminder that can become internalized over time and be used by students as they grow toward independence. The checklist has a physical and intellectual proximity to the contents of the portfolio.

FIGURE 5
A Sample General Checklist for Conducting a Scientific Observation

_____ I understand the focus of the observation.

_____ I understand the purpose of the observation.

_____ I conduct my observation according to the steps we learned in class.

_____ I sit quietly so as not to disturb the animals.

_____ I observe as much activity as possible.

_____ I do not make sudden movements or noises.

_____ I take notes during the observation, recording important information in relation to my goals.

_____ I learned the following from my observation: _____.

Note. From *Understanding and Using Reading Assessment, K–12* (p. 79), by P. Afflerbach, 2007, Newark, DE: International Reading Association. Copyright 2007 by the International Reading Association.

As students work through the checklist, they are building an account of their learning. Attending to the checklist's contents requires students to provide information from their science inquiry, and the checklist provides a framework for that inquiry. Another checklist provides ideas for reading resources for students' unit projects. This list is checked as students access different sources of information in their textbooks and at the media center. In this use, checklists within the portfolio support Jennifer's students as they explore different resources and allow them to evaluate this exploration. Such work is necessary for any student to initiate and accomplish tasks successfully and independently.

Portfolios provide a further, supportive context for student reading, discussion, and assessment. The public forum in which students and teachers discuss the portfolios' contents gives students valuable feedback on their work. Consider students who work in small groups to hypothesize about possible threats to the schoolyard ecosystem, based on their reading and class experiences. These students discuss and share their ideas about the characteristics of different ecosystems. The group focuses on temperature change as a possible threat to the ecosystem of the schoolyard and determines from diverse readings that plants and insects thrive only when climatic conditions are optimal. Students' understanding that plants and insects are integral parts of the food chain and that they must be protected derives directly from the portfolio-supported discussion.

The public forum provided by the portfolio process requires students to anticipate different audiences, communicate effectively with their classmates, and clearly reason about their learning based on the evidence provided in the portfolio. A result is that students develop important communication and social skills related to presenting their work and responding to their peers' work. Students provide constructive feedback to their classmates' ongoing enterprises and learn to be supportive of one another. Through the use of the portfolio to demonstrate their learning about ecosystems, Jennifer's students better understand the nature of peer evaluation and the value of constructive criticism. Further, the discussion and use of evaluative criteria for judging fellow students' work reinforces each student's understanding of these same criteria for judging his or her own work.

Jennifer uses portfolios to help her students learn self-assessment.

How can portfolios contribute to students' developing ability to self-assess? In Jennifer's classroom, the portfolio provides a means for her students to regularly check on their learning of key vocabulary in the ecosystem unit. All of her students are required to read, learn, and use these words, and the curriculum is designed to help students learn through repeated encounters with the words and repeated opportunities to use the words in speaking and writing. Jennifer and her colleagues are interested in how portfolios can contribute to the dual goals of having students learn new vocabulary and having students become independent in assessing their vocabulary knowledge.

The flexibility of the portfolio supports student and teacher work toward both goals. Words such as *predator, prey,* and *symbiosis* represent important concepts in the ecosystem unit that students need to learn. A section of the portfolio is dedicated to the dual goals of learning the new vocabulary that is central to understanding the ecosystems unit and students' self-assessment of this learning. The vocabulary section consists of three groupings of vocabulary words labeled "My new words," "I'm getting to know this word," and "I definitely know this word." These stages of vocabulary knowledge reflect Jennifer's understanding of how portfolios can help students develop and enrich their knowledge of word meanings (Beck, McKeown, & Kucan, 2002).

Important vocabulary words emanate from assigned and independent readings and from the ecosystem word wall in the classroom. Students write each vocabulary word on an individual note card and categorize the words according to the three labels. Students sort these words on a regular basis, with growth expected so that students manage the movement of each word card from the "My new words" group to the "I'm getting to know this word" group and eventually to the "I definitely know this word" group. Used in this manner, the portfolio supports both students' vocabulary learning and the development of their ability to self-assess vocabulary knowledge. Having students sort their words on a regular basis forces the issue of self-assessment as content is learned, and Jennifer is convinced that this is one of the most helpful aspects of portfolio assessment in her classroom.

Self-assessment can be encouraged at the individual vocabulary word level, as previously described, or with larger tasks, including comprehending texts and using what we understand to undertake and complete school tasks. Without the ability to self-assess, students will always be dependent on the teacher to tell them how they are doing in reading. A history of gaining control of the act of reading helps students develop critical understandings of themselves in relation to school learning and success. For example, the increased independence in learning and assessing vocabulary that is provided by the regular use of portfolios contributes to students' understanding of the control they have over their learning. When students perceive themselves as central players in the acts of reading and learning, they attain increased self-esteem and motivation (Guthrie & Wigfield, 1997).

Portfolio use in Jennifer's class helps her students appreciate their growth as readers. Portfolio assessment is hard work, work that when done well has great rewards. Students who are in the midst of assessment, as when they are accounting for their vocabulary learning, using checklists, and reading drafts of their writing, are attending to the immediate task at hand. The students are interested in how a particular aspect of assessment can describe and inform their achievement. Although such individual assessments can help students understand their work at a particular point in time, there may be no better venue than the portfolio for students to appreciate and understand the breadth and depth of their reading accomplishments. The portfolio also allows teachers, students, and parents to step back from and then appreciate completed student work, as well as student work that is developing or in progress.

In Jennifer's class, her students' reflection journals provide regular accounts of work completed and how this work contributes to their progress toward the goals of the unit project. The journals also help students understand the work that remains to be done. Jennifer's students learn how their schoolwork influences their daily lives. As a result of reading about pollution's effects on ecosystems, a student authors an account of how his increased sensitivity to pollution led to a campaign to turn off unused lights. The student establishes the direct connection between the reading he did to better understand pollution's effects on the environment and his newfound mission to turn off lights when they are not needed and to educate and remind others to do likewise. Establishing these relations between the reading students do and the related outcomes of reading is important in the quickly passing blur of the school day. Here, portfolios can help students build appreciation for how reading influences their lives.

Another use of the portfolio is to encourage students to consider which items best reflect their learning and growth. A legitimate concern with any such "My best work" portfolio is that it might lead students to overstate the case and brag about their work. Given the very competitive nature of some classrooms and schools, this is unsurprising. Yet, if teachers are careful in describing the goals of this section of the portfolio, if they model how students might choose their work for the section and if they provide clear guidelines for doing so, such a section can further contribute to students' ability to reflect on their work and self-assess it.

One week before the end of the ecosystem unit, Jennifer asks her students to identify their best work and reason through their writing about why it is their best work. This use of the portfolio serves two functions. First, it requires students to reflect on their work and develop an account and appreciation of their accomplishment. Second, it provides ongoing information for the teacher related to students' self-concepts. Certain students have quite different views related to their learning and accomplishment and their attributions for success and failure, and discussions of them can provide teachers with valuable information about students' self-concepts.

A final set of uses and consequences for portfolios relates to their ability to describe and encourage reader development in areas other than cognitive. Portfolios help us understand students' growth as engaged readers. Many teachers share the concern that almost all assessments focus solely on cognitive outcomes of reading instruction. There is little disagreement as to the importance of reading skills and strategies for reading success, yet successful reading instruction has many other positive outcomes. Jennifer and her colleagues are interested in the following questions and how portfolio assessment might help answer them:

- How can we measure the teaching and learning that contribute to students' growing interest in reading, as indicated by the increased diversity and frequency of their reading?

- How do we determine that our reading programs provide reading experiences that help positively shape students' personal values and behaviors?
- How might we measure the growth of the student who, at the end of the school year, is unable to imagine going through an entire day without reading?

Jennifer and her colleagues determine that consistently using reading logs, reflective journals, and reading attitude surveys will help them gather such important information within the portfolio. Students' heightened awareness of the importance and power of reading signals that valuable teaching and learning have occurred, and portfolios can be central to the documentation of such growth and development.

Jennifer's teaching colleagues are firmly committed to the idea that high-quality reading instruction enhances students' engagement with reading and the curriculum, provides motivation for future work, and demonstrates the connections between life inside and outside the classroom. Further, successful reading instruction contributes to the sense that students have increased control over their reading and learning, which in turn builds students' self-esteem and sense of agency. Yet, teachers' and students' hard work and accomplishment related to students' reading attitudes, self-esteem, and motivation are virtually ignored by traditional assessments. Portfolio assessment provides opportunities for teachers and students to document and describe these other important outcomes of teaching and learning, such as increased motivation to read, breadth of reading experience, and an increased conceptualization of oneself as a reader (for more on this topic, see Chapter 8).

Students' reflective writing, their journals of the texts they read, their accounts of how they used reading for different purposes, and their evident pride in progress are all documented in the portfolio. Portfolios reward students who make the connection between their hard work and the tangible evidence of the work that their portfolios hold. When students are in control of assessment (as portfolios demand of them), they can develop independence and a sense of agency. That is, students who use portfolios have choices in the work they focus on and the attention they give that work. These students can exercise prerogatives, including the ongoing assessment of complex projects, which are impossible when students are passive in relation to reading assessment. Students who do well with portfolios better understand the power of participating. This engagement, the power that comes from doing something well and being in control, can further evoke a strong, positive motivation to read.

Roles and Responsibilities Related to Portfolio Assessment

Our examination of the uses and consequences of portfolios demonstrates that they have considerable potential for fostering students' reading success. Success in portfolio assessment demands that the roles and responsibilities of teachers, students, parents, and administrators be clearly defined. Jennifer and her colleagues anticipate the diverse roles and responsibilities that accompany the use of portfolio assessment of reading and prepare to help each student meet them. Prior to implementing portfolios in their classrooms, Jennifer and her colleagues discussed the demands and possible outcomes of portfolio assessment. Their work was guided by a series of questions, presented in Table 9, that helped Jennifer and her colleagues determine their assessment priorities in relation to their teaching goals.

Teachers who advocate for portfolios must be knowledgeable about how to maximize the contributions of portfolio assessment and help students learn to do likewise. Jennifer knows that portfolios present challenges to many students because of their complexity. She and her colleagues conduct a task analysis of what it means to do a portfolio assessment. (For more on task analysis, see the Reading Assessment Snapshot for Task Analysis at the end of Chapter 1.) This task analysis suggests that teachers must provide students with guidance on how to develop and use the portfolio. Jennifer uses reminders and detailed instructions so that her students will develop the ability to use portfolios well, as when students use checklists to guide their science inquiry. She models the use of vocabulary cards and the sorting routine by thinking aloud about word knowledge and the means to accurately sort cards in relation to this knowledge. She provides repeated examples of how to use the checklists that assist students in their learning and assessment tasks.

Portfolios demand what for some teachers and students may be novel and unusual amounts of assessment attention and activity. The success of portfolio assessment in reading is influenced by the precedent for students taking control of assessment routines, teachers modeling good reading assessment practices, and schools and districts

---

TABLE 9
Questions to Ask When Considering a Portfolio Assessment Program

- What are the audiences and purposes of the portfolio?
- How are goals for portfolio assessment determined?
- As the portfolio and reading curriculum are aligned, what are the most productive uses for portfolios in my classroom?
- How can I help students become familiar with the materials and procedures that comprise portfolio assessment?
- What procedures related to portfolio assessment must students learn?
- How comfortable am I with modeling portfolio use for my students?
- How do I model use of the portfolio to support students' inquiry and learning?
- How does learning to use the portfolio promote students' independence and success?
- Given my available time and resources, what are the practical limitations of portfolios?

Note. Modified from *Understanding and Using Reading Assessment, K–12* (p. 84), by P. Afflerbach, 2007, Newark, DE: International Reading Association. Copyright 2007 by the International Reading Association.

providing material and intellectual support for the portfolio endeavor. Thus, it is important that teachers consider the goodness of fit of portfolios with all students and their particular needs.

Portfolios ask much of students, and some students will be better prepared than others to meet the challenges of portfolio assessment. To engage students at the point of their individual development related to making full use of the portfolio, Jennifer takes responsibility for addressing such individual differences. Teachers must be alert to the dual tasks of presenting portfolio materials and procedures to students while teaching students about the uses of portfolios and the responsibilities that accompany them. Jennifer's teaching includes frequent modeling and explanation of how to use a portfolio. Throughout the school year, teachers in Jennifer's school are involved in scaffolding the means for successful portfolio assessment for their students. The modeling and explanation that each teacher provides reflect the school's strategic plan that students will increasingly take responsibility for conducting portfolio assessment in an independent manner. With this form of reciprocal teaching (Palincsar & Brown, 1984), student and teacher responsibilities are complementary, and students are expected to grow in their ability to use the assessment strategies that are modeled and taught by their teachers. Questions for teachers who are interested in determining how well prepared their students are to take on the roles and responsibilities necessary for success in portfolio assessment of reading are presented in Table 10.

Consider two students. The first is a fifth grader who is struggling to read and develop a sense of self as reader. As he attempts to work through the reading assignments and other tasks included in the ecosystem unit, his poor self-esteem surfaces. He believes that he has little control over what happens to him in school, and he attributes his school performance to his belief that he is not smart. His inability to answer questions about the key concepts of predator and prey reinforces this belief. He feels that he is not an agent

---

TABLE 10
Questions to Help Determine the Suitability of Portfolio Assessment for Particular Students

- Is the student familiar with portfolio materials and procedures?
- Is the student familiar with the concept of self-assessment?
- Is the student active or passive when it comes to assessing his or her work?
- Is the student a confident and informed assessor of work?
- Will the student be comfortable assuming increased responsibility for assessing work?
- Can the student manage the different tasks that comprise portfolio assessment?
- Will the amount of work representing content area learning and portfolio assessment learning be manageable?

Note. From *Understanding and Using Reading Assessment, K–12* (p. 85), by P. Afflerbach, 2007, Newark, DE: International Reading Association. Copyright 2007 by the International Reading Association.

in his own learning, and his days are marked by a passive approach to school (Johnston & Winograd, 1985). This student may have a difficult time when asked to conduct the management, planning, and evaluation that are central to effective portfolio use.

Contrast this student with a classmate who regularly assesses herself in relation to school tasks and goals. She continually asks questions about her own understanding of ecosystems. She expects the portfolio to provide evidence of her progress through the ecosystem unit and serve as a forum for discussion and presentation of her work and accomplishments. The student looks forward to the daily vocabulary word sorting and assessing task, and asking her to take increasing control over the portfolio to assess her reading is natural and prone to a successful outcome.

Students who are unfamiliar with portfolio assessment may face challenges related to specific portfolio materials and processes. Their teachers must be clear and consistent in presenting models of how to use portfolios, explaining why they are valuable assessments and when to use them. Jennifer knows that discussion of the strategies that are necessary to build and maintain a portfolio should help her students increase their familiarity with portfolios. Important questions for students to ask related to their knowledge of portfolios are presented in Table 11.

The productive use of reading portfolios requires what may be an unprecedented degree of involvement on the part of students. Those with passive relationships with assessment (i.e., students who consider assessment to be someone else's work) will be challenged at different points in portfolio assessment. First, students must move from the conceptualization that reading assessment is something that someone else does (Black & Wiliam, 1998) to one that involves their active participation. Second, a significant portion of student activity must be dedicated to careful organization. Portfolios do not magically change the messiest desk in the classroom into one that represents careful thinking and structure. Yet, with guidance, students using portfolio

---

TABLE 11
Questions for Students Related to Using Portfolios

- How do you determine the goals of your portfolio?
- What are the audiences and purposes of your portfolio?
- How do they influence the manner in which you use your portfolio?
- What materials should be included in your portfolio to demonstrate your progress toward these goals?
- How do you interact with the materials in your portfolio?
- How do you use your portfolio to support your inquiry projects in class and your learning across the semester?
- How does learning to use your portfolio promote your independence and success?

Note. From *Understanding and Using Reading Assessment, K–12* (p. 86), by P. Afflerbach, 2007, Newark, DE: International Reading Association. Copyright 2007 by the International Reading Association.

assessment can develop an appreciation of organization and regularly benefit from the planning and evaluation that are at the heart of portfolios.

Our intent must be focused on helping students develop to the point where they understand that self-assessment is a helpful goal. When students experience the control that accompanies self-assessment, they grow in self-esteem and agency. This contributes to a type of Matthew effect (Stanovich, 1986), in which ongoing experience and success promote further experience and success.

Parents who are familiar with traditional means of assessing and reporting reading achievement, including test scores and report cards, may need a primer on how portfolios provide a detailed understanding of student achievement. Portfolios demand close attention from the audiences who view them, as they present evidence of student achievement in considerable detail. Jennifer and her colleagues develop a portfolio guide for parents to help them understand how to best interpret and use the information that portfolios contain. A portfolio guide can describe special characteristics of portfolios and how they offer improvement over other assessments. In addition, parents should be alerted to the fact that there will be unfinished and imperfect items in the portfolio for good reasons. Drafts of student work and ongoing developmental projects will not have the polish and final-version feel that many parents expect. Although portfolios may include a section that contains report cards, quizzes, and test scores, parents' ability to move beyond this typical description of student achievement must be supported. Most parents equate reading assessment with tests and report cards. Such parental understanding should be augmented by clear and persuasive demonstration of how portfolios provide rich reading achievement information.

The development of a successful portfolio assessment program takes considerable time, effort, and funding (Au, 1994). Schools and school districts must make a commitment to support portfolio assessment. In an environment in which reading assessment is conceptualized as a test score and expected to reflect startlingly fast improvements in reading achievement, portfolios may seem beside the point. Administrators who understand the benefits of portfolios must work in this difficult context. Portfolios most often represent a change in assessment culture for classrooms and schools, and efforts to implement portfolios must be conducted in a realistic time frame. It is imperative that those who lead a schoolwide, districtwide, or statewide effort to implement portfolio assessment establish a list of the important roles and responsibilities that accompany the development and use of portfolio assessments of reading. This list will include professional development, funding decisions, and the establishment of ongoing support for teachers and principals who are eager to learn about all of the potential contributions that portfolio assessment can make to students' reading growth. A notable feature in the strategic plans of both Race to the Top assessment consortia is that assessment is developed systemically. The following observation is from the SBAC (2010) assessment consortium: "Assessments are grounded in a thoughtful, standards-based curriculum and are managed as part of an *integrated system* of standards, curriculum, assessment, instruction, and teacher development" (p. 32). In such a system, the demands of portfolio assessment may be anticipated and met, and the promise of portfolio assessment may be realized.

Reliability of Portfolio Assessment

A goal for portfolio assessment is the establishment of consistent and useful assessment routines that yield reliable information (Moss et al., 1992). For our purposes, two forms of reliability are important to portfolio assessment. These are the reliability of teacher judgments of student work on standardized sections of reading portfolios, and the developing reliability of students' evaluations of their own and others' work.

Jennifer uses her considerable experience with portfolio assessment to inform her evaluation of her students. Across the fifth-grade school year, students develop the ability to read different science texts and synthesize the information contained in them into a coherent expository text. Teacher reliability in portfolio assessment is encouraged by training in how to score portfolios and by the determination of a core of teaching and learning goals that does not vary across students. To achieve a reliable measure of different students' reading achievement, a set of standard contents for each student's portfolio must be designated. This provides the opportunity to assess all students' work across the same reading and reading-related tasks.

Through the guarantee of similar contents across students and a similar means for assessing across teachers, the acceptable levels of reliability of the measure of portfolio assessment can be established (Valencia & Place, 1994). Teachers must practice the application of portfolio assessment procedures to ensure that acceptable degrees of reliability are attained. That Jennifer and her colleagues work in a district that advocates for the consistent use of portfolios across all grades means that teachers have regular opportunities to practice and build reliability into their portfolio scoring. In addition, professional development resources are regularly allocated by the school district to support the teachers and their responsibility for reliable scoring of portfolios.

I suggest throughout this book that the development of students' ability to self-assess their reading should be a foundational goal of all reading instruction and reading assessment programs. Because the ability to self-assess is a developmental process, we must anticipate that individual students will enter a portfolio reading assessment program with different experiences and competencies related to evaluating their own work. Here, reliability becomes both an instructional concern and an assessment concern. We are fortunate that close attention to helping students learn to use portfolios will address both.

From an instructional perspective, we are interested in providing students with the knowledge they will use to make informed judgments about the quality of their reading work in relation to individual and class goals. We must teach students the correct use of the portfolio to help them approach this level of portfolio proficiency, for instance, as they evaluate how their ecosystem graphic organizers evolve from the beginning to the end of the unit. Our instruction here should focus on providing regular and predictable examples of portfolio use. This contributes to a consistency of the assessment routines that students conduct within their portfolios, which may directly affect the reliability of the assessment. From a measurement perspective, students who practice using portfolios in a planning manner can approach an appropriate level of reliability in how they choose and appraise their portfolios' contents.

Jennifer provides repeated opportunities for her students to practice and apply portfolio assessment knowledge, which helps address both the instructional and measurement aspects of reliability. A general goal here is standardization: the standardization of contents, treatment, and experience for all students with particular items or sections within the portfolio. When teachers provide clearly stated criteria and rules for judging work, students can learn to use them and then begin to develop the ability to conduct reliable portfolio assessment. For example, sets of questions that guide students' appraisal of their ecosystem unit project may eventually become internalized as a schema of important questions to ask while doing portfolio assessment. Questions might include the following:

- What aspects and examples of your classroom work are you using in your assessment?
- Have you included the required items from your portfolio to make your assessment?
- How do these different aspects of your work specifically demonstrate your learning in relation to the goals of the assignment?

Conducting portfolio assessment in relation to these questions brings regularity and standardization to the assessment.

Validity of Portfolio Assessment

Jennifer and her fellow teachers conceptualize reading development in relation to the growth of students' skills and strategies. The teachers believe that the five core areas identified by the 2000 National Reading Panel report (NICHD, 2000) are important contributors to students' reading success. The teachers value the portrayal of reading in the Common Core State Standards (CCSSO & NGA, 2010) that focuses on the comprehension of increasingly complex text and the use of what is comprehended in related tasks. The teachers also agree that reading has clear and strong connections to students' writing and their discussions. The portfolio, with demonstrated flexibility to accommodate different assessment foci, addresses each of the facets of the construct of reading. Across the elementary and secondary grades, the portfolio adjusts to reflect those skills, strategies, and growth that are developmentally appropriate for each student. Thus, the attention to phonics in first-grade portfolios progresses to an attention to reading comprehension strategies in third grade. Also, portfolios are adaptable to students' individual differences.

Jennifer and her colleagues also believe that the successful reader is one who can choose reading materials independently, set goals and monitor progress toward these goals, ask questions of the text and author, self-assess understanding of the text, and be motivated to read further because one feels in control of the act of reading. Portfolio assessment matches well with this conceptualization of the developing, accomplished reader and thus demonstrates considerable construct validity. In addition, the aspects of engaged reading that are typically overlooked by traditional assessments, including students' motivations, self-esteem, and attributions for success or failure, can be measured and presented within the portfolio format.

This chapter focuses on portfolio assessment as it is embedded in the daily routines of Jennifer's classroom, with the portfolio assessment program developed and used in close relation to the science curriculum. This relationship contributes to the ecological validity of portfolio assessment. When portfolio assessment is conceptualized as an integral part of the curriculum, the connections between assessment, the curriculum, and learning can be most direct. The ability of the portfolio to help coordinate assessment and document achievement is clear. Portfolio assessment information follows directly from learning and instruction. Indeed, portfolios are not intrusive on class time, and they are a regular part of class routine. Students' portfolio assessment is done with a priori attention to assessment materials and procedures that both describe and support students' learning. This contributes to a high degree of alignment between students' learning during the course of the ecosystem unit and the manner in which that learning is assessed. Thus, the ecological validity is considerable.

Summary

Portfolios are a potentially powerful means of describing and supporting students' development as readers. Portfolios can reflect the detail of student learning and effort and do so over time frames that might include units of study, marking periods, or entire school years. Portfolios help tell the story of students' development of cognitive skills and strategies and describe the development of motivation, the positive effect for reading, and students' self-esteem in relation to reading. Portfolios encourage student involvement in assessment; thus, they demand students' considerable skill. Portfolios reward students with increased self-knowledge and independent work ability. True to their roots in the fine arts, portfolios are flexible in relation to their contents, their purposes, and the needs of their audiences.

The promise of portfolios is accompanied by considerable challenges. The field is not wanting for descriptions of judicious use of portfolios or the effectiveness of portfolio assessment to provide a good measure and support of learning (e.g., Au, 1994; Tierney et al., 1991). Rather, most schools and school districts are hard-pressed to commit the time, money, and teachers' professional development resources to portfolio assessment programs. Portfolios are relatively unprecedented in terms of the attention and work they demand of students and teachers. Portfolios are time and labor intensive, but as detailed in this chapter, the advocacy of portfolio assessment and the use of portfolios to help describe students' and teachers' accomplishments in reading are worth the effort required. Portfolio assessment done well provides detailed reading assessment information to different audiences over time. Portfolio assessment supports instruction and learning and becomes the supportive workplace for students who are developing as readers and self-assessors. Although examples of successful, large-scale portfolio programs are few and far between, this may change in upcoming years as the Common Core State Standards and related assessments are introduced and utilized.

ENHANCING YOUR UNDERSTANDING

1. Using Table 9 (see p. 87), "Questions to Ask When Considering a Portfolio Assessment Program," develop a rank-ordered list of the things you would like to include in a portfolio.

2. Develop a checklist that helps students who are new to portfolio assessment navigate the different sections and tasks involved in portfolio assessment. (See Figure 5 on p. 82 for an example of a checklist.)

3. Consider how you can use your own work (e.g., a course paper, personal writing, painting, a hobby) in a sample portfolio to help students understand the ways that portfolios are structured, how they work, and the contributions they make to your work.

4. Focus on one important unit, performance, or goal and consider how portfolio assessment can describe student learning.

Authentic Assessment

Authentic is a word used to describe assessments that have at least one of two characteristics. First, such assessments may be embedded in classroom routines of instruction and learning and conducted during regular activities of the classroom. These assessments are clearly related to the learning and achievement that are goals of schooling, and the inferences that we make from this information may be more directly connected to the curriculum and student learning. Second, such assessments may focus on their relationship to real-world reading. Here, authentic assessment involves students' performance on tasks that have important counterparts in the world outside the school. This authentic assessment is situated in contexts that anticipate the use of reading in the lives of students in and out of academic settings, be it for work, personal fulfillment, or academic pursuit. Authentic assessment holds great promise for describing the diverse ways in which students grow and develop in the literacy curriculum.

When our district, state, and national standards for reading specify goals of complex student learning, we must use assessments that describe and accurately measure this complexity. Authentic assessments done well provide such measures. Authentic assessment is often centered on the interactions of teachers and students, and because the assessment is embedded in instruction, the teacher must assume the role of assessment expert. Assessment that is focused on important classroom routines can provide results that are immediately useful. Teachers use the results of authentic assessment to shape instruction and provide feedback for students.

When authentic assessment reflects (and anticipates) the manner in which we read and apply knowledge gained through reading, we are able to expand our ideas about student achievement. The authentic assessment of students' literacy development may be conducted with various assessment materials and procedures, including performance assessments, portfolios, interviews, observation forms, and teachers' questions. Other dynamic forms of authentic assessment include running records and reading inventories, in which teachers gather information about students' oral reading, silent reading, and comprehension. However, the characteristics of the assessment materials and procedures are not the only determinants of whether the assessment is authentic. Rather, it is the manner in which an assessment is used, how it connects to the curriculum, and what it demands of students that contribute to authentic assessment.

CHAPTER 5

Performance Assessment

We are surrounded by performances related to our reading. When we read instructions to assemble a child's toy, read a recipe to make dinner, or read a set of directions for taking medicine, reading and action are intertwined. In school, students read earth science articles downloaded from the Internet and craft a three-dimensional diorama representing plate tectonics. Students create a dramatic skit based on their interpretation of characters in a short story. Students read two history texts that pose competing and conflicting accounts of slavery and determine which text is more accurate and trustworthy. All of these students are using the knowledge they gain through reading to perform important tasks.

Starting in elementary school, performance assessment can help us determine not only what students understand from reading but also how they use what they understand. Performance assessment helps describe student development in relation to complex, curricular goals. The knowledge that students gain from reading is not inert, and reading assessment should not treat it as such. Performance assessments situate students' reading in relation to important work in school, as students read to construct meaning and use it. In many classrooms, performance assessment represents a sea change in how assessment is conceptualized and conducted. Performance assessment is demanding of resources and teacher expertise but has many features that are worth the expense and effort.

A Brief History of Performance Assessment

The close connection between reading and performance tasks is as old as reading itself. However, current interest in performance assessment is attributable to several converging factors. First, ongoing research on how people read, think, and learn describes the complexity of reading, and areas of student growth and achievement related to reading (McNamara & Magliano, 2009; OECD, 2010; Pajares & Urdan, 2006; Pressley & Afflerbach, 1995; Snow, 2002). Second, the reading standards developed by professional organizations, states, and school districts in relation to this new research knowledge require assessments that capture and describe complex student achievements, such as those expected by the Common Core State Standards (CCSSO & NGA, 2010). Third, traditional reading tests do not give a full account of how well students read and use what they understand from reading (Wiggins, 1998), and these tests may be negative influences on curricula and teaching (Frederiksen, 1984). Fourth, efforts to develop large-scale and consequential performance assessment programs have demonstrated their viability (National Center on Education and the Economy, 1998). Finally, performance assessments can be used in the teaching and learning of course content and to help students learn to self-assess (Black & Wiliam, 1998).

Accompanying the development of performance assessments is the belief that reading assessment can better reflect what is known about academic reading and inform educators of students' progress related to reading in college and professional life (PARCC, 2010; SBAC, 2010). There is a considerable disconnect between the breadth and depth of students' learning in a high-quality reading curriculum and the narrow focus of many reading assessments (Davis, 1998). There must be the commitment to reducing the gap between what students learn and how we assess this learning. As we expect reading standards to reflect our most current understandings of reading, we should expect the same of the assessments used to measure student progress. It is difficult to understand the detail of a student's achievement when reading assessment results are a letter grade of B, a raw score of 53, or a ranking in the 82nd percentile, and performance assessments provide illustrative and educative details that complement the general statement made by such single, summative assessment markers.

Most recently, performance assessment has been the focus of broad initiatives to improve teaching and learning in U.S. schools. The Common Core State Standards (CCSSO & NGA, 2011) present an ambitious set of learning goals. A major focus is on students using what they understand from reading in content areas. Thus, the Common Core State Standards represent a challenging curriculum that requires a new generation of reading assessments, and such assessments are promised by two assessment consortia, the PARCC and the SBAC. Assessments developed by these consortia will regularly require student performances to measure and report the complexity of learning that is demanded by the Common Core State Standards.

The SBAC (2010) describes general criteria for reading assessments (i.e., criteria that align with performance assessments): "Assessments must be carefully structured to improve teaching and learning. This means establishing summative assessments that reflect the challenging CCSS [Common Core State Standards] content, emphasizing not just students' 'knowing,' but also 'doing'" (p. 37). Similarly, the PARCC (2010) describes assessment as the following:

> In…ELA/literacy…in grades three through high school, students will take focused assessments…and participate in an extended and engaging performance-based task…students will be given extended time to identify or read relevant research materials and compose written essays based on them. Afterwards, students will publicly present the results of that research and writing to their classmates, answering questions or engaging in debate, so that teachers can assess students' speaking and listening skills using a common rubric. (p. 36)

So far, 44 states and the District of Columbia have formally adopted the Common Core State Standards. With this adoption, there is the concomitant acknowledgment that reading assessment must change, and this change will be in the direction of performance assessments.

Characteristics of Performance Assessment

Our knowledge of reading is continually evolving. The vast amount of reading research conducted in the past several decades has added much to our understandings of how reading works, how reading ability develops, and the place of reading in the lives of students (Berkeley et al., 2011; Moje et al., 2004; Rogers, 2003). Performance assessments offer opportunities to describe and measure student reading and learning across the curriculum. In the content domains of science, social studies, math, English, and the arts, effective performance assessments share important characteristics. Performance assessments help us understand student growth and learning. They describe student achievement in detail. They are developed in relation to comprehensive analyses of what students must do to understand and complete the performance. Effective performance assessment uses scoring rubrics and guides that inform teachers and students as to the nature of the performance and gradations of accomplishment related to the performance.

In many cases, the nature and structure of performance assessments reflect classroom practices in the content areas. Performance assessments may focus on how students synthesize information learned from different sources, how they put to use the information learned from reading in classroom tasks, and how reading plays a role in students' growth and development. Thus, the inferences made from performance assessments may emanate from the daily routines of the classroom—a form of authentic assessment (see the Reading Assessment Snapshot for Authentic Assessment at the end of Chapter 4). Further, performance assessments' open-ended response formats can accommodate different student approaches to tasks and problem solving, reflecting students' constructed understanding of what they read.

Effective performance assessment requires the identification of key student learning and related performances, aided by consultation with research related to the demands of the performance. For example, if a performance assessment requires students to collect information from different texts and synthesize that information, the developers of the assessment may consult the research literature on synthesizing information from text (Bråten et al., 2009) and the special requirements for performing well in reading in content domains such as history (VanSledright, 2010; Wineburg, 1997). This type of research helps us understand specific students' abilities that can be tapped with performance assessment.

Effective performance assessment is enabled by a detailed task analysis of the performance that is the focus of the assessment. As the performance task is created, it is imperative that we establish an informed, a priori understanding of exactly what we are asking students to do. Task analyses involve a meticulous accounting of the things that must be done in order to perform an assessment task satisfactorily. What exactly are we asking students to do when they read the following prompt in an American history performance assessment: "Based on your understanding of the two primary source texts, develop an account of the challenges faced by the Jamestown colonists?" Later in this chapter, we observe that responding to such prompts can involve literal, inferential, and critical understanding; knowledge of source text cues; and the ability to take a critical stance toward authors and their work. Using task analysis, we can check to see that what we ask of students represents an important and legitimate assessment request.

The grounding of performance assessment in relation to reading research and task analysis helps in the development of a performance assessment's core features, including a task demand or prompt, rubric, and scoring guide. Also, the development of a performance assessment is facilitated by attention to the assessment's specific purpose, goal, and objectives. Thus, we should regularly ask questions like the following:

- Why are we asking students to do this?
- What will it show us?
- How do students demonstrate their accomplishment of the goal with observable products and performances?

The goal here is building a performance assessment in which we have high confidence and from which we can make legitimate inferences about students' development and achievement.

Worthwhile performance assessments are designed in relation to logical and understandable rubrics and scoring guides. A rubric is a description of how a student performance may vary in terms of quality and achievement. Popham (1997) describes three essential features of rubrics: (1) the criteria used to evaluate student work, (2) specification of differential quality of student work, and (3) the means to consistently and accurately score student work. An examination of Table 12 illustrates how these three factors operate with a rubric. In this case, the performance assessment focuses on two interrelated history reading goals, or performances: (1) Students read history texts to identify cues in text to determine source text status and then (2) use this source text status to evaluate the trustworthiness of the text. The criteria used in this rubric to evaluate student work are related to ability to identify cues to determine source text status and the ability to use the determination of source text status to evaluate the text for trustworthiness (VanSledright, 2002). The specification of different quality of student work is apparent in the different descriptions of performance. Following this rubric through the different levels of student performance, we are able to trace how students might move from "Not Apparent" to "Developing" to "Proficient"

TABLE 12
History Performance Assessment Rubric: Identifying Cues to Determine Source Text Status and Using Source Text Status to Evaluate Text

	Levels of Student Performance			
Category	Not Apparent (1)	Developing (2)	Proficient (3)	Exemplary (4)
Identifying cues to determine source text status	There is no apparent means for identifying and using cues to determine source text status.	Student identifies and uses one or more cues to determine source text status. For example, student uses archaic spelling and author voice to attribute source text status. However, identification of type of text cue is inaccurate, and/or determination of source text status is erroneous.	Student identifies and uses one or several cues to correctly determine source text status. For example, student uses archaic spelling and author voice to correctly determine text status as primary source.	Student identifies and uses all possible cues to correctly determine source text status. For example, student uses each and every cue contained in text to correctly determine text status as primary source.
Using source text status to evaluate text for trustworthiness	There is no apparent attempt to use understanding of source text status to evaluate the text. There is no apparent attempt to connect source text status with an evaluation of the trustworthiness of text.	Student attempts to use understanding of source text status, demonstrating connection between source text status and evaluation. However, designation of source text as trustworthy or not is erroneous.	Using understanding of source text status, student demonstrates connection between source text status and evaluation. Evaluation of text's trustworthiness is accurate and appropriate.	Using understanding of source text status, student demonstrates connection between determination of source text status and accuracy of evaluation. Evaluation of text's trustworthiness is comprehensive and appropriate, and use of source text status to evaluate text is elaborated.

Note. Adapted from "Teaching and Learning Self-Assessment Strategies in Middle School" by P. Afflerbach and K. Meuwissen, in *Metacognition in Literacy Learning: Theory, Assessment, Instruction, and Professional Development* (pp. 141–164), edited by S.E. Israel, C.C. Block, K.L. Bauserman, and K. Kinnucan-Welsch, 2005, Mahwah, NJ: Erlbaum. Copyright 2005 by Lawrence Erlbaum Associates. Adapted with permission.

to "Exemplary" levels of performance, earning respective scores of 1–4. The means to consistently and accurately score student work is tied to the clarity of the category, the detail of specification of student work of differing quality, and the assignment of that specification to particular scoring points.

Andrade (2000) describes several possible benefits of using rubrics and performance assessment. Well-structured rubrics communicate to students the expectation for learning. In effect, they tell the student what is needed to earn a particular grade. Rubrics also provide students with detailed feedback about their learning. By comparing their work with the set of expectations that a rubric presents, students can determine what has been achieved and what may remain to be accomplished.

The careful development of rubrics for performance assessments provides teachers and students with a clear and consistent means for judging student work. A rubric may also be used to help teach important aspects of the required student performance because the rubric focuses our attention and efforts on key curricular goals. Detailed performance assessment rubrics offer opportunities for scaffolding instruction. Teachers can use the different levels of the rubric to teach in reference to students' zone of proximal development (Vygotsky, 1934/1978), helping one student move from a level 1 ("Not Apparent" in Table 12) performance to level 2 ("Developing") and helping another move from level 3 ("Proficient") to level 4 ("Expert"). Indeed, Popham (1997) characterizes well-designed rubrics as "instructional illuminators" (p. 75). In the case of the history curriculum, the rubric provides a consistent model of the types of cues that students should use as they determine source text status and the manner in which they should use these cues to demonstrate thinking and learning in history.

Popham (1997) also provides two caveats. First, the performance that is being assessed must be worthy of the time and effort that are needed to develop and use truly effective rubrics. We do not need a performance assessment to understand students' literal comprehension of history facts because a multiple-choice or open-ended question might suffice. The array of student learning that is expected over an entire school year, as represented in statewide and school district learning standards, requires that we be judicious in choosing and developing performance assessments. From the start, performance assessment development must be approached with the knowledge that there are limits to how many assessments might be developed, given the intensive work they demand. Performance assessment tasks must reflect consensus on important student learning. Ideally, these assessments will focus on performances that represent convergences of student learning, incorporating skills, strategies, and the content domain learning that are the goals of effective instruction. A performance assessment rubric that is well designed but not at the core of important student learning may indicate unwise use of limited school resources. Also, the rubric must reflect a detailed understanding of the performance that students undertake, as informed by continuous comparisons of the performance rubric and task analyses. Otherwise, exceptional student work might not be in the direction of core learning goals and may be missed by assessment.

The effectiveness of performance assessment is enhanced by examples of student performances, for they help make explicit what students' final products can look like. Combined with instruction that helps students learn and perform the processes that yield such products, representative performances can clearly signify accomplishment at specific levels. These sample performances should serve as models of specific levels of achievement for both the scorers of the assessment and the students who are required to create the performance. For example, a scoring guide that allows us to assign a score between 1 and 4 can be accompanied by examples of student work that provide students with a target for their performance. Student work samples, perhaps taken from the previous year's class, help students develop a refined sense of what work scored as a 1 and work scored as a 4 look like and how they differ. Through their public display, these samples can provide students with consistent guidance as they build their performance toward successful completion. The samples in Figure 6 demonstrate a student's ability to locate and use different cues to determine the primary or secondary source status of history texts and then evaluate the trustworthiness of the

---

FIGURE 6
Example of a Proficient (Level 3) Performance Assessment Score:
Student Reading History Text, Using Cues to Determine Source
Text Status, and Evaluating Text for Trustworthiness

Text excerpt that contains cues used by student:

> As a citizen of Jamestown verginia I do my demesticall work each day. Yet, there remains little food for us, the poore distressed subjects. We are in dandger of losing our bretheren to hunger, this hunger that hath no seeming end.

Using cues to determine that it is a primary source text, student writes:

> This appears to be a primary source text because it has old spellings like "poore," "dandger," and "hath." Also, I get a good feel for the author of this text as he speaks in the first person—this makes the description more real for me.

Using determination of source text status to evaluate the text's trustworthiness, student writes:

> I believe that this is a primary source text because of the archaic spellings and the nature of the author's voice. Therefore, I believe that the text is trustworthy and that it reports an eyewitness account of some of the suffering that the Jamestown colonists experienced.

Note. From *Understanding and Using Reading Assessment, K–12* (p. 99), by P. Afflerbach, 2007, Newark, DE: International Reading Association. Copyright 2007 by the International Reading Association.

text to earn a score of 3, thus providing useful guidance to students who are learning this strategy. Over time, our use of rubrics and work samples in the classroom contributes to students developing specific schemata for what good work looks like, strategies for progress, and a schema for the ongoing self-assessment of their progress toward performance goals.

A final characteristic of performance assessments is that they often require an expanded time frame to fully realize their potential. Many standardized assessments, including reading tests, are administered in a compact time frame. However, performance assessments require time for learning to use a rubric to support learning, conducting self-assessment, and describing and measuring student learning. Performances take more time than answering simple questions. Performance assessment done well is a result of the consideration of the time needed to participate in and complete a performance, as well as the provision of a realistic time frame that is tailored to and appropriate for eliciting and accommodating students' performances.

Performance Assessment in Ivan's Eighth-Grade History Classroom

Ivan teaches eighth-grade history and has used performance assessment for five years. His enthusiastic use of performance assessment is guided by his strong conviction that students who are finishing middle school and about to enter high school must be able to understand complex texts and then apply the things they learn from reading. This belief dovetails with the intent of the Common Core State Standards (CCSSO & NGA, 2010), to help prepare students for success in college and their careers. Ivan's interest in performance assessment is shared with many teachers across the school district. Across grades and content areas, students' reading is assessed with performance assessments. Students read math word problems that require them to determine rainfall averages for each month of the school year, and science texts to help them interpret their firsthand observations of the schoolyard ecosystem. Students read history texts with competing, and sometimes conflicting, accounts of historical events and characters, from which students must construct an understanding of history and how it is created. The eighth graders are continuing their education in a school system that promotes critical inquiry into what is learned, how it is learned, and why it is learned. The history curriculum in Ivan's class reflects our most current understanding of how people read and learn about history and is replete with performances that require students to demonstrate their understanding (National Council for the Social Studies, 1994; Wineburg, 1997).

Within the history curriculum, students learn to analyze historical documents, assess primary and secondary source status of texts, and combine diverse sources to construct accounts of history. Students learn to adopt a questioning stance toward the texts they read. Students question the authors of the texts and read critically, considering competing accounts of history and discerning fact and opinion. In this curriculum, students learn how history is written, the materials that are used by authors to write history, and how one can critically read history to try to determine the reliability and trustworthiness of texts. This learning complements students' understanding of historical facts about people, places, dates, and events.

The above tasks and learning goals relate directly to the reading standards for literacy in history/social studies in grades 6–12 that are contained in the Common Core State Standards. Specifically, the performance assessment in Ivan's classroom helps students learn and perform as related to the following categories of the Common Core State Standards (CCSSO & NGA, 2010, p. 14):

Key ideas and details

- Cite specific textual evidence to support analysis of primary and secondary sources.

Craft and structure

- Identify aspects of a text that reveal an author's point of view or purpose (e.g., loaded language, inclusion or avoidance of particular facts).

Integration of knowledge and ideas

- Analyze the relationship between a primary and secondary source on the same topic.

The Nature of the History Performance Assessment

The performance assessment in Ivan's Colonial American history class requires students to read and evaluate history texts like historians. Research demonstrates that historians have specific strategies that help them determine the primary or secondary source status of history texts (VanSledright, 2002, 2010). Primary source texts may include original newspaper articles, diary entries, letters, maps, cartoons, and other documents that are contemporary with the historical period being studied. Secondary sources involve interpretation and reporting of primary sources and may include history textbooks, historical novels, and works representing syntheses of other texts. Students' critical performances in eighth-grade history require that they read three different texts about the same historical events (in this case, the founding and survival of the Jamestown Colony). The texts include a diary excerpt from a Jamestown colonist, an account from a work of fiction of how Jamestown changed the lives of Native Americans, and a newspaper article that describes how the arrival of a second group of colonists saved Jamestown from extinction.

The performance assessment prompt reads as follows:

You are to read the three texts on Jamestown. For each text, identify and use as many cues as possible that help you determine the status of the source text. Once you have identified the cues, determine text status and then evaluate each text for trustworthiness based on these determinations.

Students must locate and use cues in the three different texts to determine when the texts were written, who may have written them, and why the texts were written. Ultimately, students must determine the status of these source texts. Students use particular strategies and cues to make critical evaluations of text, including the trustworthiness of the historical account and the reliability of the author. These critical reading strategies and the intent to read text critically are key aspects of reading history that are goals of the eighth-grade curriculum.

Based on this understanding of reading history, the curriculum is designed to help students understand the texts that they read and teach students how to find and use particular cues in history texts that may help identify a text as a primary or secondary source. The different types of cues, including vocabulary, spelling, syntax, author voice, type of text, age of text, and header material (i.e., where the text comes from), derive directly from research on reading history and are then built into the curriculum and assessment (Afflerbach & VanSledright, 2001). Table 13 lists the types of cues that students can use to help determine source text status.

In the year-end performance assessment, students are responsible for identifying cues and using them to determine if the texts read are primary or secondary source documents. Next, students are expected to evaluate the texts for their trustworthiness, based on students' determination of primary or secondary source status. Ivan believes that consistent use of performance assessments to measure complex student

TABLE 13
Cues Used to Determine the Primary and Secondary Source Status of History Texts

- Age of the text
- Type of text
- Header material in text (displays author attributions)
- Author presence and voice in text
- Spelling in the text
- Syntax
- Vocabulary
- Combinations of two or more of the above cues

Note. From *Understanding and Using Reading Assessment, K–12* (p. 101), by P. Afflerbach, 2007, Newark, DE: International Reading Association. Copyright 2007 by the International Reading Association.

learning and help students better understand assessment is well worth the time and effort he spends on them. He expects that the use of performance assessments across each school year will reveal important student learning and help students build an appreciation for both their accomplishments and their increasing ability to self-assess.

Consequences and Usefulness of Performance Assessments

Ivan uses performance assessment for several reasons. First and foremost, it allows him to assess his students in a manner that honors the complexity of their learning and his teaching. Recall that this performance assessment derives from the detailed understanding of how accomplished readers read history. This understanding moves our expectations for assessment in history beyond the traditional inventory of students' memory of historical dates, places, people, and events. Learning goals and performance assessment converge as students demonstrate their knowledge about why history is written, how it is written, who writes it, and how it is read. The assessment does not discount the importance of historical dates, places, people, and events but seeks to describe how students learn and understand history. Because the performance assessment reflects the detail of what we know to be critical aspects of reading history, the assessment provides a direct view of student achievement in relation to this. The performance assessment used in Ivan's classroom demonstrates not only students' understanding of the content of history texts but also students' ability to determine primary or secondary source status of those texts.

Second, the use of this history performance assessment encourages Ivan to continually reflect on the content and process of schooling. As noted by Jamentz (1994), the establishment of clear performance goals and outcomes (and their alignment) provides educators with a window on their standards and their teaching craft intended to help students meet those standards. The performance assessment provides Ivan with detailed information about his students' progress toward major goals of schooling. For example, the source text status assessment helps him understand students' critical reading development within history and critical reading in general. Ivan is able to infer, with high confidence, what his students learn and the effectiveness of his teaching.

Third, the performance assessment provides formative and summative assessment information on student learning in relation to the rich construct of reading history. Ivan uses class time to focus on each cue that readers can use to determine the primary or secondary source status of the history texts they read. He constructs assessments, based on the unit-end performance assessment, that describe each student's ability to recognize and use the different cues. These assessments provide formative feedback on the effectiveness of Ivan's instruction and the extent of student learning. Across the school year, he knows each student's achievement in relation to learning the different cues that help the reader determine the source text status.

A fourth use of performance assessments is their means for teaching important content and strategies for reading like a historian. The detailed information included in Ivan's performance assessment rubrics, scoring guides, and sample student papers is useful for communicating to students what they must do to receive particular performance assessment scores. The rubrics and scoring guide help him focus on important curricular content, materials, and processes. A task analysis of locating cues to determine the status of history texts is used to build the performance assessment, and this analysis also reminds Ivan of the level of detail that is necessary in his instruction. For example, he knows that many of the primary source texts in Colonial American history are marked by archaic spellings, such as *wee* for *we* and *bye* for *by*. The close match between instruction and scoring rubrics allows Ivan to focus on helping students develop a strategy for identifying archaic spelling during class readings, which helps students with their task at hand and prepares them for the performance assessment.

The rubric itself focuses on the particular means for students to demonstrate their learning and is utilized as an outline for learning. For example, the rubric's focus on cues of archaic vocabulary, spelling, and syntax prompts Ivan to locate and use samples of historic writing that contain clear examples of such language. During classroom instruction, he uses texts with archaic spelling and vocabulary words that are associated with the Colonial era. Guided by the rubric, Ivan develops instruction that helps his students understand the nature of archaic language and how the presence of archaic language may be an important clue as to the age and source status of a history text. He uses this approach to scaffold instruction with each of the cues mentioned in the rubric. Thus, the instructional focus mirrored in the rubric and scoring guide moves from archaic spelling to syntax, and then on to author voice and text attributions (i.e., the information that may help students identify a text as a primary or secondary source text).

A fifth use of the performance assessment is teaching students self-assessment. Independence and success with increasingly complex reading performances are foci of the Common Core State Standards. As students develop their performances, they learn to self-check their work against the detailed information in the rubric. Here, the rubric provides the necessary scaffold for students who are learning to self-assess and judge their performances. Ivan further pursues his goal of teaching students how to read like a historian and assess their work by creating student checklists. He prepares a checklist that matches each of the particular cues that students may use and that is tied to the rubric. Students are required to use the checklist to determine if a particular type of cue is present in the history texts they read. Figure 7 is a checklist used by Ivan and his fellow history teachers to help students learn and attend to the different text cues in primary and secondary source texts.

Ivan's goal here is to help students practice using the teacher-provided checklist on a regular basis so that they eventually internalize the criteria it contains. This provides

The texts we read in history class may be primary or secondary source texts. Use the following checklist to help you remember particular cues and practice using these cues to determine if a text is a primary or secondary source.

Does this text contain cues that are normally found in primary source texts?
_____ Yes
_____ No

Check the following cues as you find them in the text:
_____ Spelling
_____ Vocabulary
_____ Author voice
_____ Print material attribution
_____ Combination of two or more of the above cues

Based on your reading and search for cues in this text, which do you determine it to be?
_____ Primary source text
_____ Secondary source text

Note. From *Understanding and Using Reading Assessment, K–12* (p. 103), by P. Afflerbach, 2007, Newark, DE: International Reading Association. Copyright 2007 by the International Reading Association.

students with the means to read and critically evaluate history texts independently. By using checklists, Ivan is helping his students build a useful schema for conducting self-assessment. When we examine national, state, and district standards, we note that students are expected to read with superior comprehension. We anticipate that they will apply what they learn through reading, and we hope that self-assessment will develop as a necessary part of their reading achievement. Ivan believes that students who do not learn self-assessment will forever be dependent on another to tell them how they are doing in reading. The use of checklists in performance assessment is not confined to the eighth-grade history classroom. In fact, the districtwide use of checklists in different content areas and grades breeds a familiarity with assessment that helps students build independent self-assessment routines.

A final use of performance assessments relates to their communicative ability. Performance assessment helps Ivan portray the richness of student learning and the quality of his teaching. As described previously, the assessment is used regularly to communicate to students both the goals of instruction and the means to reach these goals. The performance assessment also communicates to students the ways to self-assess. Seeing the benefits of performance assessment and the ability to describe in detail student learning and teacher accountability, teachers and administrators become supporters of performance assessments. These assessments demonstrate to parents and other school community members the complexity of learning and the success of teaching. The parents who fully understand the importance of their children developing as critical readers appreciate how the history performance assessment helps them move toward this ability. The detailed examples provided by performance assessment help parents understand the advantage of performance assessment relative to more traditional reading tests.

Roles and Responsibilities Related to Performance Assessment

Ivan has four priorities when using performance assessments: (1) conducting reliable assessment using rubrics and scoring guides, (2) using rubrics and scoring guides as teaching tools in history, (3) using scoring guides and rubrics to help students learn self-assessment, and (4) helping others learn and appreciate the value of performance assessment as he advocates for these assessments. The teacher who demonstrates how performance assessments assist instruction, guide student work, and provide a rich measure of students' accomplishments converts parents to this manner of assessment. Each of these priorities creates a series of roles and responsibilities.

Useful performance assessments derive from the careful consideration of what exactly students do as they undertake and complete a performance. As described earlier in this chapter, Ivan uses task analysis to create a detailed account of what students must know and do to perform assessment tasks. Also, teachers must regularly check to see that their instruction matches the learning and work that is demanded of students by particular performances. Teachers should check to determine the alignment of their instruction, learning standards, and the performance assessment and should be alert to the many different components of student performance. Otherwise, an accurate interpretation of students' reading may be confounded with other factors. A performance assessment that is created to have students demonstrate their content area learning may also involve reading skills and strategies, prior knowledge, motivation, and social interactions. Should the performance assessment be assumed to measure only reading and content area knowledge, the possibility of mismeasuring student achievement increases.

Performance assessment tasks and student performances are not, by themselves, necessarily transparent. For the student, parent, or teacher who does not understand how the score was derived, a score of 3 on a performance assessment is no less opaque than a score of 78 on a standardized, norm-referenced test. Students must have guidance in the process of conceptualizing and doing the performance so that they are working in the direction of the goal of the performance assessment. Ivan wants both the sample performances and anchor papers (i.e., papers that illustrate the essence of a particular score and are used by scorers to guide their work) to provide details to students about the differences in performance, or what determines a score of 4 and what determines a score of 1. In addition, the samples should help describe the space between, or the zones in which students can work and develop their abilities toward a better performance. Thus, a key responsibility for Ivan is to learn to use rubrics, scoring guides, and example papers productively; to teach performance; and to help uncover the "black box," or the relatively unknown ways and means of assessment, for his students (Black & Wiliam, 1998, p. 139). He works with performance assessments across the school year and has developed the ability to teach *with* the assessment and not *to* it. That is, the rubrics and examples of student work become tools for teaching in Ivan's hands. As the performance assessment mirrors important classroom learning and achievement, teaching with the assessment is an important daily routine.

Ivan's work with performance assessment, his task analysis of what it means to read history, and his knowledge of the curriculum allow him to teach in relation to curricular goals, the score points on the history source text rubric, and the Common Core State Standards. Note that the difference between a score of 2 and a score of 3 (in Table 12, these are "Developing" and "Proficient," respectively) on the rubric relates to becoming familiar with using particular strategies and then using those same strategies accurately and successfully. Ivan matches this important difference in student performance scoring points to his knowledge of the curriculum. He determines that his teaching, in relation to the score of 2 on the performance assessment, should focus on accurate identification of the type of text cues and accurate designation of the trustworthiness of the text. Here, performance assessment helps Ivan define and meet an important series of responsibilities.

Performance assessments often assume student reading ability, rather than directly assessing this ability. Although some assessments, such as standardized reading tests, can provide information about the degree of development of students' decoding, word recognition, reading comprehension strategies, and vocabulary, performance assessments may take this development as a given. Thus, performance assessments most often require an existing level of reading proficiency for entry into the task. This special aspect of performance assessments in reading demands that Ivan place his students in performance situations where they can succeed at the reading work. Students asked to perform complex tasks when they do not have the appropriate reading ability will experience prolonged failure. This undesirable scenario reminds us that task analyses should be conducted to determine what a particular performance might demand of students. Performance assessment practice must be supplemented by careful assessment of individual students' achievements and needs. Ivan does not want to misunderstand the information that is provided by the performance assessment. The fact that the history performance assessment demands that students can read at grade level is incentive for him and his colleagues to keep a close watch on individual students' reading ability. This helps prepare students for the assessment and allows for the allocation of class time to help build reading skills and strategies that are prerequisites to adequate performance on the history reading performance assessment.

Over time, students who are involved with performance assessment should experience growth in their ability to self-assess their reading. Performance assessment rubrics provide a degree of transparency to the assessment and represent an opportunity for students to gradually control the assessment of their work. The increased control of reading and performance derives from students who are active participants in their reading. The gradual assumption of control contributes to students' increased independence and success, which can stimulate motivation to read (Aarnoutse & Schellings, 2003). Ivan's responsibilities in relation to teaching self-assessment are guided by his understanding of the need to make clear the ways and means of self-assessment. In the daily routines of the classroom, what provides opportunities to model, discuss, and demonstrate self-assessment for students? As Ivan's students master using different cues to detect source text status, he introduces checklists that help students build toward independent and reliable routines for assessing their knowledge.

Ivan is fortunate to have colleagues with whom he can discuss and plan performance assessments. The performance assessment group uses a list of performance assessment goals and objectives (Moskal, 2003) that describes the responsibilities related to developing and using these assessments effectively and anticipates the assessments being developed by the Race to the Top assessment consortia:

1. The statement of goals and accompanying objectives should provide a clear focus for both instruction and assessment....

2. Both goals and objectives should reflect knowledge and information that is worthwhile for students to learn....

3. The relationship between a given goal and the objectives that describe that goal should be apparent....

4. All of the important aspects of the given goal should be reflected through the objectives....

5. Objectives should describe measurable student outcomes....

6. Goals and objectives should be used to guide the selection of an appropriate assessment activity. (p. 2)

Attention to the roles and responsibilities of performance assessment means that the school district realizes its promise and assigns suitable resources to do so.

States and school districts should use reading research to develop current and well-informed standards for reading across grade levels and content areas. The complexity of the reading performances related to the Common Core State Standards (CCSSO & NGA, 2010) reflects the complexity of reading, as described by contemporary research. One result is that administrators must attend to the call for more authentic assessment, or assessment that allows us to know how students work when they are given complex assignments or learning tasks (Wiggins, 1998). Ivan's building principal and the district curriculum administrators work with teachers to build an understanding of the challenges and benefits of performance assessments.

We are fortunate to have detailed suggestions for developing effective performance assessments, whether the development effort is local or national (Airasian, 1991; Brualdi, 1998; Stiggins, 2002). For example, Roeber (1996) provides helpful advice on administrators' critical roles and responsibilities that contribute to an effective performance assessment program. These include the development of an assessment framework in concert with a detailed assessment plan, establishment of assessment resources, and creation of the assessment blueprint. Detailed guidelines for performance assessment development in relation to administrators' and teachers' roles and responsibilities are presented in Table 14. Any school or school district that sees the value in performance assessment and is planning performance assessments as part of classroom practice needs to examine each of these points carefully. Without attention to each, the best intended performance assessment program may fail.

Performance assessment and the activity it involves often represent a significant change for students, given the passive nature of many student–assessment relationships. Students must be involved and invested in performance assessments, as with portfolios and other active assessments. To do so, students must learn the assessment. The history performance assessments in Ivan's classroom present a set of responsibilities for his students. The responsibilities are framed by students' developing understanding that performance assessments are helpful and that they hold no surprise in

---

TABLE 14
Guidelines for Developing and Using Performance Assessments

- Determine why the performance assessment is needed.
- Specify the important reading knowledge and outcomes that will be assessed by the performance assessment.
- Propose a specific performance that is composed of the reading knowledge and outcomes and conduct a task analysis.
- Based on the task analysis and in relation to research findings, specify the performance that allows students to demonstrate their learning and achievement.
- Specify the aspects of performance that will receive assessment attention and enable the identification and determination of student success.
- Determine the degrees of students' performance that will be identified using rubrics.
- Set performance levels and different levels of proficiency in relation to instructional goals and standards.
- Use the performance assessment to evaluate student learning and work, perhaps using checklists geared to important (i.e., "must have") aspects of the task, using rating scales that represent the continuum of expected student performance. Note that piloting helps fine-tune scoring guides to best cover and represent what students might do.

Note. From *Understanding and Using Reading Assessment, K–12* (p. 108), by P. Afflerbach, 2007, Newark, DE: International Reading Association. Copyright 2007 by the International Reading Association.

how students and their work will be evaluated. The students know that they must attend to the detailed rubrics to guide their work, that this attention provides guidance on the detail of good performance. For example, the students know that superior performances in the history performance assessment will involve the use of different cues to determine source text status and the evaluation of the text in relation to this determination. The students are familiar with taking responsibility for knowing where they are in a task and how they are doing. They are comfortable with being in control of assessment, providing their own feedback to ongoing efforts. Ivan's students appreciate the control and agency that result from this involvement. They understand that responsibilities taken and met can bring tangible rewards.

Like students, parents need to pay attention to the special features of performance assessments, as these differ from the assessments with which parents are most familiar. They must learn the new performance assessment and understand its benefits. When parents are introduced to a new assessment and learn of its possible benefits to their children, they can become knowledgeable and strong supporters of the assessment (Shepard & Bliem, 1995). The development of appreciation for performance assessment and advocacy for it depend on the ability of the teacher and student to demonstrate its usefulness.

Reliability of Performance Assessment

The complexity of performance assessment creates a set of reliability issues. Teachers and students must attend to the special nature of student performances, work to develop consistent routines for evaluating performances, and be aware of the numerous types of confounds that are possible with performance assessments. These assessments usually do not restrict student answers to a single correct response. Rather, the assessments reflect the fact that student performance may be individualistic while still representative of important learning. Performance assessments often set the parameters for appropriate student performances and do not dictate a single acceptable response. When there is more than one acceptable answer, response, or performance, it is imperative that Ivan and his colleagues develop the ability to reliably score them. Here, teachers' knowledge of the parameters of acceptable performance must be well developed. The scorer of a performance assessment must be able to interpret students' varied responses to a single prompt, accommodate variations on a theme, and consistently evaluate these diverse responses in relation to a scoring rubric.

Students' learning of performance assessment is developmental, and we should expect, over time, the increased ability to use performance assessment rubrics to guide student learning. When students are expected to develop self-assessment strategies, we must consider the learning curve that is involved. Ivan and his students are fortunate that school district policy focuses on the consistent use of performance assessments across grades and subjects. This contributes to the development of reliable assessment routines on the part of the students. They use rubrics and scoring guides in each subject, including history, science, and literature, to help them achieve and self-assess their performances. At the same time, teacher judgments of performance assessments provide regular and accurate information about student progress. A student's ability to judge his or her own work may be fledgling in September but better developed in May, nascent in kindergarten but maturing in fourth grade.

There are potential confounds in a performance assessment. Performance assessments, by definition, demand performances. We must be clear about what skills, strategies, and knowledge are involved in student performances so that we can anticipate how student work related to reading may influence the performance. For example, a performance assessment that requires students to write accounts based on their understanding of primary and secondary source texts introduces writing ability into the performance. A laboratory procedure that requires students to read instructions and then perform a series of measures using a balance beam involves both mathematical ability and fine motor skills. The creation of a diorama to portray what a student learns from reading about the culture of the Iroquois involves a creative, artistic component. Each of these performances not only demands successful reading but also engages other aspects of students' learning and ability. In each case, our ability to identify and anticipate the nonreading aspects of a performance assessment will provide the opportunity to evaluate students' performances in an accurate and useful manner and contribute to the reliability of the assessment. (For more on this issue, see the Reading Assessment Snapshot for Confounds in Reading Assessment at the end of Chapter 9.)

Validity of Performance Assessment

Effective performance assessment programs are the result of a careful alignment between research, standards, the curriculum, and assessment. Performance assessments offer the possibility of a rich representation of the construct and learning that we believe to be of value for our students. For example, when we determine that reasoning about the trustworthiness of a particular history text and its author is important, we must invest in assessment that accurately describes the effectiveness of our teaching and students' learning. A performance assessment allows us to create a situation in which students can demonstrate their learning in close relationship and alignment with the construct of reading as a historian. In contrast, we would be hard-pressed to make such inferences from most multiple-choice assessment items. The ability of the performance assessment to honor the construct of student learning provides the possibility of attaining high construct validity.

Earlier in this chapter, we examined rubrics, scoring guides, and sample performances. We determined that they can serve as tools of teaching, learning, and assessment. The close proximity of teaching and learning to assessment is a hallmark of performance assessment. When Ivan's students use the rubric to guide their independent work and when he teaches critical history reading strategies in relation to the rubric, these important classroom routines anticipate the end-of-unit performance assessment. The assessment tasks that students engage in to demonstrate learning are the very tasks that they have been engaged in as part of the learning process. The performance assessment's rubric and sample performances serve as a scaffold and superstructure for learning, and when assessment is this involved in teaching and learning, ecological validity is high.

Summary

Performance assessments are especially effective in describing the manner in which students use reading within the content domains of school learning. Performance assessments reflect the complexity of learning and using knowledge in school and anticipate students' uses and applications of reading beyond school. These are two of the reasons for the keen interest in performance assessments shown by curricular and assessment reform efforts (CCSSO & NGA, 2010; PARCC, 2010; SBAC, 2010). Effective performance assessments reflect a clear and detailed understanding of the things that we would like students to learn and do. This understanding is established through consultation with relevant research and task analyses that promote detailed understanding of proposed student performances.

Performance assessment can promote excellence in teaching because it presumes our attention to important curricular goals and a detailed understanding of how to reach those goals. Performance assessments come with user's guides, or rubrics, which present students and teachers with clear goals and paths for attaining those goals. Rubrics provide a means for scoring performance assessments in a consistent manner in relation to students' complex learning. Rubrics also provide a means for making transparent our curricular and assessment goals. Teachers who are familiar with rubrics can use them to teach well because they help direct attention to important learning goals. Teachers also establish consistent and reliable scoring of student performances with rubrics.

The promise of performance assessment is accompanied by different challenges. Performance assessment demands teacher and student involvement in assessment that may be unprecedented. Although performance assessments have the potential to measure and describe student growth in complex reading tasks, they must be supported by substantial commitments of school resources. We must complement our understanding of how to do a performance assessment well with the sustained commitment of resources that promote the development and use of successful performance assessment programs.

ENHANCING YOUR UNDERSTANDING

1. In relation to your personal goals for students and state and district goals, identify important school performances that may be the focus of a performance assessment.

2. Conduct a task analysis of your proposed performance assessment. What is demanded of students? What types of reading behavior are expected? What related behaviors, such as writing, creating, and discussing, are also involved?

3. Develop a rubric that delineates at least three different levels of student achievement on a selected performance.

4. Create a lesson that focuses on how students can use performance assessment rubrics to learn to self-assess their reading and reading-related work.

Advocating for Reading Assessment

Advocacy of useful reading assessment is important because high-quality reading assessments do not always find their way into classrooms. The tradition of using particular reading assessments, such as paper-and-pencil tests, creates a level of familiarity and comfort for many educators. Assessments, including high-stakes tests, are traditional in nature and firmly established. This creates an environment in which reading assessment may be conducted by habit rather than by informed choice. Thus, the most appropriate reading assessment for measuring student and teacher accomplishments may be overlooked. When particular reading assessments have the potential of increasing the value of the information we obtain, we need to consider how to best advocate for such assessments.

The advocacy process presents an opportunity to educate those whose support is needed to implement assessment change: parents, administrators, and others in the school community who have the voice and energy to advocate for change. This process may be difficult when we deal with assessments and rationales for assessments that are firmly entrenched in tradition. However, our advocacy may be welcomed. Parents who learn that performance and portfolio assessments serve the dual purpose of describing their children's achievement while supporting it may be enthusiastic in their support of new assessments. Administrators who understand that a new reading inventory provides detailed, immediately useful information that helps to both support and describe student growth will support the reading inventory.

Detailed knowledge of the different types of assessment and clear communication of their strengths and weaknesses is required to advocate for a new reading assessment. Advocacy succeeds when we are able to describe how the advocated-for assessment represents an improvement over the existing assessments. Advocacy is a critical part of a thriving reading assessment program. The requirements of advocacy must be anticipated and included in any plan that seeks to engage the school community and change an existing program, implement a new program, or maintain a successful one.

CHAPTER 6

Response to Intervention and Early Reading Assessment

This chapter focuses on the central role of assessment in RTI and on the different types of reading assessment that might be used in the early grades. The chapter includes an in-depth examination of two assessments that are used in early reading: the DIBELS Next (Good & Kaminski, 2002, 2011) and the OSELA (Clay, 2002). Also included is a consideration of strengths and weaknesses of different approaches to conducting and using early reading assessments.

Although this chapter focuses on RTI with younger students, students in upper elementary, middle school, and high school may benefit from a suitable RTI program that combines effective assessment and instruction. Such programs, like their early elementary counterparts, are sensitive to the diversity of skills, strategies, and affective characteristics that students bring to our classrooms (Brozo, 2011). These programs feature assessments and instruction that are closely aligned, distinct purposes for assessment, and student movement to different tiers of instruction, as guided by their indicated needs. It is important to remember that older students in RTI programs may bring a history of experiences in school, and with reading, that tend to be negative. Thus, our assessment and attention must be directed not only at particular cognitive skills and strategies but also at what may well be fragile self-concepts, low motivations, and disinterest.

What Is RTI?

Throughout the history of teaching reading and gauging students' reading growth, there have been different approaches to instruction and assessment. RTI is currently one of the popular approaches to conceptualizing the teaching of reading, and reading assessment. In this section, I provide an overview of RTI and then focus on the elements of RTI that demonstrate the important links between instruction and assessment: RTI is effective when instruction and assessment are well aligned and operating as partners in efforts to help students develop as accomplished readers.

Response to intervention is a ubiquitous term, one that represents an assortment of instruction and assessment strategies intended to provide all readers with appropriate instruction. According to the National Center on Response to Intervention (2010),

> Response to intervention integrates assessment and intervention within a multi-level prevention system to maximize student achievement and to reduce behavioral problems. With RTI, schools use data to identify students at risk for poor learning outcomes, monitor student progress, provide evidence-based interventions and adjust the intensity and nature of those interventions depending on a student's responsiveness, and identify students with learning disabilities or other disabilities. (p. 2)

A legal and legislative precursor of RTI is the Individuals with Disabilities Education Improvement Act of 2004. RTI is intended to determine which students need supplementary reading assistance, through a series of assessments and instruction (Fuchs & Fuchs, 2006; Lipson & Wixson, 2010). RTI is also intended to prevent the wait-to-fail syndrome, in which a student's struggling school performance is accepted until a discrepancy between his or her assumed learning potential and actual learning is demonstrated. Thus, RTI requires that struggling students be identified quickly and efficiently, as their reading challenges emerge. RTI promises focused assistance to students when they exhibit reading challenges.

Dorn and Henderson (2010) describe successful RTI as composed of four parts: (1) assessment materials and routines that reliably identify students who are struggling; (2) an intervention framework that helps guide instruction, based on evidence gathered from the assessments; (3) an organizational structure that encourages increased teacher collaboration and expertise; and (4) the linkage of RTI to a comprehensive program for ongoing, schoolwide literacy development. Undergirding RTI should be systemic support for assessment practice, reading instruction, and student performance. Successful RTI is more than a selection of assessments and reading lessons; it is a structurally sound program that provides teachers, students, and parents with important assessment information on a timely basis.

In theory, there is much in common between RTI and effective classroom instruction. RTI seeks to address students' needs, uses assessments to initially identify these needs, uses increasingly fine-grained assessment to describe the needs, and seeks to use this assessment information to inform instructional approaches to reading. A well-functioning RTI program includes detailed instruction that is informed by effective assessment.

Throughout this book, I stress the importance of formative assessment—assessment that helps shape our thinking about individual students. An appropriate analogy is this: Just as the successful reader effectively uses strategies and prior knowledge to construct meaning from text, effective teachers in RTI programs use reading assessment information and prior knowledge of students to construct meaning of their students. In doing so, the teachers use assessment to diagnose, screen, monitor, and certify student needs and learning. The scope of the assessments used in RTI influences the conceptualization of the reader: areas of need, areas of strength, and the suitability of instruction. Confidence in RTI should be tied to how well we believe in the assessment and instruction that are part of a particular approach to RTI and how well the assessment and instruction reflect the complexity of becoming a better reader.

RTI assumes teacher expertise. The provision of increasingly focused instruction, based on accurate and ongoing assessment, places the classroom teacher at the center of successful RTI (Johnston, 2010; Lipson & Wixson, 2010). The teacher, as the evaluation expert (Johnston, 1987), must be diligent in observing students in the daily routines of the classroom while making determinations of individual students' needs through the use of screening and diagnostic assessment information and then, subsequently, through the series of assessments that are part of the school's RTI regimen. Curriculum-based management is intended to provide periodic updates on the nature of student accomplishment and need, but this leaves open the question of what assessment information might be gathered and used in between curriculum-based measurement assessment events.

Tiers of Intervention and Related Assessments

RTI involves tiers of student placement and instruction. Tier 1 is situated in the regular classroom, as developing student readers have their needs addressed by the classroom teacher. Students in Tier 1 regularly progress through the reading curriculum, meeting near-term and long-term benchmarks. Tier 2 is intended as a follow-up for those students who have not progressed as expected in Tier 1. Tier 2 includes instruction provided by the classroom teacher or a reading specialist that may be intensified through increased focus on a specific need, such as sound–symbol correspondences, fluency, more time given to instruction, smaller instructional groups, or alternative methods of instruction (Scanlon, Anderson, & Sweeney, 2010). If a student does not respond positively to Tier 2 instruction, Tier 3 provides further intensive and focused instruction around the student's needs as indicated by screening and diagnostic assessments in Tier 1 and Tier 2. The relationship of the assessments to the RTI tiers is presented in Table 15.

Supporting the tiered system of RTI is an array of assessments that serve four specific functions: screening, diagnosis, progress monitoring, and outcome measurement. The screening assessment is given to all Tier 1 (i.e., regular classroom) students. The ideal screening assessment is one that reliably distinguishes between students whose reading is developing as expected and those who are encountering difficulty. Screening assessments focus on different cognitive skills and strategies of reading, and in the early grades, many RTI screening assessments focus on phonics, phonemic awareness, and fluency.

A diagnostic assessment is conducted when the screening assessment indicates that the student is struggling. Typically administered in Tier 2, the diagnostic

TABLE 15		
Assessments Used in the Response to Intervention Tiers		
Tier	Assessments	
1	Screening	
2	Diagnosis, progress monitoring, and outcome measurement	
3	Diagnosis, progress monitoring, and outcome measurement[a]	

[a]The assessments used at Tier 3 may be the same as those used in Tier 2, or they may be new assessments that increasingly focus on a student's specific needs, as informed by the already-used array of assessments.

assessment allows for drilling down into the areas that are indicated as problematic by the screening assessment. For example, a student who exhibits difficulty with reading in a fluent manner on a gradewide screening test can be given a diagnostic assessment that focuses, in more depth, on fluency in reading. In turn, the diagnostic assessment informs classroom instruction. The results are used to determine which specific skills and strategies require special attention. If a student continues to experience difficulty in Tier 2, movement to Tier 3 may be informed by the original diagnostic assessment information, or a more focused diagnostic assessment may be used to further pinpoint the student's needs to be addressed in Tier 3.

Progress monitoring focuses on how well a student is developing in relation to his or her needs, as indicated by the screening and diagnostic assessments, and in relation to the curriculum chosen as a result of these assessments. Progress monitoring is conducted frequently to check whether the student's designated areas of need are being addressed and that related reading is developing. As such, progress monitoring is a key component of curriculum-based management (Deno & Fuchs, 1987), in which students are regularly tested to gauge how well they are progressing in relation to screening and diagnostic assessment foci and curricular goals.

The final category of assessment within RTI is outcome measurement, which serves to gauge a student's development in relation to district and state benchmarks for reading development in a particular grade. For example, a reading curriculum that is closely tied to the DIBELS Next will assess outcomes of oral reading fluency instruction at the end of the school year, and the student's performance on the outcome measure will be compared with national norms for oral reading fluency.

The four types of assessment in RTI must be carefully chosen and coordinated. They must be of increasing sensitivity to students' needs as students move into the more intensive intervention levels of Tier 2 and Tier 3. Hopefully, the array of assessments reflects a rich image of reading, in which cognitive skills and strategies are used to construct meaning. The assessment regimen related to RTI is resource consuming, which means that each and every assessment component of an RTI program should be vetted for the usefulness of the information it provides for helping students become better readers.

Standard Treatment Protocol and Problem-Solving Approaches to RTI

Lipson, Wixson, and Johnston (2010) describe two general approaches to RTI: standard treatment protocol and problem solving. The standard protocol typically includes a single, scripted instructional intervention that is selected for use in a school district or school. For example, a student whose screening assessment suggests difficulty with learning sound–symbol correspondences then takes a diagnostic assessment. The combined assessment results are used to determine the student's ensuing instruction, which is often a commercial, scripted curriculum. Teachers using the standard protocol approach are expected to strive for fidelity to treatment, adhering to the scripted instruction that is associated with the demonstrated student need. Variation in instruction for individual students who exhibit the same general need is not encouraged. This can create the peculiar situation in which an individual student's specific needs are known, in as much detail as the RTI-related assessments provide, but the related RTI instruction is based on a generic approach to addressing the need. With the standard protocol approach, what is assessed as a need by the screening and diagnostic assessment becomes the focus of instruction. This illustrates the power of the screening assessment in RTI, and the need for assessment to be comprehensive.

In contrast, a problem-solving approach to RTI allows and encourages input from outside the standard assessment and instruction protocol. Reading assessment information—from a screening test, a teacher's observations of a student's performance, and running records results—can be used, all in service of portraying the complexity of the student's reading development. This complexity includes cognitive skills and strategies, and affective factors that influence reading development, such as motivation and self-efficacy. Dorn and Henderson's (2010) portrayal of the "assessment wall" (p. 136) fits well with the problem-solving approach to RTI. The assessment wall serves as a collection point for information about students' reading development, including worksheets, test results, student work, teacher observations, and the results of informal reading inventories. The wall serves as a place for discussion among teaching colleagues of students' accomplishments and needs, encouraging the use of interim assessments to change instruction, if needed (Goertz, Oláh, & Riggan, 2009). The problem-solving model for RTI assumes active engagement of teachers, the honoring of all legitimate evidence of the state of students' reading development, and the benefit of multiple assessment perspectives on students' progress.

Instruction in the problem-solving model for RTI is informed by a broad array of assessments. These assessments can serve to triangulate; information gathered through screening and diagnostic assessments may be supported, modified, or challenged by careful classroom-based assessments and the information they provide. The problem-solving approach also allows for broad consideration of the factors that influence students' reading development. For example, it is doubtful that exclusive attention to cognitive skill and strategy development is all that struggling readers need. Affective factors, such as a reader's self-esteem, self-concept, and motivation to read, can create powerful incentives or disincentives to read. Learning about these important factors through assessment can result in a more broad-based, inclusive, and successful RTI program (Johnston, 2010). Problem-solving approaches to RTI can help us avoid the assessment trap of RTI, in which aspects of reading development that we know to be important—and critical to the struggling readers' progress—are not initially assessed and, therefore, not attended to.

The preceding descriptions of the standardized protocol and problem-solving approaches to RTI represent two ends of a continuum. In many cases, classrooms, schools, and school districts evidence hybrid models of RTI. These models are selected, or settled on, based on a range of factors that include available resources, the degree of a consensus view of early reading development, state and school district initiatives, and the organizational structure of the schools. In the next section, I sketch two cases along a related but different continuum: whether or not the RTI system of assessment is closed, limited to a single assessment or assessment type that informs instruction and placement, or open, seeking all relevant information that contributes to an understanding of individual students and their needs.

Closed and Open Systems of Assessment and Instruction in RTI

Here, I present two versions of the RTI model to illustrate how different school districts might use assessments and instruction to try to help students develop as readers. The first example focuses on a district that uses the DIBELS Next and scripted instruction in a standard protocol approach, in which teachers administer tests and deliver instruction. I characterize this as a closed system. The second district employs a problem-solving approach, in which teachers are expected to be thoughtful investigators of their students' reading development. As this system is planned to make use of all relevant assessment information, I characterize it as an open system.

A closed RTI system of assessment and instruction. In this district, all students are screened in first grade using a quick and psychometrically reliable assessment, the DIBELS Next (Good & Kaminski, 2011). The results of the DIBELS Next test are used to determine how student readers are performing in line with the norms of reading development on the parts of reading on which the DIBELS Next is based, including oral reading fluency and nonsense word decoding. Those students who are flagged by the DIBELS Next as at risk for failure are moved to Tier 2 and given a more in-depth diagnostic assessment. This assessment provides better detail related to the specific reading challenges that were indicated by the DIBELS Next screening test—in this case, oral reading fluency and nonsense word decoding.

The students in Tier 2 of RTI are then given scripted instruction in oral reading fluency and nonsense word decoding, and teachers in Tier 2 instruction are required to exhibit fidelity to treatment, meaning that they should not stray or improvise in relation to the printed reading lessons. A sameness of instruction is assumed for students who have comparable DIBELS Next results and scores, even though there may be individual differences in the needs of the students within the indicated area.

The students in Tier 2 are given regular progress-monitoring tests to determine their development in relation to the scripted reading instruction in oral reading fluency that they are receiving. A student who is keeping pace in Tier 2, based on the results of progress monitoring, will remain, whereas a student who is still struggling will be recommended for Tier 3, in which additional school resources will be provided to try to help the student catch up to grade level. The student who excels in Tier 2 may return to the Tier 1 classroom, as deemed appropriate by curriculum-based management and progress-monitoring tests. At the end of the school year, all students are given outcome measures, which gauge the students' development in relation to district and state benchmarks for reading development in a particular grade, and on the skills and strategies indicated on the original screening assessment at the beginning of the year.

The above approach to RTI represents a closed system because the initial decision to move a student from the regular classroom (i.e., Tier 1) to Tier 2 is based on the results of a single test. The system remains closed as teachers deliver scripted instruction that is developed in relation to a specified, general need. RTI is intended to cater to individual students' needs, but the closed system takes a generic instructional path for students with similar designated needs. To the degree that teachers are required to stay scripted, or not veer from the generic lessons, there is no opportunity to individualize lessons. The use of progress monitoring reinforces the closed nature of the system, as test content and ongoing instruction is developed to mimic the DIBELS Next. Thus, instruction and assessment are firmly focused on content that is related to the DIBELS Next, with the intent of improving progress-monitoring scores and, ultimately, doing well on the year-end assessment.

An open RTI system of assessment and instruction. The second district subscribes to the idea that context must be considered as RTI is implemented and refined. Lipson and Wixson (2010) state, "Different solutions may be needed in different settings, given diverse students and varied instructional resources and histories" (p. xi). In accordance, the assessment and identification of student needs is centered around an assessment wall (Dorn & Henderson, 2010). The assessment wall is a prominent feature in the RTI team meeting room, as well as a primary source of information about each and every student. The school provides time for regular meetings of all teachers, grades K–3, and during this time, there are opportunities to discuss students whose needs are apparent and to plan to further gather information about students who may benefit from Tier 2 or Tier 3 intervention. In this district, the results of the DIBELS Next screening assessment that is mandated by the state are but one source of information that is used to help determine a student's instructional program and placement.

At the beginning of the school year, teachers gather the available information to construct initial understandings of their students and their reading. This information can include student worksheets, teacher observations, records from prior years, or aspects of running records. Teacher discussions allow for the elaboration of information that is contained on the assessment wall, with the students' teachers from the prior year. The assessment wall is both a permanent record of reading development and a source of formative information that is used to identify students who may benefit from interventions. A key aspect of the wall is that it contains assessment information that is collaboratively discussed and understood. The expectation is that students' ongoing progress, over time and with intervention, is charted and publicly displayed for all involved teachers. This display certifies that particular assessments are done, that discussions about students' challenges and progress are held, and that the many efforts and results related to RTI are documented. Discussions about students are collaborative events that focus on evidence about students' strengths and needs, both cognitive and affective, and possible instructional steps to help the students.

Focus on Cognitive Skills and Strategies

The vast majority of approaches to RTI focus on cognitive skills and strategies. Given the intensive assessment routines of RTI, it is important to note that assessments become our eyes, our ways of seeing students. Consider the following scenario: A first-grade student is struggling to pronounce predictable, phonically regular, three-letter words that are encountered in stories. The teacher notices this in the first week of school. The screening test, which is given to all first graders, provides confirming evidence of the challenges that the student faces when trying to decode words. The student moves from Tier 1 to Tier 2. The student's challenges, as indicated by the teacher's observations and the screening test, require a follow-up diagnostic test. This test provides more information about the nature of the decoding challenges: The student has few sight words and little strategic knowledge to decode consonant-vowel-consonant (C-V-C) pattern words. Using this information, the teacher focuses on familiarizing the student with the C-V-C pattern and identifying C-V-C words that are somewhat familiar to the student (e.g., *cat*, *bat*). Throughout the marking period, the teacher conducts progress-monitoring assessments, which provide an account of the student learning how to decode three-letter words. The progress monitoring indicates slow but sure progress for the student in Tier 2. At the end of the year, an outcome measure, in the form of a standardized test, is used to gauge the student's overall growth and progress in relation to curricular goals.

The intensity of the instruction and assessment in RTI and their focus on reading skills should not blind us to what may be other, vital needs of our developing student readers. The DIBELS Next portrays reading as a performance on isolated reading skills (Pearson, 2006). We should not become so guided by our assessments that we fail to look outside of them to determine the related areas of reading growth that are not measured. These include both the cognitive (e.g., comprehension) and the affective (e.g., self-concept, motivation) aspects of reading development. If RTI assessment has an exclusive focus on cognitive skill and strategy development, and if we are working in a school district constrained by time and budget issues, teachers and students will be restricted to determinations of growth and success in relation to the limited assessment information.

A key to valid assessment in RTI is the breadth of the measure of students' developing reading. In most cases, RTI represents the first and most detailed examination of a student's reading development. Our assessments become our eyes, and what we see in our students is what our assessments provide. We must ask these questions:

- Does the array of assessments cover all that we know to be valuable and important in student readers' development?
- Does the assessment information that emanates from RTI tell the full story of student's reading growth?

Construct validity matters greatly here. Under current models of RTI, a student who lacks positive motivation for reading or for attending during reading instruction would not encounter a single, related assessment in the formal RTI screening, diagnosis, and progress-monitoring regimen. Thus, a clear need would be ignored by the system, not indicated early on, and not a focus of in-depth diagnosis. Following, an assessment-driven instructional program that does not indicate student motivation as an issue does not attend to motivation during instruction. The status of and change in motivation are not reported in any outcome measures.

In addition, we need to assess the parts-to-whole assumptions that underlie some RTI assessment approaches. We can assess phonemic awareness, and we can assess phonics. We can also assess fluency and vocabulary. Whether we use subtests of one assessment, such as those in the DIBELS Next, or different assessments from other tests, we must always ascertain coverage and connectivity of aspects of reading that are treated as discrete parts by many RTI assessments. Do we assess developing readers when they are required to combine skill and strategy in an act of actual reading? Construct validity matters here because a true assessment of reading involves just that: reading. We do not read to be accomplished in phonics or demonstrate phonemic awareness, and we do not read to display fluency as a particular combination of rate and accuracy. These are all important aspects of reading, yet they do not get us to the point of reading: to construct meaning.

All of our reading assessments should be considered high-stakes assessments. That is, we must assume important consequences for our assessments, or we should question why we are using them (Crooks, 1988). So it is for RTI—assessment is a cornerstone for the success or failure of any RTI program. At each stage of screening, diagnosis, progress monitoring, and outcome measurement, we must be confident that RTI is timely, detailed, and useful.

In the following section, we examine two contrasting approaches to assessing early reading and consider the models of literacy from which the approaches derive and their possible uses in RTI.

A Brief History of the OSELA

The OSELA (Clay, 2002) was developed by Clay, based on her work with New Zealand schoolchildren. The tasks included in the OSELA are "derived from a theory of how young children come to master the complex tasks of reading and writing continuous text" (p. 2), and are intended "for classroom teachers who want to be careful observers of how young children learn to read and write" (p. 1). The OSELA is suggested for use as a formative assessment that will help teachers monitor their students' development and progress across the early school years. Teachers use information from the OSELA to add to their detailed knowledge of students, diagnose and characterize student reading, and inform instruction. Clay directly addresses the need for formative assessment, as opposed to the increasingly popular high-stakes test, with the observation that

> test scores are mere approximations or estimates that do not provide good guidance to the teacher of how to teach a particular child. At times those scores present results stripped of the very information that is required for designing or evaluating sound instruction for individual learners. Standardised tests need to be supplemented at the classroom level with systematic observations of children who are in the act of responding to instruction, observations that are reliable enough to compare one child with another, or one child on two different occasions. (p. 3)

Considered in light of RTI, this description presents the OSELA as a suitable blend of formative and summative assessments, used to diagnose and then prepare to teach a student. Teachers who work with Reading Recovery and those who use running records of children's oral reading are probably familiar with the OSELA: The assessment reflects the child development theories and recommended teaching and assessment practices of its creator. Prominent is the idea that assessment should provide useful information to teachers. Information from the OSELA can be employed in a timely manner to shape our conceptualizations of individual students' strengths and needs, as well as our ideas for effective instruction.

Details of the OSELA

The OSELA is intended for use in kindergarten and first grade, with the focus on students who are beginning readers and writers. The assessment is used generally with students who are 5–7 years old. It assesses students' phonemic awareness, knowledge of letter names and letter sounds, word attack strategies, reading fluency, reading comprehension, and vocabulary knowledge. The OSELA's tasks allow teachers to assess students' concepts about print, reading skills, and strategies during the administration of running records; letter, word, and sentence dictation; and story writing. This is important coverage of the critical aspects of learning to read and also the necessary focus of RTI.

Running records require students to read aloud as the teacher observes and records their reading behaviors. A major focus of running records is miscue analysis, which helps us examine students' language processing and determine their current strengths and challenges related to reading skills and strategies. From this information, we can make well-informed inferences about students' current needs and related instruction. Within the subtests, the Letter Identification task measures students' knowledge of the printed forms of letters and the sounds of letters. The Concepts About Print task focuses on students' knowledge of print conventions, including directionality (i.e., reading from left to right and from top to bottom) and how words and letters differ. The Word Test focuses on high-frequency words, some of which may be sight words that are read aloud for particular students. The Writing Vocabulary task requires students to write down as many words as they can in a short period of time, thus providing information about their knowledge of sounds and letters, print conventions, and sight word vocabulary. The Hearing and Recording Sounds in Words task has students write two short sentences, which are then analyzed and scored for correct letters and phonemes. Combined, these subtests provide detailed knowledge about a student's language processing to identify his or her needs and inform related instructional goals and methods in RTI.

The OSELA is administered individually to students. The assessment's subtests and their approximate administration times are shown in Table 16.

TABLE 16 Subtests and Administration Times for the OSELA		
Subtest	Administration Time	Scoring Time
Running Records	10 minutes	10 minutes
Letter Identification	5–10 minutes	2 minutes
Concepts About Print	5–10 minutes	2 minutes
Word Test	2 minutes	2 minutes
Writing Vocabulary	10 minutes	5 minutes
Hearing and Recording Sounds in Words	10 minutes	5 minutes
Total	42–52 minutes	26 minutes
Total administration and scoring time	68–78 minutes	

Note. From *Understanding and Using Reading Assessment, K–12* (p. 115), by P. Afflerbach, 2007, Newark, DE: International Reading Association. Copyright 2007 by the International Reading Association.

Teachers are responsible for scoring and interpreting the OSELA. Teachers are expected to be knowledgeable about Clay's theories of language development, and most teachers require considerable training to master the details of administering, scoring, and interpreting the assessment. A positive aspect of the training is that it may bear close relationship to both the literacy instruction and assessment in the classrooms in which it is used. For example, the running records component may be conducted regularly by classroom teachers as they listen to their students read aloud. The tasks included on the OSELA and the learning they are intended to assess bear strong resemblance to instruction and learning during the school day.

The OSELA serves many teachers as a formative assessment, describing, with detail sufficient to inform instruction, the nature of students' literacy development. In addition, the OSELA can provide summative information related to students' developing reading and writing skills and strategies.

Consequences and Usefulness of the OSELA

The OSELA is accompanied by substantial consequences. The decision to use it reflects the fact that a school or school district values formative literacy assessment that is grounded in classroom instruction and learning. One consequence is that the information yielded describes students' literate behavior as contextualized in tasks that can inform instruction. The formative nature of the OSELA means that the resources placed in the assessment describe not only student achievement but also where and the manner in which teachers can work to foster students' continued literacy development.

The detailed information that is provided by the OSELA helps describe individual students' needs. This provision of immediately useful information can have positive effects on literacy instruction, suggesting for teachers the students' zones of proximal development and areas of instructional need as related to early literacy skills and strategies. Moreover, students' coordinated use of reading skills and strategies can be examined with the assessment. That is, we can observe and record how a student uses skills to decode a word as he or she is reading to construct meaning. There is no hierarchy of reading skills and strategies. Many RTI assessments assume such a hierarchy, in which the mechanics of reading, including phonics and fluency, must precede attempts to construct meaning. The OSELA is individually administered, and the individual observation done well yields information that describes how a student is progressing. Thus, the OSELA has a positive consequence of encouraging instruction that is informed by the detailed descriptions of individual students' actual needs.

Extensive training and practice are required for teachers to accurately administer, score, and interpret the OSELA. The ability to record, interpret, and use the detailed information from running records requires the substantial commitment of professional development resources for teachers (Dorn & Henderson, 2010) as they work to become assessment experts in their classrooms. A consequence is that any school or district that believes that the OSELA is suitable for informing instruction and fostering students' literacy development must consider these training demands. For RTI consideration, it is recommended that school districts consider how the OSELA might serve as a screening assessment, a diagnostic assessment, or both. The number of students to be assessed should also impact any such decision.

Finally, the time commitment for the effective use of the OSELA is considerable. Individual administration times add up across the school year. For example, at the beginning of the year, use of the OSELA in a class of 25 first graders will require, at minimum, over 28 hours for administration and scoring. A consequence is the demand for sufficient time in the school schedule to realize the potential for the OSELA. This observation should be tempered with the fact that the OSELA is often closely coordinated with ongoing instruction and because instruction and assessment share a broad conceptualization of children's reading and language development.

Roles and Responsibilities Related to the OSELA

The OSELA places considerable demands on teachers. The ability to reliably administer, score, and interpret students' performance on the assessment is developed by most teachers through considerable hours of training and practice.

The fact that the OSELA is a complex, teacher-dependent observation instrument also places large demands on administrators and school districts. Professional development to introduce the assessment and train teachers how to administer it, score it, interpret the scores, and then apply what is learned in subsequent instruction must be provided. This professional development means the commitment of considerable time and school district resources. Funding to provide professional development so that teachers can achieve reliable use of the OSELA may directly compete with district and school funds already dedicated to standardized testing.

Reliability of the OSELA

The intricacies of administration and interpretation of the OSELA pose a reliability challenge. There is information to be learned about the contents and procedures of the assessment, as well as the means to take its results and use them in constructing accurate diagnoses and crafting related instruction. For example, the running records portion of the OSELA requires that a teacher observe, record, code, and interpret oral reading behaviors and patterns of behavior that show themselves in running record transcripts. The time and training needed for teachers to become reliable administrators and interpreters of the assessment are considerable. The individual teacher, school, or school district that is contemplating use of the OSELA estimates the resources involved in training for reliable use. Also, the OSELA yields voluminous data that must be carefully coordinated, analyzed, and acted on by teachers.

Validity of the OSELA

The OSELA comprises six measures: (1) text reading, (2) letter identification, (3) concepts about print, (4) a word test, (5) writing vocabulary, and (6) hearing and recording sounds in words. These individual tasks and the composite of information they provide anticipate the claim of construct validity for the instrument. The OSELA asks students to demonstrate important subskills of reading and writing, such as letter identification, phonemic awareness, and concepts about print. The OSELA also requires students to attempt to read and comprehend text and produce an account of the words they know in the text through writing. Together, the tasks included in the assessment reflect a conceptualization of early literacy as involving reading skills and strategies and their coordinated application. The OSELA also frames reading as an act of constructing meaning, placing decided value on comprehension. Further, the instrument seeks information about students' procedural knowledge of literacy: the nature of reading, how books work, and the conventions of printed language. The nature of these assessments and their relation to literacy instruction and learning in the classroom contribute to their construct validity.

In RTI, use of the OSELA reflects a comprehensive conceptualization of early reading development. This should increase the confidence in the inferences made from the results about the nature of students' literacy development and related instructional priorities. Finally, the ecological validity of the OSELA is strong in those classrooms where the language instruction and the assessment philosophy and practice are aligned.

A Brief History of the DIBELS Next

The DIBELS was developed at the University of Oregon in the 1980s and has since undergone a series of revisions. It was recently augmented by the DIBELS Next (Good & Kaminski, 2011), on which the following review is based. Good and Kaminski (2011), the authors of the DIBELS and the DIBELS Next, characterize their assessment as follows:

> Over the last decade, *DIBELS* (*Dynamic Indicators of Basic Early Literacy Skills*) have changed the educational landscape—providing accurate, timely benchmark and progress monitoring information to ensure students receive targeted instructional support. This premier universal assessment system has been embraced by educators across the country and used as a tool to help thousands of students reach their full academic potential. (p. iv)

I am not sure that all educators who choose or are forced to use the DIBELS share this enthusiasm, but many would agree that the DIBELS has "changed the educational landscape." As a result of its favored status among Reading First programs, the DIBELS Next is part of the literacy assessment experience of over two million students in U.S. schools (Samuels, 2007). The Center on Education Policy (Scott & Fagin,

2005) found that the DIBELS Next is used in 37 states as all or part of individual school districts' early reading assessment. Five other states list this test as an assessment that is approved for use. The DIBELS Next is widely used as an RTI screening test and as a progress-monitoring measure. In cases in which it is the sole or favored RTI screening assessment, the DIBELS Next may set the parameters for the content of RTI instruction, focusing on the mechanics of reading development. Indeed, Good and Kaminski (2011) note that there are specific, intended uses for the DIBELS Next and that the data yielded is limited:

> As indicators, *DIBELS* measures are not intended to be comprehensive, in-depth assessments of each and every component of a basic early literacy skill. Instead, they are designed to measure key components that are representative of that skill area, and predictive of overall reading competence. (pp. 2–3)

Details of the DIBELS Next

Good and Kaminski (2002) cite research syntheses as a basis for the construct of reading around which they developed the DIBELS:

> The measures [in DIBELS] were developed upon the essential early literacy domains discussed in both the National Reading Panel (2000) and National Research Council (1998) reports to assess student development of phonological awareness, alphabetic understanding, and automaticity and fluency with the code. Each measure has been thoroughly researched and demonstrated to be reliable and valid indicators of early literacy development and predictive of later reading proficiency to aid in the early identification of students who are not progressing as expected. When used as recommended, the results can be used to evaluate individual student development as well as provide grade-level feedback toward validated instructional objectives. (p. 1)

Good and Kaminski (2011) provide data related to the proposed validity and reliability of the DIBELS Next instrument and assessment procedures. From their description, it is clear that the authors focus on an important subset of early literacy strategies and skills and are interested in the relation between a student's performance on the DIBELS Next and his or her future reading performance. The DIBELS Next comprises six separate measures, each related to early reading development:

1. *First Sound Fluency (FSF):* The assessor says words, and the student says the first sound for each word.

2. *Letter Naming Fluency (LNF):* The student is presented with a sheet of letters and asked to name the letters.

3. *Phoneme Segmentation Fluency (PSF):* The assessor says words, and the student says the individual sounds for each word.

4. *Nonsense Word Fluency (NWF):* The student is presented with a list of VC and CVC nonsense words (e.g., sig, rav, ov) and asked to read the words.

5. *DIBELS Oral Reading Fluency (DORF):* The student is presented with a reading passage and asked to read aloud. The student is then asked to retell what he/she just read.

6. *Daze:* The student is presented with a reading passage where some words are replaced by a multiple choice box that includes the original word and two distractors. The student reads the passage silently and selects the word in each box that best fits the meaning. (pp. 1–2)

The DIBELS Next requires a relatively short time for administration and scoring. Table 17 shows the times needed to administer and score the tests as beginning-of-year, midyear, and end-of-year assessments.

Depending on students' performance, the entire battery or a subset of tests is recommended for administration three times a year: at the beginning of the school year, midyear, and at the end (Good & Kaminski, 2011). In addition, the time required for training teachers or others to administer the DIBELS Next ranges from one to four hours. Training is recommended for a wide range of school personnel, including paraprofessionals, student teachers, and administrators. The assessment accuracy checklists provide the means to assess the administrator's adherence to the DIBELS Next's assessment guidelines and to provide feedback on the "accuracy and consistency with standardized administration and scoring procedures" (p. 113).

The creators of the DIBELS Next offer computerized scoring and maintenance of student records in individual student performance profiles, which allow for charting each subtest in relation to the grade-level DIBELS Next benchmark goals. Using the computerized scoring and classification system, the DIBELS Next can provide teachers and schools with progress monitoring in relation to the assessment goals, performance levels, and the particular RTI program.

Student results are compared with existing DIBELS Next benchmark goals for each of the subtests, and students' performance results are then categorized as benchmark, strategic, or intensive. Students whose performances are at or above the benchmark are described as follows:

The odds are in the student's favor (approximately 80%–90%) of achieving subsequent early literacy goals. The student is making adequate progress in reading and is likely to achieve subsequent reading benchmarks with appropriate and effective instruction. The student needs continuing effective curriculum and instruction. (Good & Kaminski, 2011, p. 25)

TABLE 17
Total Administration and Scoring Times for the DIBELS Next

Grade(s)	Beginning of Year	Midyear	End of Year
Kindergarten	3 minutes	6.5 minutes	5 minutes
1	5 minutes	8 minutes	5 minutes
2	8 minutes	6 minutes	6 minutes
3–6	12–13 minutes[a]	12–13 minutes[a]	12–13 minutes[a]

[a]Time includes 5 minutes for group administration of the comprehension measure and 1–2 minutes for scoring.

Students whose performances are "below the benchmark goal and at or above the cut point for risk" (p. 25) receive the "strategic" label. Such students are described as follows:

> The odds of achieving subsequent early literacy goals are roughly 40%–60% for a student with skills in this range. The student typically needs strategic, targeted instructional support to ensure that he/she makes adequate progress and achieves subsequent reading benchmarks. (p. 25)

Finally, students whose performance is "below the cut point for risk" (p. 25) are labeled as "intensive" and given the following prognosis:

> The odds of achieving subsequent early literacy goals are approximately 10%–20% for a student whose performance is below the cut point for risk. The student is unlikely to achieve subsequent reading benchmarks unless provided with substantial, intensive instructional support. (p. 25)

Consequences and Usefulness of the DIBELS Next

As previously mentioned, the use of the DIBELS Next results in profiles of students' literacy that derive largely from measures of development in phonological awareness, knowledge of the alphabetic principle, and fluency with connected text. Each of these areas is associated with successful reading. However, a consequence to be avoided is the assumption that the DIBELS Next is *the* necessary literacy assessment. Because it is limited in describing students' comprehension of text and vocabulary knowledge, the test's focus on mechanical aspects of reading creates a need for additional assessments that tell us how students are progressing in their attempts to construct meaning from text. The DIBELS Next is a general indicator regarding students' specific needs and related instruction within the skills it assesses. It provides little formative assessment information, even though it is used frequently in the progress-monitoring stage of RTI. Further, the DIBELS Next provides little or no information about how students coordinate skills and strategies to achieve the goal of reading: the construction of meaning.

Results from the DIBELS Next can help identify students who have clear needs for additional instruction and academic intervention in the mechanics of reading. The test can figure prominently in decisions to move students among the three RTI tiers, although it may lack fine-grained descriptive information as to what exactly should be taught and learned. For example, a first-grade student who does poorly in the First Sound Fluency subtest receives the label "at risk." The assignment of this label is followed by instruction that focuses on the student's needs. Yet, "at risk" is only a general determination, not a detailed accounting of the specific need. There is certainly not enough information yielded by the DIBELS Next to make specific and comprehensive instructional recommendations. When used as a screening device in RTI, a DIBELS Next designation of "at risk" would be followed by diagnostic testing, which should provide more detailed and instructionally useful information. The DIBELS Next results may also be used as converging evidence that students have met key instructional goals or that they will benefit from additional instruction.

A final set of consequences relates to how the DIBELS Next may impact other aspects of schooling. The widespread use of the assessment combined with the need to demonstrate adequate yearly progress may bring with it the temptation to use the DIBELS Next as a blueprint for instruction (Pearson, 2006). In this scenario, schools using a particular RTI model may overly focus on students' reading development as narrowly defined by the DIBELS Next, on doing things quickly (e.g., oral reading fluency), while ignoring a major goal of reading: the construction of meaning. In addition, such a high-stakes test can send powerful messages to teachers, parents, and students about the nature of reading, reading development, and assessment. Van Kraayenoord (2010) notes that "the focus on the assessment of fluency via CBM [curriculum-based measurement] will quickly provide a message to students and parents that this is what counts as reading and reading assessment" (p. 372).

Roles and Responsibilities Related to the DIBELS Next

As noted earlier, the DIBELS Next can be administered by almost all school personnel with minimal training. It is a test that places low demand on expertise or knowledge of literacy development for administrators or scorers of the test. In fact, its ease of administration is appealing for districts that must screen entire grades of students. An important responsibility for teachers and administrators who use the DIBELS Next is to regularly supplement its results with other assessments that focus on a broad conceptualization of literacy development. The DIBELS is an extremely popular assessment, and in earlier versions, it has given relatively slight attention to students' ability to construct meaning. The DIBELS Next reflects the developers' concerns that reading comprehension is better addressed. However, users of the DIBELS Next should look for opportunities to augment it with more detailed examinations of how students construct meaning. This may help prevent comprehension blindness, or the pursuit of the improvement of subskills of reading without attention to the goal of reading, which is understanding texts that are read.

The DIBELS Next is an assessment that is chosen at state department of education levels and is most frequently used as a gauge of progress in federally funded Reading First programs. As such, it may be a widely used but not well-understood test. We should learn about the DIBELS Next to help make the determinations of how and if it reflects our own conceptualizations of elementary school students' reading development. We should examine the test for its attention to important aspects of reading development and consider educating parents and administrators as to its nature.

Reliability of the DIBELS Next

The DIBELS Next is a relatively straightforward test, one that can be administered by school personnel after just a few hours of training. As a standardized test, the DIBELS Next administration procedures and assessment accuracy checklists may work to enhance the reliability of test results. Challenges to the reliability of the DIBELS Next could come from the novelty of the subtests' contents and procedures for young children, as well as the fact that students with particular dialects and accents may be misinterpreted as they make the verbalizations required by the subtests. It is notable that the creators of the DIBELS Next also coproduced a Spanish-language test of basic early literacy skills, the *Indicadores Dinámicos del Éxito en la Lectura* (Baker, Cummings, Good, & Smolkowski, 2007), which is intended to reliably assess the early reading skills and strategies of particular English learners.

One further concern for reliability is the nature of the maze procedure (Gillingham & Garner, 1992) that is included in the Daze test. On this portion of the DIBELS Next, students are required to choose the appropriate word from three possible choices, twice in each sentence, to create a syntactically and semantically acceptable sentence. The following is the sample item provided in the *DIBELS Next Assessment Manual* (Good & Kaminski, 2011, p. 101):

The student's task is to choose the two words that complete the sentence so that it is syntactically correct. As illustrated by this task, it is possible that students who are unfamiliar with the maze procedure are confused by it, which could influence their performance and subsequent decisions based on the student's score. A task analysis of this item reveals that the student must deal with an extremely novel sentence and assessment task.

Validity of the DIBELS Next

The DIBELS Next is accompanied by documentation related to concurrent and predictive validity. The development effort for the test included procedures in which the DIBELS Next scores were compared with scores on existing literacy assessments that measure similar early literacy skills. This provides a measure of concurrent validity.

A second important psychometric feature of the DIBELS Next is its claimed predictive validity, or its ability to relate students' current scores on mechanics of reading measures to measures of their future reading performance. The DIBELS Next manages to predict, with some accuracy, students' future development as readers, although the degree of accuracy is debated (Pressley, Hilden, & Shankland, 2006). A concern with the test is the power of its predictive ability and the trade-offs that may be involved with construct validity. For example, the DIBELS Next uses psychometric formulas to predict an approximate level of future reading performance, but the test does so by using only some of the reading skills and strategies necessary for successful future (or current) reading and portrays such skills, including fluency, narrowly (Samuels, 2007).

That relatively little attention is given to comprehension in the DIBELS Next leads some educators to question the construct validity of the instrument. Clearly, the DIBELS Next provides information related to important mechanics of reading, including phonics and fluency. Yet, the test does not provide for observation and interpretation of these mechanics as they occur in actual reading. When we examine the DIBELS Next, we may conclude that early literacy skills relate to developing phonemic awareness, decoding words from print to sound, and reading orally at a suitable rate of speed and accuracy. What sort of construct, then, is the DIBELS Next measuring? It is a construct that tangentially involves word meaning and comprehension. It may be that the DIBELS Next is an assessment of part of the construct of early literacy, for it does measure important parts of learning to read. However, it is not a robust reflection of the construct of reading.

The recent addition of two measures to the DIBELS Next demonstrates that the creators of the test are aware of user concerns. The DIBELS Oral Reading Fluency and Daze tasks are included partly as a response to educators' feedback that previous versions of the DIBELS did not attempt to assess students' achievement in relation to the goal of reading: comprehension. According to the developers of the DIBELS Next, the DIBELS Oral Reading Fluency subtest is now included because they do not want students to assume that speed reading is the goal of reading, as opposed to comprehending what is read. The addition of this subtest is intended to assuage some teachers' concern that a one-minute measure of oral reading fluency is not as important as a measure of comprehension.

As stated by Good and Kaminski (2011), "Passage retell provides an efficient procedure to identify those students who are not able to talk about what they have just read" (p. 80). The following is a sample oral reading fluency/retell passage from the DIBELS Next:

> Four baskets were filled with fish. Now it was time to take them to the market. Ken helped his father load the baskets onto the family's boat. Ken's family lived on a large island off the coast of Africa. They used the boat to sail to market. (p. 111)

Student retelling is then judged with the following score scale:

Quality of Response:

(Note: If the student provides only a main idea, it is considered one detail.)

1   Provides 2 or fewer details

2   Provides 3 or more details

3   Provides 3 or more details in a meaningful sequence

4   Provides 3 or more details in a meaningful sequence that captures a main idea (p. 111)

Users of the DIBELS Next should examine the oral fluency/retell reading passages, and the scoring of these passages, to determine how closely they meet standards for construct validity. In addition, although the Daze measure is incorporated into the DIBELS Next in an attempt to address the comprehension issue, the Daze measure does so by using an item format that is limited to sentence-level comprehension and is potentially confusing to developing readers.

Points of Comparison: The OSELA and the DIBELS Next

To say that the OSELA and the DIBELS Next have both ardent supporters and strident detractors might be the early literacy assessment understatement of this decade. In this final section, I examine these tests as they each relate to the training required to administer the assessment, the nature of the information provided by the assessment, and the validity of the assessment. Each of these points is worthy of consideration when determining a particular school's approach to RTI.

Training Required to Administer the Assessments

The OSELA requires a substantial amount of training and teacher expertise to conduct. A central feature of the assessment is running records, which require of teachers the ability to place students appropriately in a reading situation, observe and record students' reading miscues, use miscue analysis to develop a series of inferences about students' reading skills and strategies, and use these inferences in the planning and providing of reading instruction. These teacher abilities are developmental in nature and normally require substantial learning and practice by the teacher. Reliably administering, scoring, and interpreting the OSELA for use in RTI is tied to comprehensive training and also to particular instructional theory (Clay, 2002). In this sense, administering and interpreting the OSELA effectively is related to teaching effectively, and many teachers who use the test may otherwise use related materials and procedures as part of their instruction.

Estimates of the time needed to administer, score, and interpret the OSELA and the DIBELS Next, as provided by the developers of the two assessments, differ substantially. The OSELA requires upward of one hour per student for administration and scoring, whereas a single student or an entire class can take the DIBELS Next in under 30 minutes. As with all assessments, it is important to gauge the time and resources needed in relation to the usefulness of the assessment information.

The OSELA requires teachers to assess both the processes and products of reading, as described in Chapter 2. Thus, teachers are able to make inferences about students' reading based on their retellings and answers to questions in relation to actual stories. Teachers also conduct assessments through direct observations of students' reading processes. Both are resource-consuming practices, but a potential balance to the considerable demands on teacher training is the fact that the observation, recording, and interpreting of students' literacy behaviors on the OSELA are things that accomplished reading teachers already do. One minute of oral reading with the DIBELS Next yields a fluency score (words correct per minute) and a retell fluency score. Both are product measures. In contrast, oral reading in the OSELA yields oral reading behaviors or processes that help us understand the nature of students' reading strengths and needs, as well as product measures.

As demonstrated in the previous description, there are differences in the amount of time and training required to administer, score, and interpret the OSELA and the DIBELS Next as intended. The DIBELS Next materials suggest that less time is needed for a person to learn to administer the assessment. The different training times are indicative of different approaches to assessment: The DIBELS Next is limited in the information it can provide to teachers, whereas the OSELA yields detailed information on student development. Thus, we get what we train for, as the information yielded by these two assessments demonstrates.

Nature of the Information Provided by the Assessments

In spite of similar foci on important aspects of reading development, including phonics (Torgerson, Brooks, & Hall, 2006) and fluency (Kuhn, Schwanenflugel, & Meisinger, 2010), the information yielded by the OSELA and the DIBELS Next differs considerably. This should not be surprising, given the differences in the types of tasks that each assessment presents to students and the amount of time that each assessment requires. The OSELA yields process and product data. In general, the grain size or degree of detail provided by each assessment is greater with the OSELA. This is due to the fact that it is an assessment designed to yield information to inform our understanding of students' present needs and challenges and teachers' related instruction.

Validity of the Assessments

An examination of the OSELA and the DIBELS Next suggests that they are based on different conceptualizations of early literacy, sample different parts of the construct of literacy, or both. Construct validity is the most important form of validity (Messick, 1989). With construct validity, we are assured that an assessment bears direct and strong relation to the theoretical construct that it would measure and from which students' reading behaviors are inferred. For example, a test of reading comprehension may include items that focus on a reader's literal, inferential, and evaluative comprehension. To the degree that we concur that reading comprehension is composed of literal, inferential, and critical understandings of the texts we read, we can conclude that there is construct validity to the test.

How do the OSELA and the DIBELS Next rate in terms of construct validity? How might they influence the nature of RTI in schools and classrooms? Each assessment focuses on particular reading skills, strategies, and knowledge, including phonemic awareness, letter names, and fluency. Thus, if our construct of students' reading development includes phonemic awareness and knowledge of letter names, then the tests may have construct validity. The OSELA's assessment items and tasks represent a more broad sampling of the skills, strategies, mind-sets, and knowledge that developing readers need to become independent readers. Thus, the OSELA represents a more robust conceptualization of the construct of reading.

The DIBELS Next is noted for its predictive validity. The test briefly samples some of students' developmental and important reading skills and uses students' results to then describe students' anticipated, future reading performance. Consider this description related to the DIBELS Next:

> The most researched, efficient and standardized measure of reading proficiency is Oral Reading Fluency. It is the culminating measure of the DIBELS assessment system. The ORF measure has students read an unfamiliar passage of grade-level material for one minute. The final score is the number of words read correctly in that minute. With this robust measure, we can readily determine how a student's reading development is progressing and whether that student is on the path to becoming a proficient and fluent reader. (University of Oregon Center on Teaching and Learning, n.d., para. 3)

This description illustrates not only Good and Kaminski's goal of creating a test with high predictive ability but also a trade-off. Defining a student's reading as proficient without carefully checking on the student's comprehension called into question the construct validity of earlier versions of the DIBELS (Good & Kaminski, 2002). We read to construct meaning, not to attain a high rate of words read correctly per minute. Can the revisions present in the DIBELS Next (Good & Kaminski, 2011) help better determine a "student's reading development" through adequately assessing comprehension? Van Kraayenoord (2010) notes that the DIBELS presents an account of reading development in which the mechanics of reading are the first focus. Thus, the preponderance of measures focuses on letters, sounds, and other mechanical aspects of reading development. This ignores the fact that children expect meaning from language in the early grades, just as they have in the first five years of their lives.

The DIBELS Next may predict performance on statewide reading tests. The predictive validity of the DIBELS Next is considered a strength by some, as it may alert schools and teachers to the need for a student to receive subsequent instruction that focuses on a broadly indicated need. The concern here is that the DIBELS Next may prompt the privileging of test preparation over teaching to the full construct of reading. The DIBELS Next then becomes a determinant of reading instruction and reading programs (Pearson, 2006).

Lessons Learned About Early Reading Assessment

Each child comes to school with a history of language and learning. Some students are well prepared to fit in with expectations of schooling and have prior knowledge and experiences that greatly enhance their ability to learn to read. Some students will begin school knowing how to read, whereas others face significant challenges to reading development. The examination of the DIBELS Next and the OSELA and their possible use in RTI puts us in a good position to consider a common set of issues that relates to most, if not all, early reading assessments. There is a multitude of assessments available for our critical analyses and eventual use (Meisels & Piker, 2001). Informed choice related to these assessments is imperative and can be influenced by the issues raised in this section.

Coverage of the Construct of Reading

A concern related to choosing appropriate early reading assessments is the model, or understanding, of reading on which the assessment is based. From this model derive the core abilities, skills, and strategies that are the focus of the assessment. Our assessments should reflect, at minimum, those things that we believe to be vital to growth and development in early reading. As exemplified by RTI, we attend to the things that are indicated by our assessments. If they do not focus on particular important aspects of early reading development, such as comprehension, and our instruction is assessment driven, we are at risk for missing aspects of students' strengths and needs.

Exclusive Focus on Skills and Strategies

The preponderance of early reading assessments in RTI focuses on reading skills and strategies. These assessments are capable of providing accounts of what our early readers need in terms of phonemic awareness, phonics, and fluency. Chapter 8 focuses on "the other" in reading and reading assessment, and it is never too early to establish our focus on important reader characteristics such as motivation, self-concept, and agency. Our early reading assessments should seek increased specificity of students' needs. If our initial assessment is silent to critical aspects of reading development, including motivation to read and self-concept as a reader, our conception of student need is correspondingly narrow.

Second and Third Opinions on Students' Needs and Strengths

Our confidence in an accurate diagnosis of students' needs may be raised when we have more than one assessment. Early reading assessment results should be triangulated. In research, triangulation relates to the establishment of two or more points of reference, from which we can make inferences about the effectiveness of instruction. Our goal is high confidence in the decisions we make based on early reading assessment information. However valid and reliable, a single assessment provides just one sample of students' reading-related information. Second and third assessments will serve to reinforce the understanding established in the first case or will challenge us to rethink our ideas about student readers. In all cases, it is better to have several samples of students' reading work and performance than just one.

Assessment Programs as Closed or Open Systems

Early reading assessment may be conducted in closed or open systems. A closed system uses sets of data collected from predetermined assessments. Instruction is driven by assessment data and addresses indicated student needs. The nature and role of the utilized assessments is predetermined. The assessments in a closed assessment system dictate our understanding of students' reading. An open system uses predetermined assessments in much the same manner but encourages teacher collaboration related to classroom observations, personal insights, and classroom-based assessment. The system is open to contributions and discussions about student progress.

What do we learn about students as we interact with them on a daily basis? How can our evolving understanding of students, outside an RTI assessment regimen, inform our teaching? A value here is that open systems of assessment broaden the opportunity to problem solve, using diverse types of assessment information. We must avoid the myopia caused by an assessment system that restricts the view of the developing early reader. We begin to understand our developing readers, in part, based on the results of our assessments. If our assessment system is closed and restricted to isolated skill and strategy measures, we construct a meaning of the student as one who can or cannot do isolated skills. We may teach, and teach successfully to an indicated skill and strategy need, but we may be missing the forest for a select few trees. A related outcome is that we mistake the successful skill or strategy user as a successful reader.

Focus on Individual Student Differences

Once a student's needs and strengths have been identified in RTI, we can provide instruction according to a standardized treatment protocol or a problem-solving approach. If RTI is about instruction that is increasingly sensitive to students' individual differences, then assessment must lead this effort. Instruction may be based on what works for the general student population, but a student's individual differences can demand an alternative approach. For example, not all students who struggle with rate and accuracy of their oral reading will need exactly the same instruction. Our screening assessments should be broad, and they should be followed by a diagnostic assessment that provides an appropriate level of detail that allows us to best understand our students' individual differences.

Skills and Strategies in Isolation and in Real Reading

All successful readers, whatever their age or degree of development, coordinate reading strategies and skills to construct meaning. Many early reading assessments do not focus on the construction of meaning; rather, they attend to letters and sounds, and rate and accuracy as separate components of reading. Yet, there is the perennial need for developing readers to use reading strategies and skills in the larger scheme of constructing meaning. We comprehend text when we are able to orchestrate all relevant skills and strategies. It is an unwise practice to assume that the young reader's mastered individual skills and strategies equate with reading success. Thus, early reading assessment should strive for inclusion of measures that assess students' comprehension, be it reading or listening.

Summary

RTI uses a series of assessments to identify students who need help early in their careers as readers. Assessment serves four purposes in RTI: screening, diagnosis, progress monitoring, and outcome measurement. As RTI is a tiered approach to appropriate reading instruction, assessment provides information that is used in decisions to move or maintain students at different tiers. In best practice, assessment continually informs instruction. This chapter describes the OSELA and the DIBELS Next as clearly different instruments, based on different ideas about the connections that assessment should have with teaching and learning; different ideas about the primary purposes of assessment; and different models of literacy, teaching, and learning. Lessons learned from comparing the two assessments demonstrate that great care must be taken when choosing an early reading assessment. Whether or not such early assessment is to be used in an RTI program, the assessment should represent a robust construct of reading, provide for different measures of students' developing reading, and maintain foci on the developing skills and strategies of early reading, the construction of meaning, and the affective lives of developing, young readers.

ENHANCING YOUR UNDERSTANDING

1. Identify an assessment that is used in your grade or school district. Determine the match between how you view students' reading development and how the assessment views reading development.

2. Explore the means by which assessments come to be used in your school and school district. How important is teacher input in the decision-making process for creating or selecting reading assessments?

3. Consider joining an assessment-related initiative in your school or school district.

Technology and Reading Assessment

The evolution of technology has important implications for what and how we assess. Our students are digital natives, born into a world of Google, Facebook, and Twitter. Reading in the 21st century is impacted by technology, and reading assessment must follow suit. Consider technology and *what* we assess: When students use Google or another search engine to locate possible texts to read, knowing how search engines operate and privilege particular links and accurately reading the brief URL descriptions are all important, reading-related skills. Thus, it is important to determine how our student readers negotiate their ways through the countless texts that may be offered during an online search. Claims that the Internet has lowered the bar for publications can be debated, but there is no doubt that the amount of information on the Internet has raised the bar for critical appraisal and comprehension of texts that we encounter online. Thus, our reading assessments should include items and tasks that help us best understand how students evaluate text sources, information, and messages across acts of reading. We need assessments that describe both naive and sophisticated approaches to students' critical Internet reading.

When students embark on an online reading task, we must be sure that our assessments are capable of describing all that is needed for a successful experience, beyond the skills, strategies, and prior knowledge that are useful when reading traditional, printed texts. Given the need for students to manage their attention to the reading goal, their search for appropriate Internet links, the narrowing of their search from a virtual universe of possible texts, and their monitoring of comprehension as each text is read, do our assessments focus on metacognition? Given the diverse information sources that may be present within a single online text (e.g., text, graphics, embedded video and audio), are our assessments capable of describing what sources our students readily understand and what sources are problematic? Finally, when students encounter such information-rich texts, can our assessments describe what is going well and what is challenging, in relation to synthesizing the diverse information sources?

It is the rare classroom in which students know less about particular forms of technology than the teacher, and it is around technology that there is probably no stronger potential for students to contribute to classroom discussions and knowledge bases. Thus, understanding what our students know about technology, above and beyond what we bring to the classroom, is valuable, technology-related assessment information.

Next, consider the influence of technology on *how* we assess: Effective classroom-based assessment includes the regular collection and integration of formative information. When teachers circulate around the classroom with a handheld device that contains up-to-the-minute profiles of each student's reading needs and strengths, this information can contribute to enhanced teaching and learning. The assessment information is immediately available anywhere in the school or classroom. When the handheld makes it easier to input, store, and combine reading assessment information, technology is making a tangible contribution to our education efforts. Such approaches to classroom assessment help teachers conduct progress monitoring and triangulate related assessment information from different sources.

The accurate and timely collection of assessment data is always paramount in successful systems. Technology can reduce the time needed to input, retrieve, analyze, and synthesize the assessment information of our student readers. Likewise, digital portfolios allow students to create copies of reading-related work that otherwise would be challenging to store and display. A single CD or DVD can store digitized copies of students' writing, quizzes and worksheets, videotaped performances, artwork, and complex projects across time and across different media, serving as rich assessment sources and indicators of students' learning.

The disconnect between what we know about the construct of reading and the manner in which high-stakes tests assess reading is apparent. The nature of high-stakes reading tests is attributable more to the need for quick and reliable scoring than it is to a robust representation of the construct of reading. Many of our high-stakes tests are limited in the number of short and extended constructed-response items they include because assessing these items requires human scorers. Human scorers are costly, especially when compared with multiple-choice items scored with a Scantron scanner. The technology of large-scale reading assessment has acted to constrain the construct validity of the assessments. We do not get many opportunities to assess critical reading or higher order thinking in reading because multiple-choice test items are limited in their ability to describe such complex human behaviors. When a large majority of test items must be multiple-choice format because of the cost involved, we have a clear indication of reading assessment technology constraining what we learn from the assessments.

However, recent handwriting recognition and text analysis software may be assessment-changing technologies. With such software, student writing may be quickly and reliably scored. Imagine if all students in a particular classroom, grade, or school were given the prompt to critically evaluate source texts in social studies and provide an account of their reasoning in this critical evaluation. Handwriting recognition software can make quick and accurate work of almost all students' writing, and related text analysis software can intelligently and reliably score students' written responses for both content and form.

CHAPTER 7

High-Stakes Reading Tests

Tests are considered high stakes when their results are used to make important educational and life decisions. Current high-stakes tests focus on cognitive skills and strategies that are important components of students' reading success. NCLB and its related adequate yearly progress are initiatives that rely on high-stakes tests to show accountability. The power and ubiquitous nature of these tests are matched by the controversies related to their use and intended and unintended consequences. In 2010, the U.S. Department of Education awarded grants to two assessment consortia, the PARCC and the SBAC, and charged them with developing assessments that best describe students' ongoing needs and summary achievement levels. These assessment efforts, reflecting the content and goals of the Common Core State Standards (CCSSO & NGA, 2010), will include the newest generation of high-stakes tests.

A Brief History of High-Stakes Tests

The phenomenon of high-stakes testing is approximately a century old. The creators of the first high-stakes tests wanted to create a means to rapidly and accurately sort test takers into groups based on their test scores. Early large-scale tests were intended to help screen slow learners from the general student population and place them with appropriate instruction. In fact, the founder of the Educational Testing Service believed that multiple-choice tests could be given to all citizens and that their scores could help determine the vocation and employment to which they were best suited (Lemann, 1999). Thus, tests were perceived as contributing to a just and efficient society. Large-scale testing became commonplace for college admission and the sorting of military personnel, and this testing had high-stakes consequences: determining whether one could attend college or determining one's role in the armed forces. The past 60 years illustrate individual states' growing interest in conducting large-scale testing of students at particular grade levels, often in the pattern of one grade tested in late elementary school, one grade tested in middle school, and one grade tested in high school (e.g., reading tests administered at grades 4, 7, and 10). These tests were most often used to give a general description of the state of reading achievement at school, district, and state levels (Afflerbach, 1990).

In the 1960s, the inception of the NAEP marked the beginning of regular, nationwide assessment of students' reading achievement (Hamilton, Stecher, & Klein,

2002). NAEP, also called "The Nation's Report Card," is administered to representative samples of 4th-, 8th-, and 12th-grade students and is considered a barometer of reading achievement in the United States. NAEP results allow for a comparison of general reading achievement levels across different years.

Concurrent with the development of the NAEP as a national measure of reading achievement, many states began to institute minimum competency testing. Minimum competency tests are intended to provide a measure of accountability: how well a particular school district prepares students for future schooling and life. As such, these tests are most often administered in later grades. The tests were encouraged, in part, by lawsuits from parents who claimed that schools had promoted their children while failing to teach them how to read. Thus, minimum competency tests are used to certify that a student can read at a basic reading level and to describe how schools and teachers are faring in their efforts to teach each student to read. By providing this accountability measure, schools may demonstrate that they are doing their job (Supovitz, 2009). Combined, the NAEP (to provide general descriptive data on reading achievement), statewide testing (to get a sense of student achievement at the elementary, middle school, and high school levels), and minimum competency testing (to pinpoint failing students and demonstrate teacher and school accountability) contributed to the increasing use of high-stakes reading tests (Afflerbach, 1985, 1990).

The last 25 years have seen a dramatic increase in the use of high-stakes testing of reading at the state level (Afflerbach, 2005; Kober, Chudowsky, & Chudowsky, 2008). In 1983, the publication *A Nation at Risk: The Imperative for Educational Reform* (National Commission on Excellence in Education, 1983) portrayed education in the United States as severely deficient in preparing students to succeed, in school and out. The alarmist tone of this publication provided for some policy makers the rationale for increased individual testing of students. The report contributed to popular perceptions that more testing leads to better schooling and that students' reading test scores are a reflection of teacher and school performance. What better way to promote increased student learning than more testing? Concurrently, international comparisons of student achievement, accomplished with tests such as the PISA (OECD, 2010), are gaining in popularity and influence.

Contemporary accountability movements continue to value and use a student's single test score as a trustworthy account of the student's reading achievement. The mandated testing of reading required by NCLB to demonstrate adequate yearly progress continues the preeminence of high-stakes tests in reading assessment. The use of tests is also increasing in the early grades, despite the protestations of professional groups that work with and advocate for young children (IRA, 1999; Johnston et al., 2010; NCTE, 2000). These tests focus on aspects of reading related to phonemic awareness, phonics use, letter-naming speed, nonsense-word pronunciation, fluency, and knowledge of vowels and consonants. The results of these tests are often used for screening and placement, as in RTI, so that children might receive appropriate instruction. However, the developmental appropriateness of such tests for young children is questionable (National Association for the Education of Young Children & National Association of Early Childhood Specialists in State Departments of Education, 2003). A new generation of reading tests is being developed in relation to the Common Core State Standards (CCSSO & NGA, 2010). The PARCC and SBAC assessment consortia propose high-stakes testing that is used to gauge accountability, assess higher order thinking skills, and complement formative reading assessments.

The Popularity of High-Stakes Reading Tests

In general, the public supports high-stakes testing, but why do these tests enjoy such popularity? First, many people believe that high-stakes tests treat all students fairly. Under typical standardized testing conditions, no student receives preferential treatment. The possibility of teacher bias and teacher favoritism entering into the act of assessment is minimized. Such standardization of assessment has become a standard itself, but there are important caveats to consider. However well a test achieves a sameness of treatment of each student, we should not confound that with the fact that students in high-stakes testing situations are different. Students' lives at home and in school, opportunities for test preparation, familiarity with testing, and familiarity with the language of testing all vary. We should not make the erroneous assumption that a standardized test levels the playing field for all students because no test can do so.

A second reason for the popularity of high-stakes testing is the belief that tests are scientific. The vast majority of reading tests involve considerable expenditures of time, effort, and expertise invested in creating them. The development teams for high-profile, high-stakes tests, including most popular commercial tests of reading and many statewide reading tests, often consist of trained and experienced measurement professionals whose sole task is to create tests. Test development team members specialize in locating or creating suitable reading passages, developing test items, reviewing passages and items for potential bias, and choosing items based on their ability to discriminate among readers. Most tests exhibit rigor in relation to psychometric formulas and guidelines. Through adherence to what are for most people abstract notions of validity and reliability, tests create an aura of science as being rational, logical, and inscrutable. Tests have the ability to reduce and summarize the complexities of reading to single raw scores and percentile rankings, and in doing so, tests appear almost magical (Afflerbach, 2002b).

In addition, test scores are a frequently used outcome in "scientific" studies of reading. Experimental research designed to investigate reading instruction effectiveness uses test scores as the primary, and often only, outcome of students' reading achievement. Test scores are the dependent measure in many studies, figuring largely in meta-analyses of reading program success and in the derivation of effect sizes attributable to instructional programs. Finally, high-stakes tests are familiar. There are few adults who have not experienced firsthand the culture of testing in schools. Throughout our school years and into college and graduate school, high-stakes tests have been part of our lives. That our current generation of students receives at least as much standardized testing as we did is unsurprising. Testing appears natural, a core experience of schooling, given our assessment traditions. The familiarity of high-stakes tests contributes to their ongoing popularity and the often unquestioning acceptance of their use and power.

It is clear from the current debate around high-stakes reading tests that many educators would not make these tests their first choice in reading assessment (Calkins, Montgomery, & Santman, 1998; Goodman, 2006). Given this fact, why are they used so frequently in schools? To explore this question more deeply, we must consider reading assessment in the context of U.S. society. Teachers and students are largely left out of the educational policymaking process that mandates standardized, high-stakes reading assessments. Teachers are rarely consulted about the types of reading assessment that would best serve their purposes. A most recent example can be found in the passage of NCLB, which was supported in the U.S. Senate by a vote of 91 to 8. This legislation demands that each student be tested in reading for six consecutive years (grades 3–8), as if there was not enough testing taking place prior to the passage of NCLB. The tests and their results are used to hold teachers and schools accountable.

In contrast, it is possible that politicians, business leaders, and the general public too often focus on test-based accountability without full accounting (and full funding) of the educational programs that would help schools help students become better readers and best prepare for high-stakes reading tests (Berliner & Biddle, 1995; Kohn, 2000). It is also possible that high-stakes test results are used to deflect attention (and full responsibility) toward schools and away from the greater society of which schools are a part. For example, the number of children in the United States who live in poverty is increasing, with 13.3 million children representing a U.S. childhood poverty rate of 18% (Moore, Redd, Burkhauser, Mbwana, & Collins, 2009). Both of these figures, the number and percentage of children living in poverty, have increased since the first edition of this book printed in 2007. The U.S. Census Bureau (2011) sets the poverty level for a family of four at $21,756 or below for a family of four. Children of poverty may want for the nutrition, health care, personal safety, reading materials, and models of literacy that help prepare and support other students for school success (Hart & Risley, 1995; Moore et al., 2009). That an economic and political system cannot help provide, or guarantee, these things for every child may be considered by some a failure of that system. By this standard, society in general could be assigned a failing grade for neglecting to support the reading development of all students. High-stakes assessments are used to focus responsibility for students' failure and success on schools, which has the effect of placing the entire burden for students' education and well-being on parents and teachers rather than the social system that contributes to the poverty that influences students' reading development in the first place.

The designation of any reading assessment as "high stakes" should cause us to pause and reflect. Who is assigning that label, and what are the high stakes when it comes to teaching and learning reading? I believe that any assessment that has the potential to contribute to students' reading development should be considered high stakes. For example, our knowledge of students' interests and hobbies, gained through classroom discussions or the use of an interest inventory, can help us guide students to recreational reading choices that contribute to increased motivation for reading. In turn, this may contribute to increased reading fluency, content area knowledge development, and student self-perception as a successful reader. Likewise, we may determine that a reader is struggling with a cl– consonant blend, based on our ability to accurately observe and record oral reading miscues during diagnostic reading instruction. The subsequent use of this knowledge to help the student become adept and confident in using the cl– blend certifies our work as high-stakes assessment. The point here is that our focus must be on reading assessment that has consequential, positive outcomes for our students. If we regularly ask the question, What are the high stakes related to this assessment? we will be in the position to make the most of the assessments we use. In any case, the designation of a reading assessment as high stakes should cause us to scrutinize an assessment for the usefulness of the information it may provide.

A change in high-stakes reading test tradition is promised by the PARCC and SBAC assessment consortia that receive Race to the Top funding. That is, the consortia are developing summative (i.e., high-stakes) assessments as they develop complementary formative assessments. The information from formative assessments will be used by teachers to inform instruction as students work toward the related summative assessments.

Characteristics of High-Stakes Reading Tests

High-stakes reading tests are exceedingly familiar to most adults and children. As adults, we can recall testing experiences from our student careers, such as the reminders the day before to make sure to get a good night's sleep, eat a good breakfast, and have two #2 sharpened pencils. We listened carefully to the instructions as they were read by the teacher. We worked quietly and independently. As we worked through the test, the teacher kept account on the blackboard of the time elapsed and the time left. We encountered a stop sign when we came to the end of a section. Upon finishing, we handed in our answer sheets and were praised for our hard work. Schoolwide, the tests were collected, bundled, and sent to scoring centers. At these centers, the tests were largely machine scored, providing the opportunity to move thousands of tests through a scoring facility in a short time. Months later, we were reminded that we had, in fact, taken the test when the scores arrived at the school.

Throughout this chapter, I focus on those reading assessments that match the most popular conceptualization of high-stakes assessments in reading: tests that share the characteristics of being standardized, norm-referenced, and administered to large groups of students, such as districtwide or statewide administration at a particular grade level. These tests are typically composed of a series of short reading passages accompanied by multiple-choice items that are machine-scored with occasional, short fill-in or constructed-response items. In addition, these tests may contain vocabulary items that require the test taker to determine word meanings in isolation and as they occur embedded in text. In the case of RTI, the most widely used test, the DIBELS, focuses on the mechanics of reading, with little attention to reading comprehension.

High-stakes reading tests are standardized; that is, in the ideal, they are administered to all student test takers under exactly the same conditions. Sireci (2004) notes, "The idea behind standardization is to keep the measurement instrument and observation conditions constant so that any differences observed reflect true individual differences, rather than measurement artifacts" (p. 7). Standardization conditions typically include time allowed to take the test (i.e., each student has exactly the same amount of time to complete the different sections of the test) and a scripted interaction between the administrator of the test (usually the classroom teacher) and the test-taking students. Certain students with special needs may receive accommodations during high-stakes testing, including the allowance of extra time to take the test. Other students may receive a language accommodation, in which directions and the texts and items themselves are read to the student by the teacher, or test administrator, or provided in another language. (For more information on accommodation in assessment, see Chapter 9.)

It is assumed that each student will take the test in an environment that is well suited to the task, including classrooms that are quiet, well lit, of appropriate temperature, and free from distractions. Each student test taker interacts with test items that are identical or psychometrically determined to be of similar focus and difficulty. No talking is allowed, and students' questions during testing regarding the form, process, and content of the test are generally not allowed. A teacher's response to a student's question would invalidate the standardization of the test. These procedures and regulations are regarded by many as proof that all students are treated the same when taking the standardized high-stakes test.

The majority of high-stakes reading tests are norm referenced, or developed in relation to a sample norming population of students. The tests are developed to portray students' reading achievement scores in relation to one another. In the test development phase, pilot versions of the reading test are given to sample groups of students who are demographically representative of the general student population. Based on these students' performances on the pilot testing, particular scores are assigned places along a normal curve distribution. This practice allows test results to be reported as both raw scores and percentile rankings and for students to be rank ordered. It is important to note that one student's performance on the test influences the characterization of another student's performance. In contrast, a small proportion of high-stakes reading tests are criterion referenced: Students' performances are scored in relation to a criterion task. With criterion-referenced testing, all students may receive the same score, as the scores are representative of reaching a particular performance or meeting criteria in the reading test task and not contingent on the scores of other students who are taking the test.

The content and format of high-stakes reading tests are predictable. Vocabulary is a staple of reading tests, as it correlates highly with reading achievement and general intelligence. Separate vocabulary items include words of varied frequency and difficulty. The vocabulary words included on high-stakes reading tests are chosen in relation to their relative frequency of occurrence in written language, and the more difficult vocabulary items focus on words that are not commonplace. Other vocabulary test items focus on words that are central to understanding and passage comprehension. The vocabulary words may be central or tangential to the theme, topic, or main idea of the passage. Particular vocabulary words may be chosen more for their ability to discriminate among test takers and allow for rank ordering students than for their importance in the reader's understanding of a passage. These vocabulary items may focus on the usage and meaning of words as contextualized in a particular passage.

Comprehension items typically measure students' literal and inferential reading comprehension. Students silently read the reading passages, which may or may not be available for students to access as they respond to questions. The status of text availability influences whether the test is focusing on readers' comprehension, memory, search ability, or some combination of these. The comprehension items are intended to allow for making inferences about how well students understand the reading passages included on the test. Some tests include items that focus on students' critical reading comprehension, but this enterprise is made difficult by relatively short reading passages, a lack of reading passages with content that supports asking truly critical questions, and the time allotted for reading. In general, the comprehension items are constructed to allow students to demonstrate their ability to determine main ideas, identify themes and author purposes, summarize text, find supporting details, and make inferences. The majority of reading comprehension items are multiple choice or short constructed response, which often restricts the ability of tests to tap complex comprehension processes. Such processes include those at work when students bring considerable prior knowledge to the reading act, read more than one passage on the same topic and must synthesize an understanding across texts, and engage in critical and evaluative reading tasks.

The reading passages found on high-stakes tests are generally short, although the length and text complexity of reading passages usually increase with the grade level of the test. Regardless of grade level, there may be a discrepancy between the type and length of passages that students are expected to read in school and the average length of texts contained in the test. The texts on tests are generally of two types: narrative and expository, or informational. This duality of text type is intended to reflect the types of texts that students are expected to read in school. In the last decade, the percentage of expository text passages on many standardized reading tests has increased, reflecting the idea that students must become increasingly adept at constructing meaning from informational text as they progress through school (National Assessment Governing Board, 2009). There is some attention to a third text type, the hybrid text, reflecting the fact that students read texts that are not easily categorized as either narrative or expository, such as biographies. Such hybrid texts are composed of integrated textual, graphic, or visual information and may combine narrative and expository characteristics within a single text. Finally, tests may include online and hypertext reading experiences for students, in which the ability to find, select, comprehend, and use particular texts is assessed (Leu, 2007).

High-stakes reading tests typically use sets of multiple-choice items and brief constructed-response items to measure vocabulary and comprehension. Multiple-choice items have standard components, including prompts, distracters, and correct answers. Prompts are the questions, demands, or statements that require student thinking and responses. Distracters are plausible yet wrong responses that are provided to student readers in any multiple-choice item. Examples of multiple-choice items, brief constructed-response items, and extended constructed-response items are provided in Table 18.

Multiple-choice items include a correct answer that is presented along with several incorrect answers. Other test items present students with questions that demand a student-constructed response. In general, constructed-response items are regarded as more demanding because they require the student to devise an answer rather than choose the correct answer from given alternatives. In many high-stakes tests, the mix of multiple-choice and constructed-response items is consistent across the test, whether the test is measuring vocabulary or comprehension. Payne (1974) notes that "test items are probably read more closely than any other type of nonlegal written communication" (p. 99). This is as it should be because high-stakes test items figure largely in important inferences that we make about student reading. High-stakes tests demand high scrutiny; critical analysis of test items can increase the quality of the items, the results we get from students, and the inferences we make about students.

Test items are typically sequenced in an easy-to-hard order. The items encountered earlier in a test are, in general, less challenging than those encountered later in the test. This ordering of items by difficulty is intended to provide more students

TABLE 18
Sample High-Stakes Reading Test Items

Test Item	Sample Question
Multiple-choice item with a prompt, a correct answer, and distracters	What year was the Jamestown Colony founded? (prompt) A. 1577 (distracter) B. 1607 (correct answer) C. 1776 (distracter) D. 1637 (distracter)
Brief constructed-response item	What was one reason that colonists sailed to what is now known as the Jamestown Colony? (The test form provides 6 lines for the student's response.)
Extended constructed-response item	Describe one theory for why the Jamestown Colony ceased to exist and provide at least three details that support your response. (The test form provides 12 lines for the student's response.)

Note. Modified from *Understanding and Using Reading Assessment, K–12* (p. 138), by P. Afflerbach, 2007, Newark, DE: International Reading Association. Copyright 2007 by the International Reading Association.

with experiences of success on items early on in the test in order to support motivation and decrease the number of students who experience failure early in the test. Item difficulty is established relative to other test items and particular levels of student reading achievement. Computer-adaptive testing allows for the sequencing of test passages, items, and tasks in relation to a student's ongoing performance on the test. For example, if a student obtains a perfect score on the first two reading passages, computer-adaptive testing may automatically revise the test so that the third reading passage is more challenging than had the student performed poorly on the first two passages.

Most high-stakes reading tests are administered, collected, bundled, shipped to a scoring facility, and scored, and the results are then returned to the school districts or states. In contrast, more immediate scoring and availability of test results can be accommodated through computerized test administration, as software for scoring student work and use of the Internet streamline the process. Scores may be reported as individual and group raw scores and percentile rankings. Raw scores represent the actual number that is assigned to an individual student's performance (or a school's or a state's average performance). Percentile rankings, a special feature of norm-referenced tests, allow for raw scores to be represented in relation to a normal distribution curve. The raw score indicates the performance of the student in relation to the high-stakes test itself, whereas the percentile ranking indicates the performance of the student or a group of students in relation to other students. A score in the 57th percentile means that the test taker performed better than all but 42% of all other students taking the test.

All high-stakes tests have a decided product orientation. This means that the information yielded by high-stakes tests, typically answers to questions, is one product of the student's reading and thinking processes. From these products, we must try to infer the processes, robust or developing, that the student used to construct meaning. As is the case with all product assessment information, we must use what I refer to as backward inferencing to try to determine students' areas of strength and challenge in reading. In essence, we try to reconstruct the process of reading from a score to understand how the product, represented by the score, was created.

There are several promising aspects of high-stakes testing related to technology. First, a refinement in handwriting recognition software (or a movement toward student keyboarding to respond to open-ended questions) may result in test items that maintain the feature of ease of scoring while allowing for the inclusion of test items that demand complex responses. As test items are much more quickly and economically scored by machines (e.g., Scantron scanner, computer), the development of more sophisticated means of machine scoring may contribute to items that better represent the kinds of questions (and related student thinking) that we want to ask in relation to reading. Second, computer-adaptive testing uses ongoing patterns of student response (i.e., correct vs. incorrect) to configure subsequent test item sequences. For example, the student who answers the first five items on a test well may then get a more challenging question, whereas such challenge occurs later in testing for the student who is struggling with literal-level, relatively simple items. In both cases, the application of new technology to reading assessment promises to make more efficient the scoring of increasingly complex student responses. The incorporation of such new technologies will be hastened by pressures from new standards initiatives, such as the Common Core State Standards. Optimistically, the next decade will witness such beneficial changes to high-stakes testing items and their scoring.

Consequences of High-Stakes Reading Tests

One of the greatest challenges related to high-stakes reading tests is to fully anticipate their consequences. For example, increased performance on high-stakes reading tests will earn a school more money in some school districts, while decreased performance will have the same effect in other districts. When a school does not meet adequate yearly progress targets for several years, students can move to other schools, effectively reducing the funding available to that school. Note that I assign considerably more possible negative consequences to the use of high-stakes tests because (1) they are assigned from outside the classroom and are hardly ever a teacher's first choice for a reading assessment that provides useful information; (2) the very nature of most high-stakes tests (i.e., short reading passages with a single, predetermined correct answer to be picked in a multiple-choice format) reflects an outdated conceptualization of reading and how to measure it; and (3) high-stakes tests may be clumsily paired with political rhetoric about the necessity for accountability, rhetoric unaccompanied by sufficient education funding levels to help schools approach nationwide standards of universal literacy (Afflerbach, 2005).

Possible positive consequences of high-stakes testing. One positive aspect of high-stakes tests is that they can help us understand the performance of particular subgroups of students who take the test. This means that if we are interested in how students of different genders, ethnic groups, socioeconomic statuses, or geographical regions fare on a particular test, we can so designate the scores of students from these different groups, disaggregate these scores from all scores, and then analyze the disaggregated scores. We may determine that particular subgroups of students are performing well and that others are not as a result of using such disaggregation. For example, the NAEP determines that there is a significant and consistent gap in the reading achievement of urban, minority youths and other students. An example of how high-stakes test results can be disaggregated to provide comparisons between particular groups of students—in this case, eligibility for free or reduced-cost school meals, a proxy for socioeconomic status—is presented in Figure 8.

To the extent that we use this information to inform educational decision making, including school funding decisions, we may claim positive consequences from a test. For example, the funding of reading instruction initiatives for particular groups of students who have demonstrated histories of underachieving (in comparison with other students) may contribute to their increased reading achievement.

High-stakes tests may also serve a large-scale diagnostic function. As tests are administered at year end for several years, the results provide a regular and standardized description of some of a school district's reading program strengths and weaknesses. For example, high-stakes test results may demonstrate that a reading program helps students develop vocabularies of frequently used words but does not work as well in preparing students to determine the meaning of less common vocabulary as encountered in the context of school reading. With this information, adjustments to the reading instruction curriculum may be made at the school district level. In addition, an individual teacher's close attention to annual scores may show patterns of student achievement and suggest particular instructional foci related to the results and the use of particular reading instruction materials and procedures. Consistently high or low student test scores in vocabulary or comprehension can help teachers understand their effectiveness and should signal programmatic strengths and weaknesses.

High-stakes tests may motivate students to do well in school prior to taking the tests. The inclination to work with good effort is increased for some students who know that a major test is awaiting them. However, students' motivations related to reading and testing are quite complex and emanate from different sources (Guthrie & Wigfield, 1997). Tests also provide students with information on their reading

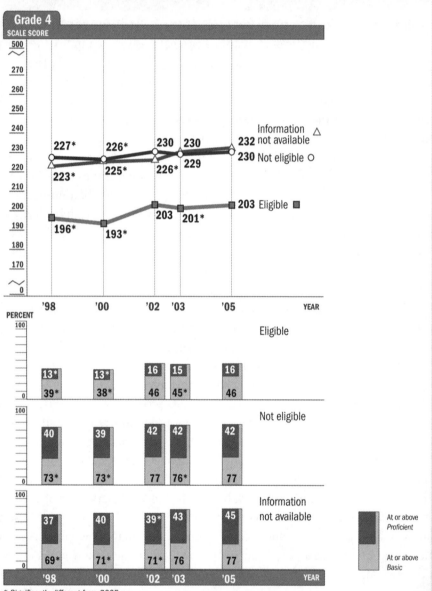

FIGURE 8
Example of Disaggregated Reading Test Results
From the National Assessment of Educational Progress

* Significantly different from 2005.
SOURCE: U.S. Department of Education, Institute of Education Sciences, National Center for Education Statistics, National Assessment of Educational Progress (NAEP), various years, 1998–2005 Reading Assessments.

Note. From *The Nation's Report Card: Reading 2005* (NCES 2006-451, p. 8), by M. Perie, W. Grigg, and P. Donahue, 2005, Washington, DC: National Center for Education Statistics, Institute of Education Sciences, U.S. Department of Education.

achievement and their performance relative to others, and in this sense, tests may provide students an awareness of their accomplishment. Scoring high on a high-stakes test is a good experience for most students.

Community trust and support can be built through the sharing of high-stakes test results. Taxpayers, real estate agents and home buyers, elected officials, and legislators pay attention to test scores. Given their prevalence and value, scores from such tests have considerable weight with many of those in the school community who are interested in student achievement. Yet, as we determine later in this section, one school's experience with the positive consequences of high-stakes test scores may be contrasted with another school's negative experiences and consequences.

High-stakes test scores can serve as a common vocabulary that is used in decisions related to grouping students and helping set goals for them. When students move, entry into a new school and related initial placements can be helped with the common information provided by the standardized test score. Being standardized, there may be some degree of faith that these test scores mean similar things for each student. This faith must be tempered by the following questions: What does a single standardized, high-stakes reading test score actually mean? How much of the story of reading instruction quality and student achievement can a single high-stakes test score tell, and what other sources provide important information?

Of course, each of the potentially positive consequences of high-stakes testing can cut other ways. The notion that these tests provide diagnostic information about reading achievement and program quality can be countered with the argument that there is very little return of useful information on the massive investment of time and money that is spent on these tests. For each student who is motivated by a good test score to read more, there may be one whose motivation to read decreases because of low test scores. The trust and support of schools that may be a consequence of high-stakes tests in one community may contrast with suspicion and lack of support in another community. Finally, although standardized test scores provide a common vocabulary across school districts, the scores are limited in what they describe.

Possible negative consequences of high-stakes testing. The possible negative consequences of using high-stakes tests are numerous, including negative effects on students; the reading curriculum and learning; teacher professionalism; and student, teacher, and school morale. Some students always do well on tests. In contrast, there are students who never do well on tests. These students are too familiar with the routine of their reading failure made public, as they struggle through hours of high-stakes testing. When a test is norm referenced, a large portion of students taking the test will be determined to be below average. A less able student's improvement in reading achievement, while substantial, may be reflected by a large change in percentile ranking (say, from 27% to 43%) but no change in the "below average" label. Test scores, be they percentile rankings or raw scores, are assigned to individual students, creating communities of haves and have-nots when it comes to reading achievement. It may be difficult for the accomplished reader to comprehend the threats to self-esteem and motivation (Wigfield & Eccles, 2000) for students whose continuing experience with high-stakes reading tests is negative. Yet, current testing practice guarantees that significant numbers of less accomplished readers will face threats to their self-esteem and future willingness to read. Labels from test results are accompanied with myriad related consequences, such as lowered expectations, differential treatment in the reading classroom (Allington, 1983), and decreased perseverance for those labeled as low-achieving readers.

In classrooms everywhere, there is tremendous pressure to improve test scores, which leads to additional negative consequences. A reading curriculum may be chosen on the sole merit of being closely related to the content and form of the high-stakes reading test. In such cases, tests contribute to the constriction, or shrinking, of reading curricula (Frederiksen, 1984). If the majority of standardized high-stakes reading tests were worth teaching to, this would not be an issue. The point is that most high-stakes tests have narrow foci on particular reading skills and strategies. These skills and strategies are important to reading, but by no means do the skills and strategies sum up to what is practiced and learned in a broad-based reading curriculum. Moreover, they do not provide students with all that they need to succeed as readers. In addition to the negative consequence of high-stakes tests constricting the reading curriculum, they may also take considerable time away from the teaching of reading. For every school hour spent on reading test preparation, an hour is taken from the instructional day. Time given to practicing and administering tests is time that could be spent on pursuing diverse instructional goals related to reading. When schools devote time and effort to testing and preparing students to take tests, considerable sums of money are spent to do so. Initiatives to support testing take away from other, worthy initiatives. Money might be spent in other ways, including an enriched curriculum and teachers' professional development related to assessment (Stiggins, 2002).

Teachers may suffer numerous negative consequences from high-stakes testing. First, teachers are often conflicted about the stance they must adopt in relation to the test and their students (Calkins et al., 1998). What about the teacher who does not endorse high-stakes testing but knows that his or her students must be adequately prepared to take such tests? What about the teacher who has worked for years to develop an array of engaging reading instruction lessons and is forced to give them up to teach to a test? When testing concerns override teacher professionalism, curricular decisions are made according to a test format rather than teachers' knowledge and prerogatives. A further consequence for teachers is that they prepare students to take the tests, they administer the tests, and they serve as the conduit to parents and others for test results. Thus, teachers serve a vital role in communicating and interpreting the results of high-stakes tests, whether or not they have faith in them. Each of these comprehensive and time-consuming tasks creates practical and ethical dilemmas for those teachers who do not fully endorse how high-stakes tests are constructed and used (Johnston, Afflerbach, & Weiss, 1993).

Usefulness of High-Stakes Reading Tests

Different members of education communities may provide starkly different accounts of the usefulness of high-stakes assessments. A state legislator believes that tests provide all of the necessary information related to how well schools and teachers are helping students develop as readers. In contrast, a classroom teacher is convinced that the same test consumes precious school funds and school time while yielding little or no information that is instructionally useful. This section examines the usefulness of high-stakes reading tests from such diverse perspectives.

High-stakes tests are used as a tool for demonstrating accountability. Taxpayers pay taxes, taxes are used to fund schools, and schools are held accountable. In U.S. society, the primary means of teachers and schools demonstrating their accountability to audiences outside the school is to have students with good high-stakes test scores. The fact that high-stakes tests are standardized contributes to their use as a standard measure of reading achievement across states, districts, schools, and classrooms. A problem arises when we find accountability at cross-purposes. Imagine a school with a corps of accomplished teachers and with students who have a history of achieving. Their high-stakes test scores are a consistent source of pride for the school and the community. Recent mandates at the national, state, and district levels have resulted in subtle and then nontrivial forced changes to reading instruction. New regulations require that significant blocks of time be dedicated to test preparation exercises for all students. The teachers in this school have a long tradition of accountability to their students—and to themselves as professionals. This attention to accountability is lived out each school day through the respect, caring, and attention to students' individual differences that characterize teaching and learning in successful schools. The imposition of test preparation, in the name of accountability, is in opposition to what the teachers believe is best for their students. There is a conflict in the use and usefulness of reading assessment.

High-stakes test results are used for making comparisons. Whenever reading scores are released in counties, school districts, and states, we find corresponding color-coded maps in newspapers that take compilations of student scores and present them to the public. The blue-shaded schools do better than the yellow-shaded schools, which do better than the red-shaded schools. The comparison of particular schools and districts may be useful for governmental agencies to provide funding for those schools, reward them in other ways, or take punitive action. Test scores may also prove useful in acknowledging the hard work and success of teachers and schools. The NAEP provides scores for different groups of students by geographic region, gender, ethnicity, and socioeconomic status (National Assessment Governing Board, 2009). In doing so, the NAEP can guide federal legislation and funding that is directed at help-ing groups who demonstrate consistent underachievement when compared with other groups. These comparisons are also conducted at international levels. The PISA and the Progress in International Reading Literacy Study (TIMMS & PIRLS International Study Center, 2011) are conducted to compare the reading and literacy achievements of students across countries. International comparisons may be used to suggest that reading initiatives in particular countries are successful or needed.

Classroom teachers may use high-stakes reading test scores as one piece in an array of evidence that suggests certain levels of student achievement and possible in-structional strategies. In the decision-making processes of a talented reading teacher, determining a convergence of evidence that different reading assessments provide and trends in that evidence are critical abilities. High-stakes test scores in reading comprehension and vocabulary words that reflect the nature of a student's work across the school year can contribute to a teacher's increased confidence in making deci-sions. (It is important to remember, however, that high-stakes test results may be months old when they arrive at the school administrator's actual or virtual mailbox.) In the meetings that are held to determine whether students would benefit from place-ment in a particular remedial reading or gifted and talented program, high-stakes test scores can have great influence because they are one form of reading assessment that most students have in common. In the extreme, reading test scores may trump other important sources of information about a student's reading achievement. Again, test scores' reputation for being a standard and reliable measure leads many to defer to them in such situations.

Roles and Responsibilities Related to High-Stakes Reading Tests

Many talented teachers resent the incursion of high-stakes tests into their classrooms and teaching routines. For such teachers, suggestions that tests should be accommo-dated in the classroom and that valuable class time should be given to them (above and beyond the time needed for administration) may seem like folly. Test scores may underrepresent student and teacher accomplishments, yet scores are overused. A logi-cal conclusion to what some may perceive as acceptance of these tests, or complacency in regard to them, is an absence of time and ability to work for constructive change in high-stakes testing. I acknowledge that for high-stakes tests to change, advocates for change must be supported and have time to do this important work. Yet, working to change the high-stakes testing system will not immediately change the reality of test-ing for our current students.

High-stakes tests bring with them an array of responsibilities that require our careful consideration. A first responsibility is to become knowledgeable about the strengths and shortcomings of these tests. This knowledge serves several important purposes. Knowledge about high-stakes tests helps us determine our stance toward such tests: how we regard them, how we use them, and how they figure in the life of the classroom. When we are educated consumers of the results of high-stakes tests, we place ourselves in a more powerful position. Our knowledge about these tests also influences the nature of our teaching and our classrooms. This knowledge allows us to interpret the test results and use them when appropriate. This knowledge also allows us to deal with the considerable intellectual and emotional challenges that high-stakes tests may present and should help our work as professionals around what are often conflicting sets of assessment issues and agendas.

A second responsibility for teachers is to help educate others, including students and their parents, about the nature of high-stakes tests. Most parents have knowledge about testing as a result of their own experiences with taking tests, and media is a second source of information about high-stakes tests. These sources may combine to suggest to parents that test scores are the only measure of their children's reading achievement that matters. Here, our informed explanations of the strengths and limitations of high-stakes tests, especially in relation to other forms of reading assessment, will demonstrate to parents our professional knowledge on an issue of great concern about their children (Dreher & Singer, 1985). Our words may also influence parents' understanding of teaching and testing to the point where parents regularly seek the teacher's opinion on testing-related issues. Our ability as teachers to demonstrate a detailed understanding of high-stakes tests should gain us an appreciative audience when we describe the strengths and shortcomings of these tests and their appropriate and inappropriate uses.

A third responsibility, test preparation, accompanies the influx of high-stakes tests (Popham, 1997). Teachers are responsible for determining the value that such test preparation may provide, the manner in which test preparation is conducted, and the parameters of ethical test preparation. Teachers must decide the amount of time, if any, that they are willing to take from the instructional day to devote to test preparation. In other cases, these decisions are imposed on teachers and students. Regardless of our personal position on high-stakes testing in reading, our students must take these tests. Students' scores on high-stakes tests matter in profound and consequential ways, and we must communicate the importance of taking them seriously to both students and parents.

If we believe that test preparation is suitable for our students, it is important to develop an understanding of the ways and means of effective test preparation. Popham (1991) and Calkins et al. (1998) provide guidelines for selecting test preparation materials and procedures that focus on common features of high-stakes tests. We can make the distinction between teaching *to* the test and teaching *about* the test. Appropriate test preparation may include helping students learn how tests work, how test items are constructed, and how to manage limited time during testing. In addition, we should be responsible for helping students develop a serious approach to test taking. We must never underestimate the influence that our attitudes toward high-stakes tests may have on our student test takers. Students who respect their teachers take them at their word. If we make disparaging comments about an upcoming high-stakes reading assessment and students do not take it seriously, we may then fail the task of being responsible teachers, undercutting the effort and attention that students might otherwise give.

With high stakes may come high anxiety. Certain students have considerable anxiety about tests throughout their school careers. When a test is featured on the news, when parents talk about it at home, and when the teacher spends considerable class time helping students prepare to take tests, test anxiety is increased for some students. A reading test performance debilitated by test anxiety is an unworthy source of information from which to make important educational decisions. Thus, a key responsibility for teachers is to provide thorough preparation for students prior to any high-stakes test encounter. This and our continuing reassurance should serve nervous students well.

Reliability of High-Stakes Reading Tests

Tests must be accurate and consistent in measuring student work. We want all assessments to be designed and conducted so that they place students in the best (and equitable) position to demonstrate their reading achievement. Developers of tests, like those who develop other types of assessment, must strive to determine that test materials and procedures do not favor a particular student or group of students. Test developers must determine that no student or group of students is privileged by a particular reading passage, a specific type of reading test question or item, or the directions that are read to students at the beginning of the administration of a high-stakes test. Each of these components of testing can have a subtle or strong influence on student performance and test scores, which would render the test results unreliable. We must be sure that what is measured in a reading test is directly related to a student's achievement in reading comprehension and vocabulary.

The content of reading passages represents a continual challenge for test developers. Passages present content that may be closely or remotely related to students' prior knowledge. Should a reading passage on a high-stakes test contain material that is familiar to some students, they will have an unfair advantage over those students who are unfamiliar with the material, independent of reading achievement level. As noted in Chapter 2, some students may be able to answer test questions correctly without having read or understood the reading passage. This phenomenon is known as passage independence, or the ability to answer assessment items correctly without reading. Conversely, the selection of reading passages that contain material with which few or no students are familiar also poses a problem because we know that prior knowledge plays an important role in constructing meaning from text (R.C. Anderson

& Pearson, 1984). A reader who constructs meaning with little or no prior knowledge for a text may claim a notable achievement, but it is also a rare form of reading and not one that reflects good classroom practice or common classroom reading tasks. This fact of reading makes it difficult to account for the prior knowledge of content that some students have (and others lack) for a particular reading passage on a high-stakes test, which directly influences the reliability of the tests.

As noted earlier, the standardization procedures for test administration might serve to reduce or eliminate certain types of bias. As a result, standardized reading tests may exhibit increased reliability. However, the notion that standardization of any assessment removes all extraneous factors from the testing situation is misguided. Would we claim that a student who lost sleep the night before a high-stakes test because of test anxiety is on an equal footing with the other students who had a relatively peaceful night's sleep? Would we expect two students of similar reading achievement levels who have great and little prior knowledge of trains, respectively, to perform similarly on reading comprehension questions that follow a passage about trains?

Validity of High-Stakes Reading Tests

High-stakes tests can be examined through several validity lenses, and in this section, we consider ecological, construct, and concurrent validity. Ecological validity helps us consider the relationship between what students are asked to read and do on high-stakes reading tests and the reading and reading-related work that is typically done in the classroom. The type of reading that students do on high-stakes reading tests is rarely representative of the types of reading done in school—unless, of course, the reading curriculum consists of the short paragraphs and multiple-choice questions that comprise test preparation curricula.

It is important to determine the relationship of test reading to typical classroom reading. One could argue that the steady diet of high-stakes tests makes students quite familiar with what to expect on tests. Indeed, most students have considerable prior knowledge and experience that can influence their performance on tests. The inevitability and familiarity of tests, however, do not create an argument for their validity or continued use. When the content and form of classroom reading and reading instruction differ greatly from the nature of the test that is intended to measure learning, we must question the ecological validity of the test. High-stakes tests that consist of short reading passages and a preponderance of multiple-choice items will be challenged by the following questions, related to the regular classroom and thus ecological validity:

- Do students regularly read entire chapters and entire books?
- Do students do so over substantial periods of time?
- Are students encouraged to read critically?

- Do students feel it is their responsibility to question the author or critique the style of a text and the apparent trustworthiness of the information it contains?

- Do students regularly engage in higher order thinking in relation to texts and tasks in the classroom?

- Are students reading multiple texts, from which they are expected to synthesize information?

Next, construct validity of a test is a measure of how well a test reflects and measures reading and what are agreed upon as the core reading abilities. These may include the five target areas identified by the National Reading Panel report (NICHD, 2000) or some suitable subset of these areas. Some educators suggest that the ability to question the author, determine the truthfulness of sources, and monitor one's reading progress are equally important reading abilities (McNamara & Magliano, 2009; Muspratt et al., 1997; Pressley & Afflerbach, 1995). We are the beneficiaries of considerable research that continues to describe the complexity and diversity of what it means to read and student development as a reader. Research descriptions of reading continually evolve, and we happen to know much about the cognitive, motivational, affective, and prior knowledge factors that influence each and every act of reading (Alexander, 2005; Guthrie & Wigfield, 1997; Snow, 2002). Our knowledge of reading is cumulative, with new research findings adding to or revising our existing understandings of reading.

It follows that reading research evidence should influence how we think about reading or the construct of reading. This construct, which represents state-of-the-art summaries of our best and most recent understandings of the complex thing we call reading, should guide the development of standards for learning. In turn, standards for reading should influence a reading curriculum. Also, this curriculum should be honored by reading assessments that are closely aligned with the curriculum, standards, and constructs. How do high-stakes assessments relate to our current understandings of the construct of reading? We could conduct a familiarity test to begin to answer this question: Does the high-stakes test used in your classroom this year, whether elementary, middle school, or high school, look very different from the high-stakes tests you took while in the same grade in school?

The majority of high-stakes reading tests continues to present reading as information processing. Students read short passages and are expected to give back information when answering questions. Thus, our current knowledge of the constructive nature of reading comprehension is not fully represented in most high-stakes reading tests. Passages are chosen so that students' prior knowledge for the text content is expected to be fairly distributed: Either almost everyone knows something about the text topic, or only a few know a little about the topic. This consideration of students' prior knowledge for text content is done with the good intention of trying to ensure that no student or group of students is privileged due to knowledge of content brought to the test. Yet, this very practice works against the fact that reading comprehension occurs when readers combine text information with relevant prior knowledge (Pressley & Afflerbach, 1995).

Scrutiny of a test's construct validity often leads to the determination of a partial validity. Tests focus on lower level reading skills and strategies (e.g., they help us understand how well a student decodes words or establishes literal and lower level inferential comprehension) but lack items that focus on more complex reading and higher order thinking (Afflerbach et al., 2010). For example, most reading tests fail to investigate and describe student readers' ability to synthesize information from multiple texts, critically evaluate complex texts, or apply their understanding of text to solve problems. The challenge of moving beyond a partial construct validity may be addressed by the new assessments being developed by assessment consortia in the Race to the Top effort.

Another factor that influences a test's construct validity is the economics of testing. For example, requiring students to construct their own responses to a reading assessment prompt allows for potentially rich and detailed information from which we may infer students' reading accomplishments and achievements. Yet, students' written responses are difficult to score by machine, and hiring people to score reading test items is an expensive proposition relative to the machine scoring of tests. To sacrifice the quality of high-stakes tests by ruling out the use of multiple, longer text passages and extended constructed-response items because of their scoring costs may seem to some indefensible.

Finally, concurrent validity also influences the nature and popularity of high-stakes reading tests. The majority of these tests are developed by for-profit companies. Given the strong tradition of using standardized, multiple-choice reading tests, commercial publishers of tests must always anticipate their market and what will sell. Publishers must present their reading tests as dependable and useful instruments and must make their test sales pitch in particular social and political contexts. In these contexts, familiarity is more often important than innovation. The producers of high-stakes reading tests must explain how their tests measure important aspects of reading and also demonstrate a connection to the current array of high-stakes tests. This leads to the practice of using concurrent validity to demonstrate test worth. By this, we mean the degree to which a new reading test correlates with or resembles an existing reading test. High concurrent validity between two tests indicates that they measure similar aspects of reading. However, high concurrent validity also means that a new test resembles existing tests rather than reflecting our most recent and detailed understandings of reading.

Summary

High-stakes reading tests are omnipresent in school society. They are most often used against the best advice of the people who construct them. That is, they are used as *the* single indicator of student achievement, teacher effectiveness, and school accountability instead of using several indicators. These tests are accompanied by many possible consequences. Some are intended, whereas others are not. Positive consequences from the use of high-stakes reading test scores may include increased funding and the establishment of a common reading measure for most students. That some unintended negative consequences occur with high-stakes reading tests should be unsurprising because most of these tests are mandated and imposed from outside the classroom. This creates a situation in which accomplished classroom teachers must adapt to the high-stakes system in an effort to help their students demonstrate their reading achievement, regardless of the teachers' professional knowledge and values related to the tests.

ENHANCING YOUR UNDERSTANDING

1. Educate yourself about and prepare a listing of the strengths and weaknesses of high-stakes tests.
2. Describe how high-stakes tests offer one perspective on reliability in assessment.
3. Determine what teachers can do to help prepare their students to take high-stakes tests, paying particular attention to acceptable and unacceptable test preparation practices.
4. Develop an account of how present-day testing practices influence your teaching and your students' learning.

Consistent Assessment in Schools

Student learning is often enhanced when course content is presented in an engaging and predictable format. Knowing this, we are in a good position to examine reading assessment materials and procedures that may vary from grade to grade and from one content area to another. In many schools, there is variation in the types of assessment used, and the use of assessment is uncoordinated. Instructional programs are developed in the different content areas by a single faculty member, groups of faculty, administrators, or curriculum development companies. With so many sources, it is unsurprising that many students encounter inconsistent and uncoordinated assessment materials and procedures.

This diversity of assessment across content areas and grades may convince students that there is no commonality to the assessments they experience during the school day, except that they must be done. In such a situation, there may be missed opportunities to use assessments that provide complementary information and that reflect a grade-, school-, or districtwide consensus on the purposes and uses of assessment. Further, there is reduced opportunity for students to learn to self-assess when they are required to use inconsistent forms of assessment in their classrooms.

There are considerable benefits that emerge from reading assessment that is consistent across grades and content areas. First, the consistency provides teachers with many opportunities to practice assessment and develop expertise in classroom-based assessment. For example, performance assessments and rubrics, common to all classrooms and used from kindergarten through high school and across content areas, can provide students and teachers with repeated opportunities to become familiar with assessment. Second, consistent assessments help teachers understand what their students accomplished in previous grades and classrooms. Assessment results from year to year are comprehensible from teacher to teacher. This affords a clear understanding of the student's strengths and needs and the appropriate instructional focus. Third, common assessments provide a consistent teaching target: Those teachers who are committed to helping their students become better at self-assessment can consistently model assessment uses for students across grades and content areas.

Students benefit from the consistency of assessment, which helps them practice how to become independent readers and learners. For example, working with consistent forms of checklists (e.g., What is your goal for reading? Did you understand the paragraph, section, or chapter well enough to help you reach your goal? Did the author provide evidence to support this claim?) helps students learn the common aspects of reading and self-assessment across content areas. Students are not required to spend extra time learning new approaches to assessment at each grade and in each content area, except when needed. Consistent materials and procedures for reading assessment present the opportunity for students to build accurate self-impressions of their achievement throughout their school careers. When assessment is coordinated, students become familiar with the means of assessing and evaluating their work, and they get repeated reinforcement for learning in each of the content areas.

CHAPTER 8

Assessing "the Other": Important Noncognitive Aspects of Reading

What are the important and enduring outcomes of effective reading instruction? Do they include students' understanding that reading is a valuable tool, a means to achieve goals, a manner of relaxing, and a key to personal growth? Do the outcomes include students identifying themselves as readers? In this chapter, we explore assessment of "the other," that is, important factors that are both contributors to and outcomes of reading success. These factors include readers' motivation and engagement, self-concepts, agency, interests, and attitudes, as well as the attributions that readers make for their performances in reading. We consider the factors from a formative perspective, examining how they develop and either support or impede reading development. We also consider the factors from a summative perspective, as they represent a range of positive or negative outcomes of our reading instruction. The factors are central to a student's reading success and are interrelated. Yet, they are largely neglected in contemporary reading assessment, thus their designation as "the other." Consider the narrative report card in Figure 9 and how it describes some of the positive, important outcomes that are possible when reading instruction is effective. The figure also provides a sampling of things we know to be important yet often fail to assess.

A Brief History of "the Other" and Reading Assessment

How did we arrive at this point in time, knowing that there are many ways to judge successful reading programs yet only assessing students' cognitive skill and strategy development and their content area knowledge gains? For over a century, reading instruction has clearly focused on teaching reading skills and strategies (Afflerbach et al., 2008; Huey, 1908; Thorndike, 1917). Despite variation in how reading instruction has been conceptualized (Verhoeven & Snow, 2001) and efforts to increase attention to the noncognitive aspects of students' development (Afflerbach, Cho, Kim, & Crassas, 2011; L.W. Anderson & Bourke, 2000; Athey, 1985; Mathewson, 1994; McTigue, Washburn, & Liew, 2009), there is a lack of assessment attention to "the other." Recent federal

---

FIGURE 9
Sample Narrative Report Card

Rowan Mill Elementary School
Narrative Report Card
Student: Jamal Turner   Teacher: Ms. Nan Fleming   Date: March 15, 2011

Jamal continues to develop as an enthusiastic reader. He chooses to read when given choices for independent work in the classroom. He identifies himself as a reader. He understands that he is in control of reading and that his effort and persistence influence the outcomes of his work. Compared with the beginning of this school year, Jamal is a motivated reader. I attribute this to the fact that he now understands the value of reading: how it helps him reach learning goals, how it can enrich his life, and how it helps him prepare for the future. Jamal's hard work at learning the needed reading strategies is clearly paying off. At the beginning of the school year, he did not believe that he was in control of his reading and had a poor attitude toward reading. Through a series of lessons, hard work, and the development of a positive attitude and motivation, Jamal has learned that understanding text is something that is under his control. He demonstrates the sense of agency that is so important to successful readers. The ability to begin, work through, and complete reading on his own contributes valuable lessons about his hard work and his ability to succeed and act on the world in a positive manner. In summary, Jamal now sees himself as a reader, one who experiences success and values the outcomes of his reading.

Note. All names are pseudonyms. From *Understanding and Using Reading Assessment, K–12* (p. 154), by P. Afflerbach, 2007, Newark, DE: International Reading Association. Copyright 2007 by the International Reading Association.

---

law (e.g., NCLB) has reinforced the idea that we need to look no further than skill and strategy development as the positive outcomes of reading instruction, and the hallmark of lifelong reading, using assessment that focuses on cognition.

The hyperfocus on skills and strategies and the uneven treatment or neglect of "the other" can be illustrated in many ways: through school district curricular guides, reading programs, and state education standards. Consider how the California Department of Education (1998) characterizes accomplished student reading in the state's grade 6 English language arts content standards:

> Students read and understand grade-level-appropriate material. They describe and connect the essential ideas, arguments, and perspectives of the text by using their knowledge of text structure, organization, and purpose. The selections in *Recommended Literature, Kindergarten Through Grade Twelve* illustrate the quality and complexity of the materials to be read by students. **In addition, by grade eight, students read one million words annually on their own** [emphasis added], including a good representation of grade-level-appropriate narrative and expository text (e.g., classic and contemporary literature, magazines, newspapers, online information). In grade six, students continue to make progress toward this goal. (p. 35)

Students are not physically able to read one million words annually on their own in school. Thus, underlying this goal is the idea of readers who choose to read voraciously when they are not in school. Such readers are significantly motivated to such reading, but motivation is neither an instructional focus nor an assessment focus.

Similarly, the English language arts learning standards of the New York State Education Department (n.d.) include the following: "Students will read, write, listen, and speak for information and understanding. As listeners and readers, students will collect data, facts, and ideas; discover relationships, concepts, and generalizations; and use knowledge generated from oral, written, and electronically produced texts" (paras. 2–3). These state standards clearly portray reading as an important set of information processing and thinking activities. Our knowledge of cognition helps us assess the ways, simple and complex, that readers construct meaning from text. Yet, the preeminence of cognition means that other important aspects of reading are overshadowed.

A final example comes from the Introduction to the Common Core State Standards (CCSSO & NGA, 2011). The following description is notable in that it includes the ideas of reader engagement with text and that close, attentive reading is necessary for enjoying complex works of literature, which students who meet the standards are prepared to do. However, the focus remains on cognitive skills:

> Students who meet the Standards readily undertake the close, attentive reading that is at the heart of understanding and enjoying complex works of literature. They habitually perform the critical reading necessary to pick carefully through the staggering amount of information available today in print and digitally. They actively seek the wide, deep, and thoughtful engagement with high-quality literary and informational texts that builds knowledge, enlarges experience, and broadens worldviews. They reflexively demonstrate the cogent reasoning and use of evidence that is essential to both private deliberation and responsible citizenship in a democratic republic. In short, students who meet the Standards develop the skills in reading, writing, speaking, and listening that are the foundation for any creative and purposeful expression in language. (p. 3)

With the Common Core State Standards description, we can envision students who "actively seek the wide, deep, and thoughtful engagement" with texts, but engagement is not necessarily a focus of reading assessment.

Do students become accomplished readers only because they have mastered the skills and strategies of reading? Do students become lifelong readers simply as a result of our teaching and their learning cognitive skills and strategies and our careful assessment of the same? Do students choose to "read one million words annually on their own" only because they have learned the five pillars of NCLB and thus possess the appropriate cognitive skills and strategies? Or, is there more to the notion of student readers' development and more to consider when we assess outcomes of reading programs? When viewed from the perspective of Pellegrino and colleagues' (2001) model of assessment, current assessment practice privileges cognition, largely ignores affective development, and therefore does not account for student development relative to the full construct of reading. If we are successful in advocating for the importance of these present and future outcomes, we may be able to change the status quo in reading assessment.

Successful student readers are motivated, have a positive attitude, possess a good self-concept, and are capable of making accurate attributions for their performances.

Yet, the centrality of these factors to school success is largely ignored in influential educational policies and documents, including NCLB legislation and the related report of the National Reading Panel (NICHD, 2000). A resultant risk is that high-quality reading instruction is conceptualized as teaching only the target areas of phonics, phonemic awareness, fluency, vocabulary, and comprehension, with less or no attention paid to the affective lives of student readers. Every finding from scientific research and every classroom observation that demonstrates the power of motivation, self-concept, attitude, interest, and attributions in students' reading development should call the question, Why don't we assess these important aspects of the teaching and learning of reading? (Boekaerts & Corno, 2005; Guthrie et al., in press; Pajares & Urdan, 2006).

The good news is that there is building research evidence, and our classroom experiences that can help us advocate for assessing these important facilitators and outcomes of reading. Likewise, there are assessments that describe student development in relation to reading self-esteem, reading motivation, and reading habits. However, the continued focus on assessing only the cognitive outcomes of the teaching and learning of reading is problematic. Schools and classrooms already overburdened by testing will find it difficult to accommodate another series of reading assessments. School budgets, already placed at risk by mandated testing costs, have little or no monies for more assessments. This makes the challenge twofold: We must advocate for the centrality and importance of "the other" in how our student readers develop, and we must find ways to assess "the other" in an already crowded reading assessment program.

What About "the Other" Needs to Be Assessed?

How might we conceptualize the successful student reader? Accomplished student readers share important characteristics that are related to, but different from, their cognitive skills, strategies, and achievement (Afflerbach & Cho, 2010). The narrative report card included earlier in this chapter touches on a number of these characteristics. Successful student readers are strategic, resourceful, and motivated and have generally good self-concepts. These students have life interests that can be founded in and examined and extended through reading, interests that can influence a reader's stance toward a reading task. These students possess positive attitudes toward reading and identify themselves as readers. Reading fits into the lives of successful student readers in many ways. It helps them plan and achieve school-related goals and establish and grow in areas of personal interest. Reading is something worth doing: It rewards, enriches, informs, and transforms. Many students learn to read, but many choose not to read as they leave school and live their lives. This aliteracy may be explained not by a failure to learn to read but by a failure to realize the full value of reading.

Factors such as motivation and self-esteem are possible outcomes of becoming a better reader. Each is also a potential facilitator or obstacle to students' ongoing reading development. Consider this less accomplished reader: A struggling fourth-grade reader may already have five years, or half a lifetime, of below-average reading performance. He has a history of reluctant reading, in part because when his reading is on public display, his self-concept and motivation suffer. Thus, he has developed routines that help him avoid reading situations. These routines have mixed effects. His routines may result in not only avoiding embarrassment but also in missing opportunities that could help his reading development. He has a generally negative attitude toward reading and is not interested in reading on his own. He is not motivated to do things with which he repeatedly experiences failure, which is unsurprising. That a teacher can change such a student's motivations to read is a powerful form of accountability. A reluctant reader who approaches acts of reading with a history of failure and then learns to build and maintain motivation has accomplished much. The reluctant reader who is motivated to agree to read in school and then elects to read outside of the classroom demonstrates a possibly life-enhancing change. This change should be assessed and described.

A Closer Look at "the Other" Factors That Facilitate and Reflect Becoming a Better Reader

In this section, I provide overviews of the possible contributions of five reader characteristics to reading success:

1. Motivation with reading (For example, moving from a single interest in reading about football to reading in general and motivation to read in the face of challenge are learned habits of good readers.)

2. The reader's self-concept (How we view ourselves as readers influences what, when, and how we read.)

3. Reader attitudes, which can enhance or inhibit reading from the start

4. Reader interest, which may be topic specific or general

5. Reader attributions (To what student readers attribute their success and failure can have a great influence on their reading.)

An important point is that any and all of these factors may be symbiotic or enmeshed with reading development. They encourage the student's ongoing growth and development as a reader. These factors may contribute to what Stanovich (1986) calls "the Matthew effects" (p. 360), in which those students who are already experiencing success with reading are in a good position to further grow as readers. While Stanovich focuses on cognitive skills and strategies and their relationships, consider the possibility of a Matthew effect in relation to readers' affective characteristics. A reader who experiences success in reading in school may be motivated to continue to read in school. In other instances, the factors may present an obstacle to reading growth. These factors can have interactive and additive relationships to reading development. Consider, again, the student who is a struggling reader. He has a history of not reading well but is put on the spot in class—an immediate threat to his self-esteem and self-concept as a reader. Why would he be motivated to read? Such students may experience a reverse Matthew effect: a deliberate effort to avoid reading, with the result of the poor getting poorer. The task, then, is to describe the potential contribution of "the other" to reading success, the relation of "the other" to reading, and the possible means to assess these important factors and outcomes.

Assessing "the Other" in a Fourth-Grade Classroom

Nan is a fourth-grade teacher who is focusing on her students' motivations to read, their self-concepts, their interests and attitudes related to reading, and their attributions for reading success or failure. Her focus is determined, in part, by the availability of assessment tools that help her examine and describe each of these important aspects of student reader development. Nan is what I call an opportunistic assessor of her students' reading. She consistently looks for opportunities to assess her students during reading class. She also searches for and uses available assessments, created by herself, colleagues, or others, that help her know and tell the full story of her students' reading development. This opportunism has led Nan to focus on specific "other" outcomes of reading and on assessments that help her best understand related student development.

Helping Nan are portions of four different instruments: the Elementary Reading Attitude Survey (McKenna & Kear, 1990), the Motivation to Read Profile (MRP; Gambrell, Codling, & Palmer, 1996, Pitcher et al., 2007), the 30-item version of the Reading Self-Concept Scale (RSCS-30; Chapman & Tunmer, 1995), and a reading interest survey (Hildebrandt, 2001). Each of these assessments is aligned with areas that Nan and her colleagues consider important in the development of lifelong readers. Each assessment has the further appeal of being readily available: Nan and her colleagues are happy to use existing assessment instruments that are well suited to their needs, thus avoiding the demands of having to create a new assessment.

Nan must be judicious in her choices of assessment materials and procedures, for her time is at a premium, and a considerable portion of the school district's assessment effort focuses on federally mandated testing. Thus, she is careful to choose assessments that focus on what she knows to be important: influential factors of students' reading development. Nan and her colleagues do considerable legwork to identify possible resources, including existing assessments, that can help them meet their goal of assessing "the other." The teachers conduct searches of alternative assessments using graduate course materials, recommendations from colleagues, and the Internet.

Student Readers' Motivation

Our motivations can have a subtle or obvious influence on our work. They can be weak or strong, positive or negative. They are often related to our past experiences. Nan is familiar with students whose lack of motivation stems from their prior experiences: little or no perceptible reward for their efforts, difficult public performances, and unpleasant memories. When Nan thinks of her struggling readers, she tries to empathize. Their experiences with reading could lead to a lack of motivation that is similar to her lack of motivation to have a root canal or visit the Department of Motor Vehicles. In contrast, she is quite motivated to read. Nan identifies herself as a reader and can read most things that she encounters and develop an understanding of them. Her prior experiences are positive, and they motivate her to return to acts of reading because they bring rewards.

Nan's experiences and those of her students are related to a robust research literature on motivation (Guthrie et al., in press; Pintrich, Marx, & Boyle, 1993). This research demonstrates that motivation can serve as a facilitator of students' reading achievement and that increased motivation to read is an outcome of effective instruction and learning. Simply put, motivated readers are willing to persevere when reading is challenging, they choose to read in the face of attractive alternatives, and the positive motivation sets student readers up to do more reading. Thus, motivation can contribute to the increased reading that in turn contributes to increased reading achievement.

Motivation can turn students toward or away from acts of reading. A related phenomenon, engagement, reflects a "merger of motivation and thoughtfulness" (Guthrie, 2001, para. 1). According to Guthrie, "Engaged readers seek to understand; they enjoy learning and they believe in their reading abilities. They are mastery oriented, intrinsically motivated, and have self-efficacy" (para. 1).

Engaged readers exhibit four characteristic behaviors: They are well-motivated, they approach reading strategically, they are knowledgeable about reading and content areas, and they interact socially in relation to their reading. According to Guthrie, McGough, Bennett, and Rice (1996), engaged readers are motivated as they read to pursue varied personal goals, and they use different strategies and their prior knowledge to construct meaning from text. Engaged readers interact socially as they construct and use meaning. Further, engaged readers use a beneficial combination of affect, language, and cognition as they read.

To better understand their students' motivations to read and aspects of engagement, Nan and her colleagues use items from the MRP (Gambrell et al., 1996). The MRP consists of two parts: a self-report reading survey, which is administered in groups, and an individual conversational interview. The survey assesses two dimensions of reading motivation—student readers' self-concepts and how students value reading—whereas the interview explores individual aspects of students' motivation to

TABLE 19
Sample Items From the Motivation to Read Profile

Reading Survey

1. Reading a book is something I like to do.
    a. Never   b. Not very often
    c. Sometimes   d. Often

2. I tell my friends about good books I read.
    a. Never   b. Not very often
    c. Sometimes   d. Often

3. I think libraries are _____ to spend time.
    a. A great place   b. An interesting place
    c. An OK place   d. A boring place

Conversational Interview

1. Did you read anything at home yesterday? If so, what did you read?
2. Tell me about your favorite author.

Note. The questions are modified from *Elementary Students' Motivation to Read* (Reading Research Report No. 52), by L.B. Gambrell, R.M., Codling, and B.M. Palmer, 1996, Athens, GA: National Reading Research Center.

read, such as their personal interests in reading. Nan and her colleagues select a subset of items from the MRP, as shown in Table 19.

The use of the items from the MRP helps Nan and her colleagues combine their classroom observations with focused questions that further describe students' reading motivations. These sources provide Nan with valuable information for planning instruction, suggesting reading materials, and focusing on the motivational aspects of becoming a better reader and supporting reading. In teaching, she strives to join cognitive skill and strategy instruction with tasks and activities that motivate and help her students understand their progress.

Student Readers' Self-Concepts

Each of us carries with us an extensive set of self-concepts. These are developed as we experience life and think about ourselves in relation to these experiences. For example, Nan's limited experiences with playing tennis, combined with watching matches from Wimbledon and the U.S. Open, lead her to conceptualize herself as a novice tennis player. She does not have a problem with this self-concept because she believes it to be accurate, and it helps her recognize when she might, or might not, be a suitable tennis partner for another person. Also, she has other self-concepts that are not so impoverished. For example, her experiences with reading suggest to her that she is a fairly accomplished reader. She understands the vast majority of things she reads. Both of these self-concepts influences the approach that she takes to different aspects of her life. Nan has a high self-concept as a reader and is willing to take on often challenging reading tasks because she sees herself as one who can meet those challenges. Unfortunately, her tennis game and her self-concept as a tennis player lead her to decline invitations to play. Such high and low self-concepts likely exist in each classroom among our different developing readers.

Research demonstrates that a positive self-concept contributes to students' achievement, whereas a negative self-concept can interfere with or prevent academic progress (Chapman & Tunmer, 1995). From this research, we understand that all the effective skill and strategy teaching in the world may not translate to reading success if a student's self-concept is needy and unchanged as related learning and growth occur. To explore the development of students' self-concepts as readers, Nan and her colleagues utilize sections of the RSCS-30 (Chapman & Tunmer, 1995), which includes items that focus on students' self-concepts related to reading competence, attitude, and difficulty. The items selected by Nan and her colleagues from each of these areas are shown in Table 20.

As is the case with information provided by the MRP, Nan uses the results of the RSCS-30 to elaborate on the information she gathers through classroom observations and discussions with students. For example, she has learned to identify students who appear to possess negative self-concepts as readers. She knows that many students reading below grade level develop a low self-concept from the consistent messages they receive about the nature of their below-average reading and that even above-average student readers may have a weak self-concept because of pressures they receive or place on themselves to do better than they already are. Assessing students' self-concepts provides Nan with valuable information. She is able to consider both the content and the context of her reading lessons, working to boost students' skills and strategies while also attending to their very real needs for positive reading experiences and increased self-concepts as readers.

TABLE 20
Sample Items From the 30-Item Version
of the Reading Self-Concept Scale

Competence Subscale	• Can you work out hard words by yourself when you read?
	• Are you good at remembering words?
Attitude Subscale	• Do you look forward to reading?
Difficulty Subscale	• Do you make lots of mistakes in reading?
	• Are the books you read in class too hard?

Note. The questions are from "Development of Young Children's Reading Self-Concepts: An Examination of Emerging Subcomponents and Their Relationship With Reading Achievement," by J.W. Chapman and W.E. Tunmer, 1995, *Journal of Educational Psychology,* 87(1), pp. 166–167.

Students' Attitudes Toward Reading

Reading attitudes are closely related to reader motivation and reader self-concept. Nan thinks of her students: Who has a strong, positive attitude toward reading? Who has a less than positive attitude toward reading? How consistent are these attitudes? As Nan develops a mental model of her student readers with a positive attitude, she notes the following traits:

- I have a generally good attitude toward reading.
- I expect to find reading rewarding.
- I expect to succeed.
- I know that when I encounter difficulties, I will probably be able to overcome them.

Nan knows that, in contrast, students with a history of failure in reading are often further hindered by a poor attitude toward reading. The less able students identify reading in school with experiences of failure and public demonstrations of weakness.

To meet the challenge of identifying and addressing students' diverse attitudes toward reading, Nan and her colleagues use the Elementary Reading Attitude Survey (McKenna & Kear, 1990), in which students are asked to circle a cartoon character (Garfield) whose drawn expression most closely represents their own feelings. Sample items are shown in Table 21.

This survey helps Nan further detail her students' attitudes toward different aspects of reading and sharpen the focus of her instructional efforts. She finds the survey especially useful because it helps differentiate between her students' academic reading and their recreational reading. When Nan finds discrepancies between student attitudes in these two types of reading, she tries to locate an area in which a student has a relatively positive attitude toward reading. For example, when she determines that a student has a very positive attitude toward recreational reading because there is choice

---

TABLE 21
Sample Items From the Elementary Reading Attitude Survey

Recreational Reading Scale	• How do you feel when you read a book on a rainy Saturday?
	• How do you feel about getting a book for a present?
	• How do you feel about reading instead of playing?
Academic Reading Scale	• How do you feel when the teacher asks you questions about what you read?
	• How do you feel about reading your school books?
	• How do you feel when you read out loud in class?

Note. The questions are from "Measuring Attitude Toward Reading: A New Tool for Teachers," by M.C. McKenna and D.J. Kear, 1990, *The Reading Teacher*, 43(9), pp. 630–634.

involved, she provides the student with choices in academic reading in an attempt to convey the already existing positive attitude into academic reading.

Students' Reading Interests

Nan and her colleagues believe that knowing and using students' interests to help plan reading instruction can positively influence student reading. Nan is concerned that several of her students are disinterested readers. Assessment that helps her pinpoint student interests within and outside the classroom is worth the time and effort. She googles "interest inventory reading," which leads her to Hildebrandt's (2001) reading interest inventory. This survey seeks information on school reading interests, reading habits, and special areas of interest for each child, as shown in Table 22.

Nan compares the information provided by the reading interest inventory with what she understands of her students through her reading of their work and listening to their discussions with classmates. When she sees clear areas of student interest, she notes the opportunity to gather resources to try to meet individual students' needs, within a context that is already motivating and interesting to the students. For example, Nan determines that a student is quite interested in science fiction and space exploration and uses this information, with the help of the school media specialist, to develop a suggested reading list for the student—one that focuses on things for which the student has an affinity, so reading progress may occur.

Students' Attributions for Success and Failure

Each of us builds theories about our work in the world: Why did this day go well? What could I have done differently to change things? Why did I get a C in reading? Why are my peers better readers? Students, like adults, think about the outcomes of things they do. School performance is important and consequential for most students. High or low grades (and scores) get students thinking about why a grade is high

---

TABLE 22
Sample Items From the Reading Interest Inventory

- What are some of the books that you have read lately?
- List the topics or subjects that you might like to read about.
- Do you have a hobby? If so, what is it?
- Put a check mark next to the kind of reading that you like best. (The options provided include history, sports, romance, science fiction, adventure, novels, humor, folk tales, poetry, biography, how-to books, mysteries, and plays.)

Note. The questions are modified from "'But there's nothing good to read' (in the library media center)," by D. Hildebrandt, 2001, *Media Spectrum: The Journal for Library Media Specialists in Michigan, 28,* pp. 36 and 37.

or low, how the grade was determined, and why it is expected or unexpected. This thinking leads to theorizing about performance and the development of attributions for our performances (Berkeley et al., 2011; Hiebert, Winograd, & Danner, 1984). We can believe that external factors, such as luck, the difficulty of the reading task, or the teacher liking or not liking us, causes the outcome. We can make an internal attribution that we gave much or not enough effort to our reading task, or that we are intelligent or not intelligent. Each attribution has the potential to become a habitual way of thinking about oneself in relation to reading and reading success or failure.

Students' theories of their performances may or may not be accurate, but their theories are powerful. Built on students' prior experiences with reading, these theories can influence present and future reading experiences. The theories color the students' approaches to reading, and particular reading outcomes are expected. Students may attribute their past reading performances to not being smart and believe that all future reading outcomes will reflect this fact. Students with such attributions are supremely challenged: "Not being smart enough" is seen by most students as a fixed and permanent attribute. From the perspective of the student, reading is best avoided, and when it cannot be, the student may be resigned to failure (Johnston & Winograd, 1985).

Nan uses a series of questions and observations to determine to what students attribute their successes and failures. The questions reflect Nan and her colleagues' knowledge of the research literature on attributions and their ongoing concerns with students' attributions (Dweck, 1999; Van Keer & Verhaeghe, 2005). For example, Nan is interested in the attributions that her students make about their reading performances, including scores on a quiz, how they understand and discuss stories, and their detailed portfolio work. She also would like to determine if students' attributions are consistent across all the reading they do or if attributions vary related to the subject matter, the type of text, and the nature of the assignment. The questions she asks include the following:

- Why do you think you got this grade?
- Why do you think you understood this chapter?
- Why is your portfolio structured this way?
- Do you feel that you will be more successful with certain reading tasks? Which ones? Why?

Students can change their ideas about the etiology of reading failure and success, which is called retraining attributions, so that new understandings may include "I worked hard and gave my best effort, and as a result, I read better, learned, and achieved." Nan wants to learn the details of her students' attributions so that she can support the development of positive attributions and help students change any negative attributions they possess into positive ones. Given the potential power of the theorizing that students do about their successes and failures, she asks, "Shouldn't we be in the habit of assessing and understanding attributions?"

Assessing "the Other": Portrait of a Struggling Reader

It is not enough that we seek to identify the potentially powerful influences on reading and the outcomes of reading. We must have a plan that helps us take information from the assessment of these factors and address, in a formative manner, students' individual needs. Nan uses assessments that provide formative and summative assessment information related to "the other" factors. At the beginning of the school year, she uses assessments in the form of surveys and questionnaires to gather information on the noncognitive aspects of her students' lives. These assessments provide complementary information to the cognitive information gathered with a comprehensive reading inventory. Combined, this formative assessment helps her understand the challenges her students face and the strengths they possess, both of which can figure greatly in how well students learn reading skills and strategies.

Nan talks with her colleagues about their students in relation to their motivations, self-concepts, interests, attitudes, and attributions. Each week, she focuses on a particular group of students in her class, using observation and questions to update her understanding of the students. She also learns about each student from her teaching colleagues: what they do when they are with their groups of friends at lunch and in physical education. In addition to the beginning- and end-of-year assessments, Nan writes narrative reports on her students' development, one of which is included earlier in this chapter (see Figure 9). She uses checklists and series of questions regularly throughout the school year to keep track of her students' affective and cognitive growth. Assessment in Nan's classroom is conceived to yield both formative and summative information about "the other" in reading. This part of the assessment program supplies valuable information that describes students' current status as readers and is used in planning reading instruction and experiences that foster reading development.

Consider Jesse, one of the less accomplished readers in Nan's classroom. Jesse makes the wrong attributions for his reading performance. The attributions are predictable and logical, but they work against his progress in reading. He believes that he is not in control of the act of reading. Thus, his success or failure in reading is perceived to be at the whim of external forces, including luck and the difficulty of the reading task. In general, Jesse is not motivated to read. He comes to Nan's classroom with a record of not reading to grade-level expectations in previous grades, and he is well aware of his status within previous classrooms as a "low" reader. In fact, there is powerful motivation for Jesse to avoid reading, as it typically shows him in an unsuccessful and unflattering light. The MRP (Gambrell et al., 1996) triangulates the information that Nan gleans from his prior years' narrative report cards. Using her assessment information, she establishes improved motivation as a key goal in fostering Jesse's reading growth. He has very little that is positive regarding his identity as a reader. He has no discernible, helpful reading habits, and his attitude leaves him with little or no opportunity to practice and learn new reading strategies or stances toward reading. If asked, he might state that across the entire school day, he feels least in control of things when he is required to read.

Using items from the reading interest survey, Nan determines that Jesse is devoted to caring for animals. She notes that he is most motivated to try to read almost anything that has to do with veterinarians, helping and rescuing animals, and saving injured animals. This motivation is clear: Jesse will take on any text related to animal care, regardless of text difficulty. Currently, this approach is yielding mixed results: Jesse is showing motivation to read, but he is often frustrated because what he wants to learn is inaccessible, too difficult to understand. Nan uses her diverse assessments of "the other" to help change his self-concept and attitude related to reading. She finds reading materials that he can understand and use; helps him understand that his motivation yields good results; and works with him to help him see the connections among his motivation, his reading, and the outcomes of his reading.

The fact that Jesse is fanatical in his devotion to caring for animals is key information for helping him begin positive changes in terms of motivation, self-concept as a reader, and reading attitude. It is also the place in which he is able to make constructive attributions for his reading performance. That is, he is willing and able to make the connections between his hard work, perseverance, and the good that comes from his reading. Nan uses this knowledge about Jesse's love of animals to provide him with reading materials from diverse sources, including veterinarian magazines, websites of organizations that care for animals, books on the lives of animals, articles about pets and wild animals, and brochures from zoos. He also becomes a participating member of an online discussion group that focuses on helping local wildlife.

With her years of experience, Nan knows that students begin each school year with reading-related motivations, a sense of self in relation to reading, attitudes, and interests that are shaped by (and can shape) their reading. In fact, her reading instruction is clearly intended to foster positive changes in these characteristics within each learner. These are incredibly important outcomes of reading instruction, for without them, attainment of reading standards and benchmarks is nearly impossible.

Consequences and Usefulness of Assessment of "the Other"

Nan knows that her assessments of these "other" factors result in several powerful, positive consequences. First, these factors provide both formative and summative assessment information. Assessment helps Nan understand her students' often complex mix of motivations, self-concepts, attitudes, interests, and attributions at the beginning of the school year, and with this information, she can develop instructional strategies that directly address her students' diverse needs. Nan can chart the change or maintenance of students' affective factors across the academic year. For example, she can demonstrate that her assessment helped her become aware of Jesse's lack of motivation and poor self-concept as a reader and then address both these obstacles through her instruction. Taking Jesse's high-stakes test scores and the detailed documentation of his growth related to motivation, self-concept, attitude, and attributions, Nan develops an explanation of her success in teaching reading—success through attention to both affective and cognitive student growth.

Nan uses assessment to help her pinpoint factors that will enhance or inhibit her students' reading development, and she charts the outcomes of her instruction that represent positive affective changes in her students. The range of assessments allows her to describe growth in her students. Although Nan and her colleagues feel immense pressure to teach reading skills and strategies, they are convinced that without detailed knowledge of their students' accompanying motivations, attitudes, interests, and self-concepts, their students' test scores will not tell the full story of learning.

Nan uses the array of assessments to develop detailed communications with Jesse's parents. She is able to describe situations in which his parents might expect him to be a motivated reader and situations to avoid. Reading materials in which people help animals are clearly recommended. She is especially concerned that his parents understand how his self-concept as a reader is gradually changing for the better and that it is an extremely fragile work in progress. With her assessments of "the other," Nan can describe Jesse's reading interests and work that should contribute to his positive self-esteem. Further, Nan and her colleagues work with parents to help their children make consistent and productive attributions for their work.

Roles and Responsibilities Related to Assessment of "the Other"

It is not an understatement to say that Nan and her colleagues have gone the extra mile in relation to using assessments to learn about critically important other aspects of students' reading development. Many teachers are challenged to develop detailed understandings of their students as information processors, or readers seen through the lens of cognitive assessments. Thus, adding to the assessment mix is work that must be supported and well planned. For Nan and her colleagues, it is an ongoing project to discuss the ideal student reader, or the characteristics of students who they would label "accomplished." A responsibility here is to continue discussions in which successful readers are defined not only in relation to the target areas of NCLB but also in relation to constructs that include the motivated reader, the reader with a positive and accurate self-concept, the reader who has a good attitude toward reading, and the reader who makes accurate attributions for his or her reading performance. Nan and her colleagues conceptualize their student readers as more than a conglomeration of cognitive skills and strategies and are committed to investigating and describing "the other": those factors that are both influences on and outcomes of successful reading.

Reliability of Assessment of "the Other"

Consistency in assessing "the other" is a goal for Nan. She works toward this goal with several strategies. First, she becomes familiar with the instruments she uses, the sets of items that are taken from each assessment, and the procedures for administering the assessments. Second, she seeks triangulation of all of her hypotheses about students' motivations, self-concepts, interests, attitudes, and attributions. To this end, Nan regularly focuses on single students to update her ideas about their reading progress and the factors that can complement or inhibit this progress. She uses classroom observations and questioning, in conjunction with the results of the items she uses from different assessments, to help her follow up on hunches that she has about individual students' motivations or attributions. The observations and questioning derive from a master list of student characteristics and questions that are designed to seek similar information about each student in a reliable and predictable manner.

Validity of the Assessment of "the Other"

Nan and her colleagues believe deeply in the need to add to people's ideas about outcomes of high-quality teaching and student reading achievement. Nan's vast classroom experience and knowledge of the research literature tell her that assessment must be a more comprehensive and accurate reflection of student reading than is provided by a year-end test that focuses on reading skills and strategies. To this end, her assessment practice not only provides valuable and valid information but also expands her idea of what reading is. Skills and strategies always matter and receive attention, but they must be surrounded by a supportive network of motivation, self-concept, and a positive attitude toward reading.

Nan's approach to assessing the more broadly conceived construct of reading provides information about factors that influence reading development and factors that are a result of reading development. For example, the formative assessment that describes students with low motivation to read is used to create motivating reading experiences, and over time, these experiences have helped created more motivated student readers. Summative assessment allows Nan to capture and describe these valuable products of her assessment and instruction.

Summary

Our use of assessment materials and procedures that focus on "the other" in reading helps fill in the gap in our understanding of how students are challenged and how they may develop. The information complements what we know about students' cognitive achievement. One result of this approach is the development of profiles of readers that move beyond their cognitive skills and strategies to describe each student's motivation to read and willingness to persevere, self-concept as a reader, reading interests, and attributions for reading successes and failures. In this sense, our understanding of affective aspects of students' reading helps us determine how skills and strategies are best used. Further, the assessments used by Nan and her colleagues best represent the integrity and reach of their reading instruction and their students' corresponding growth and achievement.

ENHANCING YOUR UNDERSTANDING

1. Create a map or graphic organizer of your goals and hopes for your students as readers. Next, describe how and how much your assessments cover this territory. What is covered? What is not covered? What needs attention?

2. Choose one aspect of students' reading development that you feel is underrepresented or missing entirely from current approaches to assessment in your school. Determine how you can begin to assess, address, and report on this aspect of reading development. Create, find, and borrow your means to do so.

3. Develop a presentation for your teaching colleagues, administrators, or parents that catalogs the things that are missed with the current reading assessment regimen. Propose the means to assess "the other" in your school, including motivation, self-concept, and attitude.

Assessing Student Collaboration and Cooperation

Important work and learning, within and outside of the classroom, often involve collaboration with other people. In school, an individual student's learning and achievement continue as a primary focus of assessment. Yet, what about the school tasks that revolve around students learning and collaborating with one another? The challenges we face in helping some students learn to work with others is mirrored by the challenge that collaborative work presents to reading assessment. For example, a school assignment that engages students in a group project to learn about a particular country's imports and exports may include specific roles and responsibilities for the members of a collaborative group. The assignment must be matched with an integrity of assessment: clearly defined measures that describe how students read and contribute to collaborative work and how they grow in terms of content area learning.

Creative solutions to assessment challenges help us make the most of the collaborative experiences that we undertake in our classrooms. One solution is to assign specific tasks within the collaborative learning team so that each member has clear goals whose attainment helps demonstrate the learning and work that takes place. Although the division of learning tasks within collaborative groups can be time-consuming work, it is necessary and beneficial. A task analysis of what is to be learned and assessed and how different collaborative group members may or may not be engaged in different facets of the project is important. At least as challenging is the measure, through assessment, of each collaborative team member's learning. We must be able to fully account for an individual student's particular learning and contribution in relation to an assigned role or task. We must also be able to chart and describe the student's growth and learning in the larger, collaborative task. Collaborative learning may join students of mixed ability levels, interests, and motivations. In each of these situations, we must be careful to clearly specify the work to be done, the division of responsibility, and the means to measure and describe collaborative and individual student contributions to accomplishments. It is important that we have a clear sense of the complexity and magnitude of the work and achievement that we expect in collaborative learning situations so that we can adjust our expectations and assessments accordingly.

It is important to note the potentially positive consequences of collaboration. Students can develop a detailed understanding of their roles and responsibilities related to collaborative learning when they are guided by assessment. In other situations, students who are responsible to one another might consult a scoring plan, such as a performance assessment and accompanying rubric, to make a priori decisions about which team members will be responsible for different aspects of learning. The assessment, in this case, can provide guidance to students. Collaborative and cooperative learning situations provide students with opportunities for valuable social learning. Outcomes of this learning may include a newfound respect for classmates and their opinions, understanding work team dynamics and using them for high-quality outcomes, taking turns, and recognizing the different learning that can occur in the collaborative and cooperative context. Our assessment efforts will do well to describe these valuable learning outcomes, above and beyond the information that they yield related to reading achievement.

CHAPTER 9

Accommodation and Reading Assessment

A ccommodation in assessment is intended to allow students to best demonstrate their reading development and achievement. Special-needs students, English learners (ELs), and others may benefit from accommodations, or modifications, of the reading assessments they take. Yet, the means by which accommodations are mandated and provided are not consistent and are sometimes controversial. This chapter focuses on the different types of assessment accommodation; the students who benefit from accommodations; and the contexts in which accommodations are considered, developed, and given.

As defined by the Board on Testing and Assessment of the National Research Council (Koenig & Bachman, 2004), *accommodation* is "the general term for any action taken in response to a determination that an individual's disability or level of English language development requires a departure from established testing protocol" (p. 1). This definition is limited to describing accommodation in standardized testing situations. For our purposes, accommodation of assessment includes, but is not limited to, reading tests. Rather, any form of reading assessment that may be modified in relation to students' needs, with the result of gathering useful and valid information, can be considered a candidate for accommodation. The guiding principle is that accommodation in reading assessment helps students perform in assessment situations to the best of their ability, which results in useful and valid assessment information.

In this chapter, we consider three general types of accommodation for students in our classrooms. The first is accommodation based on identified special needs of learning disabled students, and the second is based on the special needs of students who are ELs. The third type of accommodation, one that does not receive nearly as much attention outside of classrooms, focuses on how teachers might use their assessment materials and procedures to best accommodate all students.

A Brief History of Accommodation in Assessment

The ability to accommodate student differences is a hallmark of fairness. One group of accommodations is directly linked to the Americans with Disabilities Act of 1990 and the Individuals with Disabilities Education Act Amendments of 1997. These bodies of legislation codified both the types of challenges that make students eligible for accommodation and the particular types of accommodation that can be used to meet these students' needs. Accommodations related to this legislation can often be found in a student's individualized education plan (IEP), in which a special education need is described and documented.

A second form of accommodation may be made in relation to students' English-language status. ELs are sometimes given accommodation in high-stakes test situations. These students may have more time to take the test, the provision of a glossary of important terms, or both. Yet, the criteria for identifying such students varies from state to state, as do the time frames in which students are expected to learn English and take tests exclusively in English, unaccommodated. The assessment accommodation policies in different states generally mirror the instructional policies and expectations. For example, if students are expected to be competent in English by fourth grade, accommodation of students related to English-language learning may not be provided to any fourth-grade ELs.

The number of students with disabilities and students who are ELs, or both, totals over 9 million, fully 20% of the present student population in the United States (Koenig & Bachman, 2004). NCLB requires school districts to report high-stakes reading test scores for many subgroups within each school, including special-needs students and ELs. Thus, accommodations can help us develop the most accurate account of students' reading achievement. This current need for accommodation in assessment is paralleled by the need for ongoing research on the nature and effects of accommodation (Abedi, Lord, Hofstetter, & Baker, 2000; Fletcher et al., 2006). Most needed is research that investigates and describes the influence of accommodations on the validity of the assessment. For example, does allowing students more time to take a high-stakes test change the validity of the test? Does the rewording of test items influence validity? Do the assessment accommodations given to particular students result in bias against other students? The current situation is one in which the demand for accommodation is extremely high, but the guidance that might be provided by research on the effects of accommodation is still developing.

It is important to note that although today's accommodation of students with special needs is a legal requirement and accommodation of ELs is guided by law, helping each and every student is considered by many a moral and ethical issue. From this perspective, we want to ensure that all students are given the best opportunity to demonstrate their reading achievements and needs in an assessment situation. I add to this legal, moral, and ethical mix a practical element: We use reading assessment information to make consequential decisions. If our assessment information is faulty because an accommodation is not made, or an accommodation is inappropriate or ineffective, then we are wasting time and resources on the assessment.

Although current assessment accommodation is driven by the identification of students with special needs and the identification of students with EL status, there is a third group of students who are worthy of consideration for accommodation. These are the students who are not legally entitled to assessment accommodation but who may, nevertheless, benefit from it. These students include those who are near, but not quite close enough to, the designation of being a special-needs student or an EL and others who benefit from accommodations that may include more time to complete an assessment, a repeated explanation of the nature of an assessment, or clarification of an assessment item.

The current system requires documentation of a student's needs to mandate accommodation, needs so substantial that they earn the "learning disability" or "EL" label. Stringent criteria are used to make these designations, which leads to a situation in which there are two classes of students in our classrooms: those entitled to accommodation and those who are not. This should be a concern. How many students in each of our classes might benefit from accommodation, be it the extension of time to complete an assessment task, the simplifying of an assessment prompt, or the clarification provided by a teacher's response to the student's question? The current operating assumption is that within specific but broad parameters, students can be expected to not have major impediments to their performances on assessments because of language issues, disabilities, or both. Thus, these students need no accommodation. This assumption is worthy of challenge. What classroom of 30 students has no students who might benefit from the legitimate accommodation of extra time or the repeating of classroom assessment instructions?

Teachers who are sensitive to their individual students' characteristics and needs are continually striving to accommodate their students during reading instruction and assessment. We use our knowledge of a student's relative strengths and weaknesses to accommodate writing challenges by allowing the student to respond orally to assessment questions. Our accommodation focuses on providing the best possible environment for students to demonstrate their learning. These accommodations are not intended to help students avoid important aspects of school and learning, such as improving their writing and speaking. Rather, the accommodation is provided because we often find ourselves in situations in which we are most interested in finding out how well our students read and understand, fully aware that special challenges to our students, unaccommodated, could skew our conception of their accomplishments and continuing needs. Throughout the history of accommodating students on reading assessment, the primary goal has been to change assessment materials and procedures, not to change the construct that is measured as a result of the accommodation.

Characteristics of Accommodation

Accommodation is a change in assessment materials or procedures based on a recognized student need, without which there will be challenges to the valid assessment of the student's knowledge and skills (Thurlow & Bolt, 2001). Students who are accommodated for special needs may have hearing impairments, visual impairments, behavioral and emotional disorders, learning disabilities, autism, mental retardation, or speech and language impairments. Accommodation of ELs focuses on aspects of students' language proficiency that may interfere with valid assessment. For example, aspects of testing that demand students' English-language competency include the directions that accompany tests and the items, tasks, and prompts that comprise the test. These are primary candidates for modifying or translating the language of the assessment.

Accommodation with assessment is related to the larger efforts of inclusion and is intended to bring more students into mainstream educational experiences, be fair to all students, and demonstrate school accountability. Abedi and colleagues (2000) propose several possible advantages to assessment accommodations that are associated with efforts at inclusion:

- Inclusion provides a more accurate picture of overall student achievement and growth.
- Inclusion may provide individual diagnostic information available to parents of accommodated students, their teachers, and school administrators.
- Inclusion may allow for specific policies and funding to improve the performance of accommodated students.
- Inclusion can provide evidence that particular students have demonstrated progress and, in the case of ELs, demonstrate their development from this initial designation.

The assessment accommodations that we make for our students must have the goal of providing useful information. When accommodation is done well, the assessment is changed to accommodate the special needs and characteristics of students, yet it remains valid and reliable. It provides useful assessment information. An ongoing challenge for those considering a specific accommodation is to "validly combine assessment and accommodation" (Stretch & Osborne, 2005, p. 1).

Accommodation is done to level the playing field for all students who take a particular reading assessment. Special needs are addressed in order to allow the student to demonstrate his or her reading ability, unimpeded by the format and nature of the assessment. Without accommodation, particular reading assessment materials and procedures will not yield accurate accounts of some students' reading ability. For example, a student who is capable of demonstrating full comprehension of text but needs more time than is allotted in a standardized test may have test results that describe a student who cannot comprehend at grade level. Here, an accommodation of more time to take the test will result in a more accurate representation of the student's ability because the accommodation conditions meet the student's need for extra time. Further, without accommodation, many students are shut out of consequential assessment experiences (National Center for Education Statistics, 2010). These students are not accounted for in a school's overall achievements, which can have profound effects when schools, districts, and states contemplate their instructional priorities and funding. Having not taken a test, unaccommodated and excluded students may be unaccounted for in these decisions.

The attention to students with accommodation needs necessitates the development of a knowledge base that helps inform our accommodation processes. There is promising work (e.g., Abedi et al., 2000) that can help us determine how and when particular accommodations meet the elusive standard of changing the student–assessment interaction without changing the information yielded by the assessment. Yet, there remains much work to be done to fully understand the consequences of assessment accommodation on both students' assessment performances and students' overall development in school. A major purpose of accommodation is gathering useful assessment information. A goal for accommodation is what Phillips (1994) refers to as the differential boost. Here, the assessment accommodation lifts the performance of special-needs students more than it does the performance of students without disabilities. As such, the term *differential boost* describes an accommodation that helps the intended student while not penalizing other students.

Zuriff's (2000) maximum potential thesis posits that unaccommodated students are at their maximum level of performance when they work within the time limits of standardized tests, and accommodated students perform significantly higher on untimed tests than on tests with the standardized time allotment. Yet, many students benefit from extra time (Abedi et al., 2000), whether or not they are deemed legally eligible for extra time accommodations. This raises the issue of "timedness" and why it is an enduring feature of almost all standardized, high-stakes tests of reading. Is timed performance more important than optimal performance? If so, why? The very consideration of accommodation—in this case, the timed or untimed nature of assessment—can lead us to examine assumptions that underlie our testing and assessment for all students. If we are interested in how we can construct assessment scenarios that allow students to perform to their full potential, then we should examine assessment conditions for all students.

Accommodation must be practiced in all forms of reading assessment. Although the limited research literature on accommodation of ELs focuses on tests, each and every act of assessment should be examined for how accommodation might change, influence, and better those acts. Consider that RTI includes four types of assessment: screening, diagnostic, progress monitoring, and outcome measuring. Each deserves our scrutiny, and as noted by Brown and Sanford (2011),

> Regardless of the tools for screening and progress monitoring used within an RTI model with ELLs, these tools' effectiveness will depend significantly on the ability of educators to develop a level of expertise and proficiency in their use along with skill in investigating each child's experiential, linguistic, and cultural background—the very components that form the context within which plans must be made for appropriate instruction and intervention. (p. 19)

A related issue is how we conceptualize and care for our students. We know that continued accommodation of students may create dependencies in students' present and future lives: in the workplace, at home, and in the community. We also know that many students not designated as being entitled to accommodation do better with it. I believe that this set of issues is best addressed as teachers work to develop consistent and dependable approaches to accommodation for their students. Accommodations can be developmental in nature. For example, in our unit tests and classroom questioning, we can adjust the wait time that we provide to students who answer our questions, in effect providing the most appropriate time frame for students to think and learn. Additionally, the developmental trajectory that is expected of our students involves increased speed of doing things, such as using strategies quickly and then automatic skills, and this fact must be taken into account. Yet, if we are interested in first determining that our students can do things and then determining how quickly these things can be done, then we have created a basis and rationale for providing accommodation for any student in our classroom, as our careful ongoing assessment signals.

Accommodation for Learning Disabled Students

The most common accommodations for learning disabled students include extended time to take the test, reading the test aloud to the student, providing a scribe to take dictation from a student, paraphrasing test instructions and contents, and testing in small groups (Olson, Mead, & Payne, 2002). Specific types of assessment accommodations for these students include where the assessment takes place, when it is given, the setting of the assessment, how assessment materials are presented, the time provided to take the assessment, the assessment materials, and how students respond and interact with the assessment. Several sources (Council for Exceptional Children, 2000; Olson et al., 2002) provide helpful guidelines for accommodation, which are detailed later in this chapter. These guidelines focus on standardized testing situations rather than daily, teacher-conducted reading assessments. Nevertheless, the guidelines can help us as we consider accommodations with a variety of assessments.

First, accommodations may focus on the physical space in which the assessment takes place, such as preferential seating, a separate location, or a specialized setting. Preferential seating can accommodate students with vision and hearing needs, including the ability to accurately see, hear, and understand proctor assessment instructions and directions, and sample items. Preferential seating or a separate assessment location may be provided to students who are more easily distracted than others, and a specialized setting can be tailored to the specific needs of the individual student. For example, a student with vision needs may be seated in a brightly lit area of the classroom and receive large-print instructions in order to better see and read the assessment directions and questions.

Second, the accommodations may include modification of a single-session assessment to one that is broken up over several sessions, a reordering of particular sections of the assessment, or the specific time of day at which a student takes the assessment. In each case, the scheduling accommodation is done in relation to the student's needs, which may be related to a shorter-than-normal attention span or the need for success early in an assessment to motivate continued performance at later stages of the assessment. (Many computer-adaptive tests are already structured to promote this early success for all students.) Scheduling an assessment at an alternate time can accommodate a student who is known to be more on task at certain times of the school day.

Third, the presentation of assessment materials can be accommodated in a variety of ways, including offering different audio and visual versions of the assessment, reading the assessment items and assessment directions aloud, rereading the directions, providing cues, offering prompts to the students, responding to students' clarification questions, supplying templates and markers, securing students' papers and other work materials to the desk or work area, and providing magnifying and amplification devices. Different editions of an assessment can include Braille and large print, as well as answer sheets with large prompt and response formats (for standardized testing) or fewer items per page. Reading aloud both the assessment content and the directions to students alleviates the need for them to do so themselves. A special caveat is that reading the content of the test (e.g., reading aloud to the student the text and subsequent items) will transform a reading test into a listening test and seriously compromise the validity and reliability of the test.

Fourth, in regard to time, assessment can be accommodated through the provision of breaks within the assessment to help students who may have difficulty maintaining concentration. A second time-related accommodation is the provision of extended time to undertake and complete an assessment for students who work at a slower pace than others. In both cases, it is hoped that the time accommodation does not change the requirements of the assessment while providing students with an adequate time frame to meet the demands of the assessment. For example, the skills and strategies that students need for constructing meaning do not change, but students are given more time in which to use them.

Providing cues to students is another form of presentation accommodation, in which particular features in the assessment are highlighted. Rereading directions to students accommodates those who may not understand and remember assessment directions the first time. Prompts to students may have them continue with the assessment, pause, or rest, as indicated by the particular student's needs. Clarification accommodations mean that a teacher can answer students' questions about the assessment or give extra examples to illustrate the assessment materials and procedures. In addition, templates, or cutouts that provide a barrier to viewing all the information on an assessment, can be used to accommodate students who may be distracted by the sheer amount of print on the assessment or by a particular graphic layout. Markers, such as a plastic chip, can be used to help students keep place on an assessment. Students who may be challenged by the amount of paper involved with an assessment can have their work secured to their desks. A final accommodation of the presentation of assessment relates to the magnification of printed information or the amplification of spoken information. For example, students who have vision challenges can use magnifying glasses, and students with hearing problems can use hearing aids.

Finally, how students respond, or the response format in assessment accommodation, can vary in relation to how students use their assessment booklets, the verbal and written responses, writing instruments, reference materials, and technology. Students who cannot clearly mark and write in their assessment papers can have those answers and responses transcribed by an adult or may respond verbally to questions. The paper and pencils that students use can be modified so that students who have difficulty writing can manage with pencil grips, and those with difficulty transferring their thoughts to paper can have special paper with structured sections or more space between the lines for writing. When students are responsible for writing in relation to their reading, spelling can be an obstacle that prevents clear communication of thought. Thus, special-needs students may use spell checkers and dictionaries to help them. Further, some students may be challenged to write with paper and pen or pencil but able to write using a computer keyboard and word-processing program. Students may also be accommodated by being permitted to point to answers when testing involves multiple-choice items.

Accommodations for ELs

ELs benefit from accommodations, which may include extra time to take the assessment, linguistic modification of assessment items (i.e., making the language of the assessment more easily understood), and other language-specific accommodations, such as a glossary of key terms or translation of text. Abedi, Lord, and Plummer (1997) examined ELs' performance on short and long items from the NAEP and found that they had more difficulty with longer items because of the items' higher language demand. Also, the ELs' performance was low on items judged to be linguistically complex. Abedi and colleagues (2000) examined ELs as they took tests under different conditions that included the specific accommodations of extra time to take the test, a glossary of key concepts on the test, both extra time and the glossary of key concepts, and linguistic modification, or reducing the complexity of language in the test questions. The single accommodation that reduced the gap in test scores between EL and non-EL students was linguistic modification.

Linguistic modification is aimed at making the complexity of assessment language less of a factor in student performance in an assessment. It is important that the language of an assessment question is not more difficult than the anticipated response and that our means of eliciting student participation and response is straightforward and stripped of any unnecessarily difficult words. Linguistic modification results from analyzing the language we use in assessment situations and working to simplify that language so that it still carries meaning but may be more accessible to more students. Consider, for example, the following multiple-choice question, with the correct answer and distracters:

What word does the author utilize to describe how Elizabeth feels at the party?

A. Dizzy

B. Ecstatic

C. Frantic

D. Solemn

The prompt, or question, has a complex sentence structure and relatively difficult vocabulary. If the question's intended focus is on a vocabulary word that tells about the character's feeling, then the question might be linguistically modified as "What word describes how Elizabeth feels at the party?"

The revised version of the question is less complex and more straightforward and will have the probable result of confusing fewer students. Of course, linguistic modification is a valuable strategy to apply to all of our assessments for all of our students. Assessment tasks, items, and prompts can vary in difficulty, according to the student thinking and learning that we seek to describe. (For a discussion of how our questions can vary in complexity, see Chapter 3.) The value of linguistic modification is that it acts as a check on assessment language that is unnecessarily complex and convoluted. An important caveat is that the complexity of the questions we ask should always be intentional and gauged to the type of thinking and response we are seeking. Thus, we should be vigilant that our attempts at linguistic modification do not change the nature of the information and the indication of learning that we seek from students.

Fairbairn (2007) advocates test preparation as a form of accommodation for ELs. Students so designated may be recent arrivals in the United States and unfamiliar with the materials and procedures of high-stakes testing. Fairbairn notes, "Familiarizing students with the format of the test or of test questions is not 'cheating;' rather, it is creating the possibility for the test scores to more accurately reflect student abilities" (p. 4). Appropriate test preparation can help students build schemata for these influential assessments, on which many consequential decisions are made.

The accommodations here are intended to make testing more familiar for ELs. The accommodations may include reviewing sample test items and sections with students, explaining how and why tests are formatted, and explaining how multiple-choice questions work. This last item involves teaching students that there should be one best answer and that there may be distracters that are legitimate but not the best answers. In essence, this approach to accommodation treats high-stakes tests and testing procedures as potentially unfamiliar materials and procedures that students must learn.

Accommodation With Classroom-Based Assessments in Stephen's 10th-Grade Classroom

Accommodation With Standardized and Summative High-Stakes Tests

In Stephen's experience, accommodation of assessment is most often undertaken with high-stakes, standardized tests. This is important, as highly consequential decisions are made based on the results of these tests. Standardized tests are just that: standardized. Accommodation in testing undoes the standardization because it violates the premise that all students are treated the same while taking the test. The means to derive raw scores, standardized scores, and percentile rankings on these tests are based on piloting that adheres to strict standardization criteria. Stephen pays close attention to the tests and testing procedures that his students take part in. This provides him with information about how well particular accommodations are working for particular students and about students who are not accommodated in testing situations but struggle nevertheless. In the past, Stephen's vigilance has helped him identify several students who were not designated ELs but had little or no experience with standardized testing. This identification allowed him to provide these students with lessons intended to familiarize the students with tests. In addition, he has determined that numerous students perform well in class, where designated time limits are flexible, as opposed to the shorter time frame demanded of the standardized test.

In efforts to be fair to all of his students, Stephen must ascertain that unaccommodated students are not being treated unfairly. For example, while an accommodated student receives extra time in which to take a test, as designated in his or her IEP, Stephen is concerned that other students without such IEPs are not allowed to receive such accommodation. Most students benefit from extra time on high-stakes assessments (Zuriff, 2000), but only some students, as designated in their IEPs, have the legal right to extra time. Stephen's examination of his students and the accommodations that are required by law allow him to check on the nature of his teaching and assessment. Because accommodation forces us to face the important issue of why certain students should receive special treatment, it is often the case that we may determine that special treatment is deserved by all students. An important question to ask of any possible accommodation is, Does the proposed accommodation eliminate unfairness in assessment, or does it move it around among all of the students? Stephen must be vigilant in his efforts to advocate for accommodation when it is clearly indicated while paying attention to how one accommodation may introduce bias and unfairness to another student or group of students.

Accommodation With Classroom-Based Formative Assessments

Throughout the school year, Stephen conducts formative assessments to help him plan his instruction, gauge the effectiveness of ongoing lessons, and provide feedback to his students. Accommodation in the context of his formative assessments is geared to supplying him with immediately useful information and accompanied by a special series of issues. Stephen uses the principle of linguistic modification across the school day. He conducts task analyses of his questions and prompts, looking for language that may prove too challenging for his students, language that might get in the way of thinking and appropriate responses. In addition to the task analysis, he carefully monitors the assessments he uses. He is vigilant in his observations of how an assessment works, or does not work as planned, with his diverse students. He drafts the questions he asks students and then revises them as needed. He rephrases assessments that he believes are posing a problem to his students, not because of the students' inability to answer but because of the wording of the question or prompt. The linguistic modification is possible because Stephen continually questions his questions and conducts task analyses of the assessment language he uses.

Stephen teaches four sections of science each day. His students include several special-needs students who have IEPs: students who are newly arrived in the United States and have little spoken English and limited reading experience. His classes present a multitude of student diversities that demand his attention. Throughout the school year, Stephen strives to accommodate the needs of all of his students. This means he regularly consults the IEPs of his special education students and considers the language issues of his ELs, along with his knowledge of the other students in his classroom.

A large responsibility here is the time and effort needed to combine knowledge of students, their assessment history, and their needs for accommodation. Those students designated as learning disabled, ELs, or both have clear accommodation for the high-stakes testing that is conducted in the state and school district. As students prepare to take these tests, Stephen helps them by providing practice in test taking with the particular accommodations that the students will have. These accommodations include additional time to take the reading test, timed breaks between sections, and repeating instructions and directions that are not well understood by students in the first place. Stephen also believes that test preparation should involve activities that familiarize students with the materials and procedures of testing. Those students who are new to the school, district, and country sometimes lack any experience with tests, and Stephen accommodates this lack of prior knowledge of tests for any student who demonstrates this unfamiliarity.

Stephen amends Abedi and colleagues' (2000) four factors for accommodating ELs. Stephen uses them to consider how he might help any and all students who demonstrate a clear need for accommodation in classroom assessment in relation to validity, effectiveness, differential impact, and feasibility. The four points are addressed by the following questions:

1. Does provision of accommodation alter the construct of the assessment? (validity)

2. What accommodation strategies would be the most effective in reducing performance gaps between ELs and non-EL students that are due to language factors? (effectiveness)

3. Which student background characteristics influence accommodated assessment? (differential impact)

4. Which accommodations are more feasible, particularly in large-scale assessments? (feasibility)

Classroom-based reading assessment offers Stephen an opportunity to further his efforts in inclusion. He believes that many of his students will benefit from accommodations to his classroom assessment, and he is intent on providing specific accommodations when they contribute to students' assessment performance and provide him with useful information. Thus, his classroom-based reading assessment is diagnostic not only of students' developing skills, strategies, and mind-sets but also of how particular assessments tell or do not tell a detailed story of students' reading achievement.

Consequences and Usefulness of Assessment Accommodation

Stephen conducts reading assessments so that he may best teach his students. It follows that he must attend to the needs of all of his students. These needs include becoming a better reader as well as assessment accommodation to obtain useful information to help students become better readers. At the heart of accommodation in assessment is attention to the individual differences that students bring to our classrooms, to learning, and to participating in our assessments. We expect accommodation to be a prominent theme when we assess special-needs students and ELs. Most often there are subgroups of students who have a legal designation as learning disabled and whose IEPs specify and require accommodations according to federal law. Groups of ELs may also have mandated or suggested accommodations for reading tests, although this can vary widely depending on the state in which students live.

Stephen wants all of his students to show their best possible performances on assessments, and he focuses on those accommodations that help students do so. He is concerned about students who lack the designation of learning disabled or EL but have clear challenges during assessment situations. The nervous test taker and the slow (but not slow enough to gain special-needs status) processor are students who lack official support for accommodation but deserve it.

Roles and Responsibilities Related to Accommodation

Knowing all of his students' accommodation needs is a challenging task for Stephen. He regularly uses the guidelines for accommodation that are mandated for some of his students and beneficial for others. That is, he accommodates individual students regardless of their classification as learning disabled or EL so that his assessments provide valuable information that is worthy of the assessment effort. This is most prominent in the time frame of an assessment. Stephen first wants to know if his students can successfully complete assessment tasks and then whether his students can do the tasks under specific time constraints.

Stephen makes sure to conduct his classroom-based reading assessments in relation to his knowledge of each and every student. He needs to know if his students can do something more than he needs to know if they can do it in a short time frame. This has positive consequences, as Stephen may provide more time to students working toward mastery or provide clarification to students who do not fully understand an assessment request or demand. Thus, he views assessment accommodation in his daily classroom routines as closely connected to his understanding of individual students' development and a matter of fairness to all students.

Stephen's second set of responsibilities is to the reliability and validity of his assessments. As much as he strives to accommodate his students, he knows that inappropriate accommodation can render assessment results unusable. His inferences about student reading achievement may not be supportable when the assessment providing information is changed drastically. Thus, Stephen continually performs a balancing act in which his students' needs are balanced against his need for useful assessment information.

Reliability of Accommodation

The reliability of assessment is a paramount concern whenever accommodation is used. Recall that reliability focuses on the consistency, trustworthiness, and fairness of an assessment. Whatever our intentions and the goodwill that surround our efforts to accommodate students, we must remember that accommodation results in a change, subtle or overt, of assessment. As Sireci (2004) notes,

> In many testing situations, accommodations to standard testing conditions are given to SWD [students with disabilities] to improve measurement of their knowledge, skills, and abilities. This practice is in the pursuit of more valid test score interpretation; however, it produces the ultimate psychometric oxymoron—an accommodated standardized test. (p. 4)

Stephen's efforts to accommodate his students' individual needs are guided by his obligation to not put other students at a disadvantage. He considers the following information from the *Standards for Educational and Psychological Testing* (American Educational Research Association, American Psychological Association, & National

Council on Measurement in Education, 1999) to be important advice for both the summative and formative classroom-based assessments he conducts:

> While test takers should not be disadvantaged due to a disability not relevant to the construct the test is intended to assess, the resulting accommodation should not put those taking a modified test at an undue advantage over those tested under regular conditions. (p. 105)

Stephen does not want to be caught in an endless cycle of adjusting assessments to help some students only to find that it places other students at a disadvantage. He uses the concept of differential boost (Phillips, 1994) and the maximum potential thesis (Zuriff, 2000) to guide his thinking, and it turns out these are valuable but often difficult criteria to meet. For example, Stephen is comfortable providing extra time to students who need extra time to do their best work, and this provision is included in the IEPs of several of his students. Yet, there is a considerable number of students who do better work when given more time even though these students are not accommodated by law. Stephen appreciates that laws designate particular services and accommodations according to students' documented needs. However, he has trouble with the idea that students in the "undesignated middle" are not considered for accommodation.

At the same time, Stephen is required to provide the sameness of experience to students taking standardized, high-stakes tests. He knows that circumventing the standardization procedures will reduce the inferences that can be made from assessment results. Thus, his classroom is marked by two approaches to accommodation. The first is legally required and mandated, and it applies to the high-stakes tests that his students must take each year. The second approach is practiced throughout the year and in relation to the many assessments that Stephen conducts in the classroom. Here, he has no qualms about repeating assessment prompts to help students gain clarity on the specific demands of the assessments, nor does he withhold extra time from those students who achieve more when given extra time.

The reliability of assessment is influenced by the accommodation. With high-stakes, standardized tests, Stephen provides those accommodations that are prescribed for learning disabled students and ELs. Although he regularly questions the policy of having abrupt cutoff points beyond which many students do not receive any accommodation, he respects the fact that the test results are less helpful if reliability criteria are not met. Stephen conducts classroom assessments and is ready to shape the assessment task so that it gets him useful information for his instruction while accommodating each and every student.

With formative assessments, he is continually looking to gather information that can inform instruction—that updates his mental model of the student and describes areas of achievement and need. Stephen's standard for reliability of assessment here is different than for standardized tests. That is, if his reading assessment processes and results yield instructionally helpful information, then he is willing to modify the assessment. For example, when he wants to know that students can ably summarize chapters or articles, he rephrases or repeats an assessment prompt or question. He allows extra time for students who need it. He scrutinizes the clarity of the assessment demand and the time frame in which students are expected to meet the demand. This results in an accurate and reliable account of his students' achievement.

Validity of Accommodation

Stephen approaches validity in assessment with three related goals. First, he wants to be fair to all of his students. Second, he wants the assessment to be worthwhile and considers how accommodations may help him realize this goal. Third, he wants to be faithful to the assessment and the construct that it is supposed to measure. He is sensitive to how certain accommodations change assessment and validity. For example, reading a text to students and then asking them comprehension questions is an accommodation that changes a reading test into a listening test. Although both are receptive and related language acts, reading and listening are different constructs. Stephen is also sensitive to the fact that while accommodation is of potential help to students in the present, their future within and outside of school may be one that is not so accommodating of them. Thus, he works with students and their parents to consider long-term goals.

Central to this approach is understanding how accommodation works in relation to both assessment and students' reading development. Stephen knows that listening comprehension is related to, but different from, reading comprehension. Thus, he reads texts and questions to certain students with the knowledge that he is assessing listening, not reading. He is sensitive to the observation that test accommodation typically demands a delicate balance: Standardized tests have psychometric needs for validity, just as accommodated students have needs that are met through accommodation.

Summary

In summary, there are means of accommodating special-needs students and ELs. Ongoing and systematic investigation of these well-intentioned proposals should help create a research base that informs our use of particular accommodations. Appropriate accommodation helps students give us their best in assessment situations. As we endeavor to include and teach the diverse learners in our classrooms, assessment accommodation is warranted. Would that it were so simple! In making accommodations, we must be certain that all students continue to be treated fairly and that one type of accommodation does not have the unintended consequence of placing other students at a disadvantage. Accommodation is also complex and time-consuming, adding to the already considerable assessment tasks of classroom teachers. Our work with assessment accommodation should be energized by two facts: Accommodation represents our best efforts to treat all students fairly, and accommodation done well yields truly useful assessment information.

ENHANCING YOUR UNDERSTANDING

1. Identify an assessment routine, item, or procedure that is in need of revision in relation to accommodation of a particular student's needs. Conduct a task analysis that focuses on how accommodation is needed and the nature of the accommodation to be made.

2. Reflect on your current assessment routines. Do you make conscious or unconscious accommodations for particular students in your classroom? What is the basis for making these accommodations? Are these accommodations in the spirit of making the assessment fair while maintaining the validity and reliability of the assessment? What are the possible intended and unintended outcomes of your accommodation practices?

3. Analyze your questions and other reading assessment language. Identify language that may be too difficult or confusing for some of your students. Try to simplify the language and develop a plan for keeping track of how you do this.

4. Pay attention to how you may accommodate different students in your classroom. Keep a journal of how you come to understand students' individual differences, how you conceptualize them into accommodation, and how you accommodate these students, whether or not they have a legal determination for accommodation.

Confounds in Reading Assessment

Confounds in assessment occur when unidentified and unanticipated factors influence students' performance on an assessment. If confounds are present in reading assessment, our account of a student's true achievement may be inaccurate. We may make erroneous inferences about students' reading achievement because the assessment is influenced by factors other than students' reading ability.

Consider an assessment that requires a student to read and understand a U.S. Civil War–era history text as a prerequisite for a performance. Based on his or her understanding of the text, the student is to create a historical skit that reflects understanding of historical characters' attitudes and beliefs and present the skit to the class. Although this task promises an authentic assessment opportunity to observe how students use information learned from reading the history text, we must examine how confounds might influence our interpretation or misinterpretation of students' reading achievement. First, the student must be able to construct meaning from the text, which contains numerous references to people, places, and events. The student must also be an accomplished note taker, recording information from the text related to historical figures, their interactions, the nature of society during the Civil War, and other details that may be useful in the skit. The student must apply knowledge learned from the text to develop ideas for the skit. Next, the student must be an able writer, for this allows the transcription of knowledge gained through reading into notes and then the written text of the historical skit.

Once the skit is written, edited, and polished, the student is required to present it. Here, the student's public performance ability will influence our interpretation of achievement. The shy student who is uncomfortable in front of classmates may stumble through the skit, but the gregarious student eagerly performs his or her skit for the class. Both students read the history text and established comparable levels of understanding, but the manner of assessment introduces confounds in what is assessed.

The confounds that may arise in assessment should not be a deterrent to complex assessments. Rather, our insights into how reading fits with complex performances allows us to focus on the reading component and design appropriate assessments, while also focusing on the fact that we need to ask students to read and use that which they comprehend. In relation to the above scenario, a performance assessment could include a pure measure of reading comprehension, such as questions that require constructed responses that allow students to demonstrate what they have comprehended. The assessment might also include a checklist for note-taking that reminds students about the type of information that is useful for their purposes. Combined, these assessments enhance our faith in the conclusions we draw from them, fully aware of the confounds.

REFERENCES

Aarnoutse, C., & Schellings, G. (2003). Learning reading strategies by triggering reading motivation. *Educational Studies, 29*(4), 387–409. doi:10.1080/0305569032000159688

Abedi, J., Lord, C., Hofstetter, C., & Baker, E. (2000). Impact of accommodation strategies on English language learners' test performance. *Educational Measurement: Issues and Practice, 19*(3), 16–26. doi:10.1111/j.1745-3992.2000.tb00034.x

Abedi, J., Lord, C., & Plummer, J.R. (1997). *Final report of language background as a variable in NAEP mathematics performance* (CSE Technical Report No. 429). Los Angeles: Center for the Study of Evaluation, National Center for Research on Evaluation, Standards, and Student Testing, University of California, Los Angeles.

Afflerbach, P. (1985). *The statewide assessment of writing.* Princeton, NJ: Educational Testing Service.

Afflerbach, P. (Ed.). (1990). *Issues in statewide reading assessment.* Washington, DC: American Institutes for Research.

Afflerbach, P. (2002a). Teaching reading self-assessment strategies. In C.C. Block & M. Pressley (Eds.), *Comprehension instruction: Research-based best practices* (pp. 96–111). New York: Guilford.

Afflerbach, P. (2002b). The road to folly and redemption: Perspectives on the legitimacy of high-stakes testing. *Reading Research Quarterly, 37*(3), 348–360. doi:10.1598/RRQ.37.3.5

Afflerbach, P. (2005). National Reading Conference policy brief: High stakes testing and reading assessment. *Journal of Literacy Research, 37*(2), 151–162. doi:10.1207/s15548430jlr3702_2

Afflerbach, P., & Cho, B. (2009). Identifying and describing constructively responsive comprehension strategies in new and traditional forms of reading. In S.E. Israel & G.G. Duffy (Eds.), *Handbook of research on reading comprehension* (pp. 69–90). New York: Routledge.

Afflerbach, P.P., & Cho, B. (2010). The classroom assessment of reading. In M.L. Kamil, P.D. Pearson, E.B. Moje, & P.P. Afflerbach (Eds.), *Handbook of reading research* (Vol. 4, pp. 487–514). New York: Routledge.

Afflerbach, P., Cho, B., & Kim, J. (2011). The assessment of higher order thinking in reading. In G. Schraw & D.H. Robinson (Eds.), *Assessment of higher order thinking skills* (pp. 185–218). Charlotte, NC: Information Age.

Afflerbach, P., Cho, B., Kim, J., & Clark, S. (2010). Classroom assessment of literacy. In D. Wyse, R. Andrews, & J. Hoffman (Eds.), *The Routledge international handbook of English, language and literacy teaching* (pp. 401–412). New York: Routledge.

Afflerbach, P.P., Cho, B., Kim, J., & Crassas, M.E. (2011, April). *Toward a reconceptualization of individual differences in reading.* Paper presented at the annual meeting of the American Educational Research Association, New Orleans, LA.

Afflerbach, P., & Meuwissen, K. (2005). Teaching and learning self-assessment strategies in middle school. In S.E. Israel, C.C. Block, K.L. Bauserman, & K. Kinnucan-Welsch (Eds.), *Metacognition in literacy learning: Theory, assessment, instruction, and professional development* (pp. 141–164). Mahwah, NJ: Erlbaum.

Afflerbach, P., Pearson, P.D., & Paris, S.G. (2008). Clarifying differences between reading skills and reading strategies. *The Reading Teacher, 61*(5), 364–373. doi:10.1598/RT.61.5.1

Afflerbach, P., & VanSledright, B. (2001). Hath! Doth! What? Middle graders reading innovative history text. *Journal of Adolescent & Adult Literacy, 44*(8), 696–707.

Airasian, P.W. (1991). *Classroom assessment.* New York: McGraw-Hill.

Alexander, P.A. (2005). The path to competence: A lifespan developmental perspective on reading. *Journal of Literacy Research, 37*(4), 413–436. doi:10.1207/s15548430jlr3704_1

Allington, R.L. (1983). The reading instruction provided readers of differing reading abilities. *The Elementary School Journal, 83*(5), 548–559. doi:10.1086/461333

American Educational Research Association, American Psychological Association, & National Council on Measurement in Education. (1999). *Standards for educational and psychological testing*. Washington, DC: American Educational Research Association.

Anderson, L.W., & Bourke, S.F. (2000). *Assessing affective characteristics in the schools* (2nd ed.). Mahwah, NJ: Erlbaum.

Anderson, R.C., & Pearson, P.D. (1984). A schema-theoretic view of basic processes in reading comprehension. In P.D. Pearson, R. Barr, M.L. Kamil, & P. Mosenthal (Eds.), *Handbook of reading research* (pp. 255–291). White Plains, NY: Longman.

Andrade, H.G. (2000). Using rubrics to promote thinking and learning. *Educational Leadership*, 57(5), 13–18.

Athey, I. (1985). Reading research in the affective domain. In H. Singer & R.B. Ruddell (Eds.), *Theoretical models and processes of reading* (3rd ed., pp. 527–557). Newark, DE: International Reading Association.

Au, K.H. (1994). Portfolio assessment: Experiences at the Kamehameha Elementary Education Program. In S.W. Valencia, E.H. Hiebert, & P.P. Afflerbach (Eds.), *Authentic reading assessment: Practices and possibilities* (pp. 103–126). Newark, DE: International Reading Association.

Austin, T. (1994). *Changing the view: Student-led parent conferences*. Portsmouth, NH: Heinemann.

Bailey, J.M., & Guskey, T.R. (2001). *Implementing student-led conferences*. Thousand Oaks, CA: Corwin.

Baker, D.L., Cummings, K.D., Good, R.H., & Smolkowski, K. (2007). *Indicadores dinámicos del éxito en la lectura* [Dynamic indicators of success in reading] *(IDEL®): Summary of decision rules for intensive, strategic, and benchmark instructional recommendations in kindergarten through third grade* (Technical Report No. 1). Eugene, OR: Dynamic Measurement Group.

Baxter, G.P., & Glaser, R. (1998). Investigating the cognitive complexity of science assessments. *Educational Measurement: Issues and Practice*, 17(3), 37–45. doi:10.1111/j.1745-3992.1998.tb00627.x

Beck, I.L., McKeown, M.G., Hamilton, R.L., & Kucan, L. (1997). *Questioning the author: An approach for enhancing student engagement with text*. Newark, DE: International Reading Association.

Beck, I.L., McKeown, M.G., & Kucan, L. (2002). *Bringing words to life: Robust vocabulary instruction*. New York: Guilford.

Berkeley, S., Mastopieri, M.A., & Scruggs, T.E. (2011). Reading comprehension strategy instruction and attribution retraining for secondary students with learning and other mild disabilities. *Journal of Learning Disabilities*, 44(1), 18–32. doi:10.1177/0022219410371677

Berliner, D.C., & Biddle, B.J. (1995). *The manufactured crisis: myths, fraud, and the attack on America's public schools*. Cambridge, MA: Perseus.

Betts, E.A. (1946). *Foundations of reading instruction, with emphasis on differentiated guidance*. New York: American.

Black, P., & Wiliam, D. (1998). Inside the black box: Raising standards through classroom assessment. *Phi Delta Kappan*, 80(2), 139–144.

Block, C.C., & Pressley, M. (2002). *Comprehension instruction: Research-based best practices*. New York: Guilford.

Bloom, B.S. (Ed.). (1956). *Taxonomy of educational objectives: The classification of educational goals. Handbook 1: Cognitive domain*. New York: David McKay.

Boekaerts, M., & Corno, L. (2005). Self-regulation in the classroom: A perspective on assessment and intervention. *Applied Psychology*, 54(2), 199–231. doi:10.1111/j.1464-0597.2005.00205.x

Bracey, G.W. (2001). The 11th Bracey report on the condition of public education. *Phi Delta Kappan*, 83(2), 157–168.

Bråten, I., Strømsø, H.I., & Britt, M.A. (2009). Trust matters: Examining the role of source evaluation in students' construction of meaning within and across multiple texts. *Reading Research Quarterly*, 44(1), 6–28. doi:10.1598/RRQ.44.1.1

Brown, J.E., & Sanford, A. (2011). *RTI for English language learners: Appropriately using screening and progress monitoring tools to improve instructional outcomes*. Washington, DC: National Center on Response to Intervention, Office of Special Education Programs, U.S. Department of Education.

Brozo, W.G. (2011). *RTI and the adolescent reader: Responsive literacy instruction in secondary schools*. New York: Teachers College Press; Newark, DE: International Reading Association.

Brualdi, A. (1998). Implementing performance assessment in the classroom. *Practical Assessment, Research & Evaluation, 6*(2). Retrieved August 14, 2002, from pareonline.net/getvn.asp?v=6&n=2

California Department of Education. (1998). *English-language arts content standards for California public schools: Kindergarten through grade twelve.* Sacramento: Author. Retrieved June 21, 2011, from www.cde.ca.gov/be/st/ss/documents/elacontentstnds.pdf

Calkins, L., Montgomery, K., & Santman, D. (with Falk, B.). (1998). *A teacher's guide to standardized reading tests: Knowledge is power.* Portsmouth, NH: Heinemann.

Cazden, C.B. (1986). Classroom discourse. In Wittrock, M.C. (Ed.), *Handbook of research on teaching* (3rd ed., pp. 432–462). New York: Macmillan.

Chambliss, M.J., & Calfee, R.C. (1998). *Textbooks for learning: Nurturing children's minds.* Malden, MA: Blackwell.

Chapman, J.W., & Tunmer, W.E. (1995). Development of young children's reading self-concepts: An examination of emerging subcomponents and their relationship with reading achievement. *Journal of Educational Psychology, 87*(1), 154–167. doi:10.1037/0022-0663.87.1.154

Chapman, J.W., & Tunmer, W.E. (2003). Reading difficulties, reading-related self-perceptions, and strategies for overcoming negative self-beliefs. *Reading & Writing Quarterly, 19*(1), 5–24. doi:10.1080/10573560308205

Clay, M.M. (1979). *Reading: The patterning of complex behaviour* (2nd ed.). Portsmouth, NH: Heinemann.

Clay, M.M. (2000). *Running records for classroom teachers.* Portsmouth, NH: Heinemann.

Clay, M.M. (2002). *An observation survey of early literacy achievement* (2nd ed.). Portsmouth, NH: Heinemann.

Council for Exceptional Children. (2000). *Making assessment accommodations: A toolkit for educators.* Reston, VA: Author.

Council of Chief State School Officers & National Governors Association. (2010). *Common core standards for English language arts and literacy in history/social studies, science, and technical subjects.* Retrieved March 12, 2011, from www.corestandards.org/assets/CCSSI_ELA%20Standards.pdf

Crooks, T.J. (1988). The impact of classroom evaluation practices on students. *Review of Educational Research, 58*(4), 438–481.

Davis, A. (1998). *The limits of educational assessment.* Oxford, UK: Blackwell.

Deno, S.L., & Fuchs, L.S. (1987). Developing curriculum-based measurement systems for data-based special education problem solving. *Focus on Exceptional Children, 19*(8), 1–16.

Dorn, L.J., & Henderson, S.C. (2010). A comprehensive assessment system as a Response to Intervention process. In Johnston, P.H. (Ed.), *RTI in literacy: Responsive and comprehensive* (pp. 133–153). Newark, DE: International Reading Association.

Dreher, M.J., & Singer, H. (1985). Parents' attitudes toward reports of standardized reading test results. *The Reading Teacher, 38*(7), 624–632.

Durkin, D. (1978). What classroom observations reveal about reading comprehension instruction. *Reading Research Quarterly, 14*(4), 481–533. doi:10.1598/RRQ.14.4.2

Dweck, C.S. (1999). *Self-theories: Their role in motivation, personality, and development.* Philadelphia: Psychology.

Fairbairn, S. (2007). Facilitating greater test success for English language learners. *Practical Assessment, Research & Evaluation, 12*(11). Retrieved July 11, 2011, from pareonline.net/pdf/v12n11.pdf

Fletcher, J.M., Francis, D.J., Boudosquie, A., Copeland, K., Young, V., Kalinowski, S., et al. (2006). Effects of accommodations on high-stakes testing for students with reading disabilities. *Exceptional Children, 72*(2), 136.

Frederiksen, N. (1984). The real test bias: Influences of testing on teaching and learning. *American Psychologist, 39*(3), 193–202. doi:10.1037/0003-066X.39.3.193

Fuchs, D., & Fuchs, L.S. (2006). Introduction to Response to Intervention: What, why, and how valid is it? *Reading Research Quarterly, 41*(1), 93–99. doi:10.1598/RRQ.41.1.4

Gambrell, L.B., Codling, R.M., & Palmer, B.M. (1996). *Elementary students' motivation to read* (Reading Research Report No. 52). Athens, GA: National Reading Research Center.

Gamse, B.C., Jacob, R.T., Horst, M., Boulay, B., & Unlu, F. (2008). *Reading First Impact Study final report* (NCEE 2009-4038). Washington, DC: National Center for Education Evaluation and Regional Assistance, Institute of Education Sciences, U.S. Department of Education.

Gillingham, M.G., & Garner, R. (1992). Readers' comprehension of mazes embedded in expository texts. *The Journal of Educational Research, 85*(4), 234–241. doi:10.1080/00220671.1992.9941121

Goertz, M.E., Oláh, L.N., & Riggan, M. (2009). *Can interim assessments be used for instructional change?* (CPRE Policy Brief No. RB-51). Philadelphia: Consortium for Policy Research in Education.

Good, R.H., III, & Kaminski, R.A. (2002). *Dynamic indicators of basic early literacy skills* (6th ed.). Eugene, OR: Institute for the Development of Educational Achievement.

Good, R.H., III, & Kaminski, R.A. (with Cummings, K., Dufour-Martel, C., Petersen, K., Powell-Smith, K., et al.). (2011). *DIBELS® Next assessment manual.* Eugene, OR: Dynamic Measurement Group.

Goodman, K.S. (Ed.). (with Flurkey, A., Kato, T., Kamii, C., Manning, M., Seay, S., et al.). (2006). *The truth about DIBELS: What it is, what it does.* Portsmouth, NH: Heinemann.

Goodman, K.S., & Goodman, Y.M. (1977). Learning about psycholinguistic processes by analyzing oral reading. *Harvard Educational Review, 47*(3), 317–333.

Guszak, F.J. (1967). Teacher questioning and reading. *The Reading Teacher, 21*(3), 227–234.

Guthrie, J.T. (2001). Contexts for engagement and motivation in reading. *Reading Online, 4*(8). Retrieved July 13, 2011, from www.readingonline.org/articles/handbook/guthrie/

Guthrie, J.T., McGough, K., Bennett, L., & Rice, M.E. (1996). Concept-oriented reading instruction: An integrated curriculum to develop motivations and strategies for reading. In L. Baker, P. Afflerbach, & D. Reinking (Eds.), *Developing engaged readers in school and home communities* (pp. 165–190). Mahwah, NJ: Erlbaum.

Guthrie, J.T., & Wigfield, A. (1997). *Reading engagement: Motivating readers through integrated instruction.* Newark, DE: International Reading Association.

Guthrie, J.T., Wigfield, A., & You, W. (in press). Instructional contexts for engagement and achievement in reading. In S. Christensen, A. Reschly, & C. Wylie (Eds.), *Handbook of research on student engagement.* New York: Springer Science.

Hamilton, L.S., Stecher, B.M., & Klein, S.P. (Eds.). (2002). *Making sense of test-based accountability in education.* Santa Monica, CA: RAND.

Harris, T.L., & Hodges, R.E. (Eds.). (1995). *The literacy dictionary: The vocabulary of reading and writing.* Newark, DE: International Reading Association.

Hart, B., & Risley, T.R. (1995). *Meaningful differences in the everyday experience of young American children.* Baltimore: Paul H. Brookes.

Heath, S.B. (1983). *Ways with words: Language, life, and work in communities and classrooms.* New York: Cambridge University Press.

Hebert, E.A. (1998). Lessons learned about student portfolios. *Phi Delta Kappan, 79*(8), 583–585.

Hiebert, E.H., Winograd, P.N., & Danner, F.W. (1984). Children's attributions for failure and success in different aspects of reading. *Journal of Educational Psychology, 76*(6), 1139–1148. doi:10.1037/0022-0663.76.6.1139

Hildebrandt, D. (2001). "But there's nothing good to read" (in the library media center). *Media Spectrum: The Journal for Library Media Specialists in Michigan, 28*, 34–37.

Huey, E.B. (1908). *The psychology and pedagogy of reading, with a review of the history of reading and writing and of methods, texts, and hygiene in reading.* New York: Macmillan.

International Reading Association. (1999). *High-stakes assessments in reading: A position statement of the International Reading Association.* Newark, DE: Author.

International Reading Association & National Council of Teachers of English. (1996). *Standards for the English language arts.* Newark, DE; Urbana, IL: Authors.

Jamentz, K. (1994). Making sure that assessment improves performance. *Educational Leadership, 51*(6), 55–57.

Johnston, P. (1987). Teachers as evaluation experts. *The Reading Teacher, 40*(8), 744–748.

Johnston, P., Afflerbach, P., Krist, S., Pierce, K.M., Spalding, E., Tatum, A.W., et al. (2010). *Standards for the assessment of reading and writing* (Rev. ed.). Newark, DE: International Reading Association; Urbana, IL: National Council of Teachers of English.

Johnston, P.H. (2004). *Choice words: How our language affects children's learning.* Portland, ME: Stenhouse.

Johnston, P.H. (2010). *RTI in literacy: Responsive and comprehensive.* Newark, DE: International Reading Association.

Johnston, P.H., Afflerbach, P., & Weiss, P.B. (1993). Teachers' assessment of the teaching and learning of literacy. *Educational Assessment, 1*(2), 91–117. doi:10.1207/s15326977ea0102_1

Johnston, P.H., & Winograd, P.N. (1985). Passive failure in reading. *Journal of Reading, 17*(4), 279–301.

Kerlinger, F.N. (1986). *Foundations of behavioral research* (3rd ed.). New York: Holt, Rinehart and Winston.

Kimball, M. (2003). *The Web portfolio guide: Creating electronic portfolios for the Web.* New York: Longman.

Kingore, B. (2008). *Developing portfolios for authentic assessment preK–3: Guiding potential in young learners.* Thousand Oaks, CA: Corwin.

Kober, N., Chudowsky, N., & Chudowsky, V. (2008). *Has student achievement increased since 2002? State test score trends through 2006–07.* Washington, DC: Center on Education Policy.

Koenig, J.A., & Bachman, L.F. (Eds.). (2004). *Keeping score for all: The effects of inclusion and accommodation policies on large-scale educational assessments.* Washington, DC: National Academies Press.

Kohn, A. (2000). *The case against standardized testing: Raising the scores, ruining the schools.* Portsmouth, NH: Heinemann.

Krathwohl, D.R. (2002). A revision of Bloom's taxonomy: An overview. *Theory into Practice, 41*(4), 212–218. doi:10.1207/s15430421tip4104_2

Kuhn, M.R., Schwanenflugel, P.J., & Meisinger, E.B. (2010). Aligning theory and assessment of reading fluency: Automaticity, prosody, and definitions of fluency. *Reading Research Quarterly, 45*(2), 230–251. doi:10.1598/RRQ.45.2.4

Lave, J., & Wenger, E. (1991). *Situated learning: Legitimate peripheral participation.* New York: Cambridge University Press.

Leipzig, D.H., & Afflerbach, P. (2000). Determining the suitability of assessments: Using the CURRV framework. In L. Baker, M.J. Dreher, & J.T. Guthrie (Eds.), *Engaging young readers: Promoting achievement and motivation* (pp. 159–187). New York: Guilford.

LeMahieu, P.G., Gitomer, D.H., & Eresh, J.A.T. (1995). Portfolios in large-scale assessment: Difficult but not impossible. *Educational Measurement: Issues and Practice, 14*(3), 11–16, 25–28. doi:10.1111/j.1745-3992.1995.tb00863.x

Lemann, N. (1999). *The big test: The secret history of the American meritocracy.* New York: Farrar, Straus and Giroux.

Leslie, L., & Caldwell, J.S. (2010). *Qualitative reading inventory* (5th ed.). Boston: Allyn & Bacon.

Leu, D.J. (2007). *Expanding the reading literacy framework of PISA 2009 to include online reading comprehension.* Unpublished manuscript, University of Connecticut.

Lipson, M.Y., & Wixson, K.K. (Eds.). (2010). *Successful approaches to RTI: Collaborative practices for improving K–12 literacy.* Newark, DE: International Reading Association.

Lipson, M.Y., Wixson, K.K., & Johnston, P.H. (2010). Making the most of RTI. In M.Y. Lipson & K.K. Wixson (Eds.), *Successful approaches to RTI: Collaborative practices for improving K–12 literacy* (pp. 1–19). Newark, DE: International Reading Association.

Luke, A. (1994). *The social construction of literacy in the classroom.* Melbourne, Australia: Macmillan.

Mathewson, G.C. (1994). Model of attitude influence upon reading and learning to read. In R.B. Ruddell, M.R. Ruddell, & H. Singer (Eds.), *Theoretical models and processes of reading* (4th ed., pp. 1131–1161). Newark, DE: International Reading Association.

McCracken, R.A. (1966). *Standard reading inventory.* Klamath Falls, OR: Klamath.

McKenna, M.C., & Kear, D.J. (1990). Measuring attitude toward reading: A new tool for teachers. *The Reading Teacher, 43*(8), 626–639. doi:10.1598/RT.43.8.3

McNamara, D.S., & Magliano, J.P. (2009). Self-explanation and metacognition: The dynamics of reading. In D.J. Hacker, J. Dunlosky, & A.C. Graesser (Eds.), *Handbook of metacognition in education* (pp. 60–81). New York: Routledge.

McTigue, E.M., Washburn, E.K., & Liew, J. (2009). Academic resilience and reading: Building successful readers. *The Reading Teacher, 62*(5), 422–432. doi:10.1598/RT.62.5.5

Mehan, H. (1979). *Learning lessons: Social organization in the classroom.* Cambridge, MA: Harvard University Press.

Meisels, S.J., & Piker, R.A. (2001). *An analysis of early literacy assessments used for instruction* (CIERA Report No. 2-013). Ann Arbor, MI: Center for the Improvement of Early Reading Achievement.

Merriam-Webster. (2011a). Inventory. Retrieved June 14, 2011, from www.merriam-webster.com/dictionary/inventory

Merriam-Webster. (2011b). Portfolio. Retrieved June 5, 2011, from www.merriam-webster.com/dictionary/portfolio

Messick, S. (1989). Validity. In R.L. Linn (Ed.), *Educational measurement* (3rd ed., pp. 13–103). New York: Macmillan.

Metsala, J.L., & Ehri, L.C. (1998). *Word recognition in beginning literacy.* Mahwah, NJ: Erlbaum.

Moje, E.B., Ciechanowski, K.M., Kramer, K., Ellis, L., Carrillo, R., & Collazo, T. (2004). Working toward third space in content area literacy: An examination of everyday funds of knowledge and discourse. *Reading Research Quarterly, 39*(1), 38–70. doi:10.1598/RRQ.39.1.4

Moore, K.A., Redd, Z., Burkhauser, M., Mbwana, K., & Collins, A. (2009). *Children in poverty: Trends, consequences, and policy options* (Child Trends Research Brief No. 2009-11). Washington, DC: Child Trends.

Moskal, B.M. (2003). Recommendations for developing classroom performance assessments and scoring rubrics. *Practical Assessment, Research & Evaluation, 8*(14). Retrieved June 14, 2011, from pareonline.net/getvn.asp?v=8&n=14

Moss, P.A., Beck, J.S., Ebbs, C., Matson, B., Muchmore, J., Steele, D., et al. (1992). Portfolios, accountability and an interpretive approach to validity. *Educational Measurement: Issues and Practice, 11*(3), 12–21. doi:10.1111/j.1745-3992.1992.tb00244.x

Muspratt, S., Luke, A., & Freebody, P. (1997). *Constructing critical literacies: Teaching and learning textual practice.* Creskill, NJ: Hampton.

National Assessment Governing Board. (2009). *Reading framework for the 2009 National Assessment of Educational Progress.* Washington, DC: National Assessment Governing Board, U.S. Department of Education. Retrieved June 12, 2010, from www.nagb.org/publications/frameworks/reading09.pdf

National Association for the Education of Young Children & National Association of Early Childhood Specialists in State Departments of Education. (2003). *Where we stand on curriculum, assessment, and program evaluation.* Washington, DC: Authors.

National Center for Education Statistics. (2010). *The nation's report card: Grade 12 reading and mathematics 2009 national and pilot state results* (NCES 2011-455). Washington, DC: National Center for Education Statistics, Institute of Education Sciences, U.S. Department of Education.

National Center on Education and the Economy. (1998). *New standards: Performance standards and assessments for the schools.* Washington, DC: Author.

National Center on Response to Intervention. (2010). *Essential components of RTI—a closer look at Response to Intervention.* Washington, DC: National Center on Response to Intervention, Office of Special Education Programs, U.S. Department of Education. Retrieved July 6, 2011, from www.rti4success.org/pdf/rtiessentialcomponents_042710.pdf

National Commission on Excellence in Education. (1983). *A nation at risk: The imperative for educational reform.* Washington, DC: U.S. Government Printing Office.

National Council for the Social Studies. (1994). *Expectations of excellence: Curriculum standards for social studies.* Washington, DC: Author.

National Council of Teachers of English. (2000). *Resolution on urging reconsideration of high stakes testing.* Retrieved June 14, 2011, from www.ncte.org/positions/statements/highstakestestrecons

National Institute of Child Health and Human Development. (2000). *Report of the National Reading Panel. Teaching children to read: An evidence-based assessment of the scientific research literature on reading and its implications for reading instruction* (NIH Publication No. 00-4769). Washington, DC: U.S. Government Printing Office.

National Research Council. (1996). *National science education standards*. Washington, DC: National Academies Press.

Neisser, U. (1976). *Cognition and reality: Principles and implications of cognitive psychology*. San Francisco: W.H. Freeman.

New York State Education Department. (n.d.). *English language arts learning standards*. Retrieved June 17, 2011, from www.p12.nysed.gov/ciai/ela/elastandards/home.html

Ogle, D.M. (1986). K-W-L: A teaching model that develops active reading of expository text. *The Reading Teacher*, 39(6), 564–570. doi:10.1598/RT.39.6.11

Olson, B., Mead, R., & Payne, D. (2002). *A report of a standard setting method for alternate assessments for students with significant disabilities* (NCEO Synthesis Report No. 47). Minneapolis: National Center on Educational Outcomes, University of Minnesota. Retrieved June 14, 2011, from www.cehd.umn.edu/NCEO/OnlinePubs/Synthesis47.html

Organisation for Economic Co-operation and Development. (2010). *PISA 2009 results: What students know and can do: Student performance in reading, mathematics and science* (Vol. 1). Paris: Author.

Organisation for Economic Co-operation and Development. (2011). *Participating countries/economies*. Paris: Author. Retrieved June 30, 2011, from www.pisa.oecd.org/pages/0,3417,en_32252351_32236225_1_1_1_1_1,00.html

Pajares, F., & Urdan, T. (Eds.). (2006). *Self-efficacy beliefs of adolescents*. Greenwich, CT: Information Age.

Palincsar, A.S., & Brown, A.L. (1984). Reciprocal teaching of comprehension-fostering and comprehension-monitoring activities. *Cognition and Instruction*, 1(2), 117–175. doi:10.1207/s1532690xci0102_1

Paris, S.G. (1983). Becoming a strategic reader. *Contemporary Educational Psychology*, 8(3), 293–316. doi:10.1016/0361-476X(83)90018-8

Paris, S.G., & Carpenter, R.D. (2003). FAQs about IRIs. *The Reading Teacher*, 56(6), 578–580.

Partnership for Assessment of Readiness for College and Careers. (2010). *The Partnership for Assessment of Readiness for College and Careers (PARCC) application for the Race to the Top Comprehensive Assessment Systems Competition*. Retrieved June 20, 2011, from www.fldoe.org/parcc/pdf/apprtcasc.pdf

Payne, D.A. (1974). *The assessment of learning: Cognitive and affective*. Lexington, MA: D.C. Heath.

Pearson, P.D. (2006). Foreword. In K.S. Goodman (Ed.), *The truth about DIBELS: What it is, what it does* (pp. v–xix). Portsmouth, NH: Heinemann.

Pearson, P.D., & Johnson, D.D. (1978). *Teaching reading comprehension*. New York: Holt, Rinehart and Winston.

Pellegrino, J.W., Chudowsky, N., & Glaser, R. (Eds.). (2001). *Knowing what students know: The science and design of educational assessment*. Washington, DC: National Academies Press.

Perie, M., Grigg, W., & Donahue, P. (2005). *The nation's report card: Reading 2005* (NCES 2006-451). Washington, DC: National Center for Education Statistics, Institute of Education Sciences, U.S. Department of Education. Retrieved June 14, 2011, from nces.ed.gov/nationsreportcard/pdf/main2005/2006451.pdf

Phillips, S.E. (1994). High-stakes testing accommodations: Validity versus disabled rights. *Applied Measurement in Education*, 7(2), 93–120. doi:10.1207/s15324818ame0702_1

Pikulski, J.J., & Shanahan, T. (1982). Informal reading inventories: A critical analysis. In J.J. Pikulski & T. Shanahan (Eds.), *Approaches to the informal evaluation of reading* (pp. 94–116). Newark, DE: International Reading Association.

Pintrich, P.R., Marx, R.W., & Boyle, R.A. (1993). Beyond cold conceptual change: The role of motivational beliefs and classroom contextual factors in the process of conceptual change. *Review of Educational Research*, 63(2), 167–199.

Pitcher, S.M., Albright, L.K., DeLaney, C.J., Walker, N.T., Seunarinesingh, K., Mogge, S., et al. (2007). Assessing adolescents' motivation to read. *Journal of Adolescent & Adult Literacy*, 50(5), 378–396. doi:10.1598/JAAL.50.5.5

Popham, W.J. (1991). Appropriateness of teachers' test-preparation practices. *Educational Measurement: Issues and Practice*, 10(4), 12–15. doi:10.1111/j.1745-3992.1991.tb00211.x

Popham, W.J. (1997). What's wrong—and what's right—with rubrics. *Educational Leadership, 55*(2), 72–75.

Pressley, M., & Afflerbach, P. (1995). *Verbal protocols of reading: The nature of constructively responsive reading.* Hillsdale, NJ: Erlbaum.

Pressley, M., Hilden, K., & Shankland, R. (2006). *An evaluation of end-grade-3 Dynamic Indicators of Basic Early Literacy Skills (DIBELS): Speed reading without comprehension, predicting little.* Unpublished manuscript, Michigan State University, East Lansing.

Raphael, T.E., & Wonnacott, C.A. (1985). Heightening fourth-grade students' sensitivity to sources of information for answering comprehension questions. *Reading Research Quarterly, 20*(3), 282–296. doi:10.2307/748019

Roeber, E.D. (1996). Guidelines for the development and management of performance assessments. *Practical Assessment, Research & Evaluation, 5*(7). Retrieved February 12, 2004, from pareonline.net/getvn.asp?v=5&n=7

Rogers, R. (2003). *A critical discourse analysis of family literacy practices: Power in and out of print.* Mahwah, NJ: Erlbaum.

Samuels, S.J. (2007). The DIBELS tests: Is speed of barking at print what we mean by reading fluency? *Reading Research Quarterly, 42*(4), 563–566.

Scanlon, D.M., Anderson, K.L., & Sweeney, J.M. (2010). *Early intervention for reading difficulties: The interactive strategies approach.* New York: Guilford.

Schmuckler, M.A. (2001). What is ecological validity? A dimensional analysis. *Infancy, 2*(4), 419–436. doi:10.1207/S15327078IN0204_02

Scott, C., & Fagin, T. (2005). *Ensuring academic rigor or inducing rigor mortis? Issues to watch in Reading First.* Washington, DC: Center on Education Policy.

Shepard, L.A., & Bliem, C.L. (1995). Parents' thinking about standardized tests and performance assessments. *Educational Researcher, 24*(8), 25–32.

Sireci, S.G. (2004). *Validity issues in accommodating NAEP reading tests* (Center for Educational Assessment Research Report No. 515). Amherst: University of Massachusetts Amherst.

Slack, J.B. (1998). *Questioning strategies to improve student thinking and comprehension.* Unpublished manuscript, Southwest Educational Development Laboratory, Austin, TX.

SMARTER Balanced Assessment Consortium. (2010). *Race to the Top Assessment program application for new grants: Comprehensive assessment systems.* Retrieved June 20, 2011, from www.scribd.com/doc/53320952/Sbac-Final-Narrative-20100620-4pm

Snow, C.E. (2002). *Reading for understanding: Toward an R&D program in reading comprehension.* Santa Monica, CA: RAND.

Stahl, K.A.D., & Bravo, M.A. (2010). Contemporary classroom vocabulary assessment for content areas. *The Reading Teacher, 63*(7), 566–578. doi:10.1598/RT.63.7.4

Stanovich, K.E. (1986). Matthew effects in reading: Some consequences of individual differences in the acquisition of literacy. *Reading Research Quarterly, 21*(4), 360–407. doi:10.1598/RRQ.21.4.1

Stevens, R. (1912). *The question as a measure of efficiency in instruction: A critical study of class-room practice.* New York: Teachers College Press.

Stiggins, R.J. (2002). Assessment crisis: The absence of assessment for learning. *Phi Delta Kappan, 83*(10), 758–765.

Stretch, L.S., & Osborne, J.W. (2005). Extended time test accommodation: Directions for future research and practice. *Practical Assessment, Research & Evaluation, 10*(8). Retrieved April 5, 2007, from pareonline.net/pdf/v10n8.pdf

Supovitz, J. (2009). Can high stakes testing leverage educational improvement? Prospects from the last decade of testing and accountability reform. *Journal of Educational Change, 10*(2/3), 211–227. doi:10.1007/s10833-009-9105-2

Thorndike, E.L. (1917). Reading as reasoning: A study of mistakes in paragraph reading. *Journal of Educational Psychology, 8*(6), 323–332. doi:10.1037/h0075325

Thurlow, M., & Bolt, S. (2001). *Empirical support for accommodations most often allowed in state policy* (NCEO Synthesis Report No. 41). Minneapolis: National Center on Educational Outcomes, University of Minnesota.

Tierney, R.J., Carter, M.A., & Desai, L.E. (1991). *Portfolio assessment in the reading–writing classroom*. Norwood, MA: Christopher-Gordon.

Tierney, R.J., & Clark, C. (with Fenner, L., Herter, R.J., Simpson, C.S., & Wiser, B.). (1998). Portfolios: Assumptions, tensions, and possibilities. *Reading Research Quarterly, 33*(4), 474–486. doi:10.1598/RRQ.33.4.6

TIMMS & PIRLS International Study Center. (2011). *About PIRLS 2011*. Retrieved June 1, 2011, from timss.bc.edu/pirls2011/index.html

Torgerson, C.J., Brooks, G., & Hall, J. (2006). *A systematic review of the research literature on the use of phonics in the teaching of reading and spelling* (Research Report No. 711). Nottingham, UK: DfES.

University of Oregon Center on Teaching and Learning. (n.d.). *What are Dynamic Indicators of Basic Early Literacy Skills (DIBELS)?* Retrieved March 26, 2007, from dibels.uoregon.edu/dibels_what.php

U.S. Census Bureau. (2011). *Poverty thresholds (2010)*. Retrieved June 17, 2011, from www.census.gov/hhes/www/poverty/data/threshld/

Valencia, S.W., & Calfee, R. (1991). The development and use of literacy portfolios for students, classes, and teachers. *Applied Measurement in Education, 4*(4), 333–345. doi:10.1207/s15324818ame0404_6

Valencia, S.W., & Place, N. (1994). Literacy portfolios for teaching, learning, and accountability: The Bellevue Literacy Assessment Project. In S.W. Valencia, E.H. Hiebert, & P.P. Afflerbach (Eds.), *Authentic reading assessment: Practices and possibilities* (pp. 134–156). Newark, DE: International Reading Association.

Van Keer, H., & Verhaeghe, J.P. (2005). Effects of explicit reading strategies instruction and peer tutoring on second and fifth graders' reading comprehension and self-efficacy perceptions. *Journal of Experimental Education, 73*(4), 291–329. doi:10.3200/JEXE.73.4.291-329

van Kraayenoord, C.E. (2010). Response to Intervention: New ways and wariness. *Reading Research Quarterly, 45*(3), 363–376. doi:10.1598/RRQ.45.3.5

VanSledright, B. (2002). *In search of America's past: Learning to read history in elementary school*. New York: Teachers College Press.

VanSledright, B.A. (2010). *The challenge of rethinking history education: On practices, theories, and policy*. New York: Routledge.

Veenman, M.V.J. (2005). The assessment of metacognitive skills: What can be learned from multi-method designs? In C. Artelt & B. Moschner (Eds.), *Lernstrategien und metakognition: Implikationen für forschung und praxis*. [Learning strategies and metacognition: Implications for research and practice] (pp. 75–97). Münster, Germany: Waxmann.

Verhoeven, L., & Snow, C.E. (Eds.). (2001). *Literacy and motivation: Reading engagement in individuals and groups*. Mahwah, NJ: Erlbaum.

Vygotsky, L.S. (1978). In Cole, M., John-Steiner, V., Scribner, S., & Souberman, E. (trans. eds.) *Mind in society: The development of higher psychological processes*. Cambridge, MA: Harvard University Press. (Original work published 1934)

Wagner, R.K., & Torgesen, J.K. (1987). The nature of phonological processing and its causal role in the acquisition of reading skills. *Psychological Bulletin, 101*(2), 192–212. doi:10.1037/0033-2909.101.2.192

Walpole, S., & McKenna, M.C. (2006). The role of informal reading inventories in assessing word recognition. *The Reading Teacher, 59*(6), 592–594. doi:10.1598/RT.59.6.10

Watson, J.B. (1913). Psychology as the behaviorist views it. *Psychological Review, 20*(2), 158–177. doi:10.1037/h0074428

Webster's New Collegiate Dictionary (8th ed.). (1973). Portfolio. Springfield, MA: Merriam-Webster.

Wells, G. (1989). Language in the classroom: Literacy and collaborative talk. *Language and Education, 3*(4), 251–273. doi:10.1080/09500788909541266

Wigfield, A., & Eccles, J.S. (2000). Expectancy–value theory of achievement motivation. *Contemporary Educational Psychology, 25*(1), 68–81. doi:10.1006/ceps.1999.1015

Wiggins, G. (1998). *Educative assessment: Designing assessments to inform and improve student performance*. San Francisco: Jossey-Bass.

Wineburg, S. (1997). Beyond "breadth and depth": Subject matter knowledge and assessment. *Theory into Practice, 36*(4), 255–261. doi:10.1080/00405849709543776

Wolf, D.P. (1987). The art of questioning. *Academic Connections, Winter,* 1–7. Retrieved October 28, 2003, from www.exploratorium.edu/IFI/resources/workshops/artofquestioning.html

Zuriff, G.E. (2000). Extra examination time for students with learning disabilities: An examination of the maximum potential thesis. *Applied Measurement in Education, 13*(1), 99–117.

INDEX

Note. Page numbers followed by *f* and *t* indicate figures and tables, respectively.

H

Hall, J., 139
Hamilton, L.S., 147
Hamilton, R.L., 57
Harris, T.L., 12, 27, 74
Hart, B., 150
Heath, S.B., 13
Hebert, E., 75
Henderson, S.C., 119, 122, 129
Hiebert, E.H., 182
high-stakes reading tests, 147–170; accommodation with, 199; characteristics of, 151–167; disaggregated results from, 157, 158*f*; history of, 147–149; popularity of, 149–151; sample items in, 155*f*; term, 151
Hildebrandt, D., 176, 181
Hilden, K.R., 137
history performance assessment: nature of, 104–106; rubric for, 100*t*; scoring, 102–103, 102*f*
history texts, primary versus secondary, cues to, 104–105, 105*t*, 108*f*
Hodges, R.E., 12, 27, 74
Hofstetter, C., 191
holding pattern, 42
Horst, M., 13
Huey, E.B., 24, 53, 171

I

inclusion. *See* accommodation
independent reading level, definition of, 28
Indicadores Dinámicoas del Éxito en la Lectura, 136. *See also* DIBELS Next
individualized education plan (IEP), 191
Individuals with Disabilities Education Act Amendments, 190

Individuals with Disabilities Education Improvement Act, 119
initiate-respond-evaluate (IRE) discourse form, 53–54, 61
instructional reading level, definition of, 28
interests, 171, 175, 181; inventory of, 176, 181, 181*t*
International Reading Association, 78, 148
interpretation, in reading assessment model, 14, 16
inventory: definition of, 27. *See also* reading inventories
IRE. *See* initiate-respond-evaluate discourse form

J

Jacob, R.T., 13
Jamentz, K., 106
Johnson, D.D., 56
Johnston, P., 16, 40, 54, 89, 120, 122–123, 148, 161, 182

K

Kaminski, R.A., x, 118, 123, 131–133, 136–137, 140
Kear, D.J., 176, 180
Kerlinger, F.N., 21
Kim, J., 8, 37, 171
Kimball, M., 76
Kingore, B., 77
Klein, S.P., 147
Kober, N., 148
Koenig, J.A., 190–191
Kohn, A., 150
Krathwohl, D.R., 54
Kucan, L., 57, 84
Kuhn, M.R., 139
K-W-L strategy, 57

30t; definition of, 27; history of, 27–29; sample, 8, 9f; teacher-initiated, 38–39; using assessment information from, 40–42

reading levels: definition of, 28; and zone of proximal development, 41f

reading passages: content of, 164–165; in high-stakes tests, 154; in reading inventories, 32–35

Reading Self-Concept Scale (RSCS-30), 176, 178–179, 179f

recording devices, 40

Redd, Z., 150

reliability: of assessing Other, 186; of assessment accommodation, 202–204; in CURRV model, 17, 20–21; of DIBELS Next, 136; of high-stakes reading tests, 164–165; of OSELA, 130; of performance assessment, 113–114; of portfolio assessment, 91–92; of questioning, 70–71; of reading inventories, 46–47

report card, narrative, 172f

responses: accommodation and, 197; assessment of, 64–66

Response to Intervention (RTI), ix, 118–127; approaches to, 122–127; closed systems in, 123–124; definition of, 119; open systems in, 124–125

responsibilities. See roles and responsibilities

retelling: in DIBELS Next, 137–138; in reading inventories, 35–37

Rice, M.E., 177

Riggan, M., 122

Risley, T., 150

Roeber, E.D., 112

Rogers, R., 98

roles and responsibilities: assessing Other and, 185–186; assessment

accommodation and, 202; in CURRV model, 17, 19–20; DIBELS Next and, 135–136; high-stakes reading tests and, 162–164; OSELA and, 130; performance assessment and, 109–113; portfolio assessment and, 86–91; questioning and, 69–70; reading inventories and, 44–46

RSCS-30. See Reading Self-Concept Scale

RTI. See Response to Intervention

rubrics: definition of, 99; in performance assessment, 99–102, 100t, 107

running records, 39–40; OSELA and, 128

S

Samuels, S.J., 131, 137

Sanford, A., 194

Santman, D., 150

Scanlon, D.M., 120

Schellings, G., 111

Schmuckler, M.A., 22

Schwanenflugel, P.J., 139

scientific observation, checklist for, 82, 82f

scoring: of high-stakes tests, 155; of history performance assessment, 102–103, 102f; technology and, 146; times, for DIBELS Next, 133t

Scott, C., 131

screening assessment, in RTI, 120

scriptally implicit questions, 56

Scruggs, T.E., 15

self-assessment: checklist for, 108f; performance assessment and, 107–108, 111; portfolio assessment and, 83–84

self-concept, 171, 175; assessment of, 178–179, 179f

self-esteem, high-stakes tests and, 160

Shanahan, T., 27

Shankland, R.K., 137

Shepard, L.A., 113

showcase portfolio, 76–77

silent reading, in reading inventories, 37–38

Singer, H., 163

Sireci, S.G., 152, 202

skills and strategies: focus on, RTI and, 125–127, 141–142; in isolation versus real reading, 143

Slack, J.B., 59

SMARTER Balanced Assessment Consortium (SBAC), 76, 90, 97, 115, 151

Smolkowski, K., 136

Snow, C.E., 8, 15, 53, 96, 166

Socratic questioning, 52

Spanish-language assessments, 136

special needs. *See* accommodation

spontaneous questions, 61–62

Stahl, K.A.D., 8

standardization, 152. *See also* high-stakes reading tests

standard treatment protocol, in RTI, 122–127

Stanovich, K.E., 90, 175

Stecher, B.M., 147

Stevens, R., 53

Stiggins, R.J., 112, 160

Stretch, L.S., 192

Strømsø, H.I., 10

struggling readers, and assessment of Other, 183–184

students: care for, accommodation as, 195; collaboration and cooperation by, assessment of, 188–189; differences among, assessments and, 143; and portfolio assessment,

questions for, 89*t*; subgroups of, high-stakes tests and, 157

summative assessment, 50–51; accommodation with, 199

Supovitz, J., 148

Sweeney, J.M., 120

T

task analysis, 26, 70; in performance assessment, 98–99

teacher-initiated reading inventories, 38–39

teacher questioning. *See* questioning

technology: and accommodation, 196; and high-stakes tests, 156; and reading assessment, 145–146

test preparation, 163–164; for ELs, 198

tests. *See* high-stakes reading tests; reading assessment

textually explicit questions, 56

textually implicit questions, 56

Thorndike, E.L., 53, 171

Thurlow, M., 192

Tierney, R.J., 74–75, 93

tiers of intervention: assessments related to, 120–121, 121*t*; characteristics of, 120

TIMMS & PIRLS International Study Center, 162

Torgerson, C.J., 139

Torgeson, J.K., 13

training, to administer DIBELS versus OSELA, 138–139

Tunmer, W.E., 12, 176, 179

U

understanding questions: on accommodation, 205; on assessing Other, 187; on early reading assessment, 144; on high-stakes reading tests, 168; on performance assessment, 116; on portfolio assessment, 94; on questioning, 72; on reading assessment concepts, 25; on reading inventories, 49

United States Census Bureau, 150

University of Oregon Center on Teaching and Learning, 140

Unlu, F., 13

Urdan, T., 96

usefulness: of assessing Other, 184–185; of assessment accommodation, 201; in CURRV model, 17, 19; of high-stakes reading tests, 161–162; of OSELA, 129–130; of performance assessment, 106–109; of portfolio assessment, 78–86; of questioning, 68–69; of reading inventories, 42–44

V

Valencia, S.W., 75–76, 91

validity: accommodation and, need for research on, 191; of assessing Other, 186; of assessment accommodation, 204; in CURRV model, 17, 21–22; of DIBELS Next, 136–138, 140–141; of high-stakes reading tests, 165–167; of OSELA, 131, 140–141; of performance assessment, 114–115; of portfolio assessment, 92–93; of questioning, 71; of reading inventories, 47–48

Van Keer, H., 182

Van Kraayenoord, C.E., 135, 140

VanSledright, B., 10, 98–99, 104–105

Veenman, M.V.J., 28

Verhaeghe, J.P., 182

vocabulary, in high-stakes tests, 153

Vygotsky, L.S., 33, 41, 101

W

Wagner, R.K., 13

wait time, 63–64

wait-to-fail syndrome, 119

Walpole, S., 27

Washburn, E.K., 171

Watson, J., 52

Webster's New Collegiate Dictionary, 74

Weiss, P.B., 161

Wells, G., 65

Wenger, E., 53

Wigfield, A., 7, 10, 84, 157, 160, 166

Wiggins, G., 96, 111

Wiliam, D., 77, 89, 97, 110

Wineburg, S., 98, 103

Winograd, P., 89, 182

Wixson, K.K., 119–120, 122, 124

Wolf, D.P., 39, 66

Wonnacott, C.A., 57

word lists, and reading inventories, 31–32

Y–Z

You, W., 10

zone of proximal development, 41; and performance assessment rubrics, 101; and reading levels, 41*f*

Zuriff, G.E., 194, 199, 203